Russian Symphony

Tchaikovsky

Russian Symphony

THOUGHTS ABOUT TCHAIKOVSKY

BY

DMITRI SHOSTAKOVICH
AND OTHERS

Essay Index Reprint Series

BOOKS FOR LIBRARIES PRESS
FREEPORT, NEW YORK

Copyright, 1947, by Philosophical Library, Inc.

Reprinted 1969 by arrangement

STANDARD BOOK NUMBER:

8369-1192-X

LIBRARY OF CONGRESS CATALOG CARD NUMBER:

78-86781

PRINTED IN THE UNITED STATES OF AMERICA

CONTENTS

THOUGHTS ABOUT TCHAIKOVSKY

DMITRI SHOSTAKOVICH

THERE IS NOT a single Russian composer of the latter 19th or early 20th centuries who is not indebted in some measure to Peter Tchaikovsky. The author of six symphonies and the finest and most popular operas in the Russian repertory, Tchaikovsky was one of the founders of the great school of Russian music. His brilliant personality was a happy combination of unusual natural talent and a creative imagination that nourished his talent throughout the long years of his fruitful career. There is literally no musical genre in which Tchaikovsky's music does not occupy a place of importance. Songs and symphonies, operas and ballads, sonatas and ballets, concertos and chamber works—alike bore the stamp of his genius.

Tchaikovsky influenced his contemporaries in music regardless of their individual creative trends and conceptions. Greater still, however, was the influence the great composer exercised on subsequent generations of musicians. The traditional line of Russian musical culture handed down from Glinka to Tchaikovsky was carried on through his pupil Taneyev, and later through Scriabine and Rachmaninov. I do not know a single member of our own generation who has not felt in some way the beneficent influence of Tchaikovsky. Shaporin and Shebalin, Myaskovsky, Prokofiev, Khachaturyan and Dzerzhinsky have at

1

different times but to an equal degree been subjected to the Tchaikovsky traditions of melody and harmony. Tchaikovsky's music and philosophy have left an indelible mark on my own consciousness. Whenever I take up my pen to write some score my thoughts involuntarily turn to the methods used by this unsurpassed master of the art of composition.

Were anyone to ask me what it is that nourishes my love for Tchaikovsky I would be rather at a loss to answer. That would be the subject of an article in itself. To put it briefly, I particularly respect and admire Tchaikovsky because of his critical appraisal of his own work and the definite and profound purpose in everything he wrote.

It is not only we professional musicians who value Tchaikovsky. Like Pushkin he has become part of the Russian national consciousness. Without Tchaikovsky we could not endure our sorrows, his name is on our lips in the hour of victory and in the period of the upsurge of the Russian national spirit.

I should like to take this opportunity to clear up two controversial issues in the matter of Tchaikovsky's music. It is often erroneously thought to be touched by the spirit of pessimism, a view arising from the fact that some modern musical scholars, as well as most of the music critics and scholars of the pre-revolutionary generation, confused pessimism with a vivid sense of tragedy. Has man's conception of tragedy ever been more vividly expressed throughout the centuries than by the Greek tragedians? And yet it has never occurred to anyone to accuse them of pessimism. Tchaikovsky, like the Greek tragedians, was sensitive to the tragedy, the conflict in the development of human life, both personal and social. With the penetration of the true thinker combined with the intuition of the great artist he sensed the contradictory, dialectical path of the development of life, the world, the destiny of the individual and of mankind as a whole. Nevertheless Tchaikovsky's music was by no means marked by fatalism, gloom or faith in a blind fate. His most tragic works are permeated with the spirit of struggle, the striving to overcome the blind elemental forces.

Tchaikovsky believed in the power of creative reason, in the might and the harmony of the universe. And this radiant, intelligent faith pervades all of his musical heritage.

Another fallacious theory about Tchaikovsky is that he was akin to Chekhov and Levitan in elegiac glorification of the Russian twilight of the latter 19th century. This is as untrue of Tchaikovsky as it is of Chekhov and Levitan whose works, in spite of their wistful tenderness, are nevertheless tremendously vital. True, there is a certain affinity between the three insofar as they all cherished a poignant love for Russian landscape; their lyricism was deeply emotional and all three possessed a keen creative interest in their surroundings. One is always aware of the warm blood pulsating beneath the restrained outward form of their art. They are akin also in their sense of the tragedy of life. Tchaikovsky wrote his Sixth Symphony, Chekhov wrote "The Black Monk" (incidentally, one of the most musical pieces of Russian literature; it is written almost like a sonata); and what passion and feeling Levitan invested in his painting of a Russian storm! It should be stressed that like all the classics of Russian realistic literature and painting, it was not the idea of resignation but the theme of struggle and the overcoming of the tragic "fatum" that predominated in Tchaikovsky's most tragic compositions (*e.g.* the Sixth Symphony and "Queen of Spades").

To this day the Rimsky-Korsakov school of Russian composition has always been considered the first of its kind. It is time, however, to give due credit to the Tchaikovsky school and to appraise the wealth of his composition technique. In development of musical idea and in orchestration he has no equal. I bow to his magnificent orchestration, for as a rule he did not orchestrate his compositions after they were written, as is usually done, but composed, as it were, *a priori*, for orchestra, *i.e.*, he thought in terms of orchestra. And whenever I myself encounter difficulty in the course of my work I invariably find the solution to my problem by studying Tchaikovsky's technique.

I should like to say also that in turning to Russian literature for his subject matter Tchaikovsky was never a musical interpreter in the generally accepted sense of the word. His "Pushkin" operas cannot be regarded as poems translated into the language of music. Tchaikovsky's Tatyana, Onegin, Lensky, Herman, Mazeppa are not merely characters borrowed from Pushkin; they are congenial works of art constituting the pride of Russian national poetry.

The national character of the composer is determined by his deep understanding of his compatriots, and his fine feeling for Russian nature. His range of interests extended beyond the national boundaries, however, and Tchaikovsky frequently resorted to foreign subjects (for all of his three ballets, for "Yolanthe" and the "Italian Capriccio"). But, however "un-Russian" the subject, these compositions are no less national in spirit and character than the rest of his work.

Tchaikovsky's music is not only one of the cornerstones

of Russian musical culture, and world music too for that matter. It is at the same time a creative and technical encyclopedia to which every Russian composer has reference in the course of his own work; for example, his amazing gift for changing and varying the musical material (a striking example is the destiny theme in the beginning of the First Movement and in the Waltz of the Fifth Symphony).

Peter Tchaikovsky's musical legacy is treasured by the Soviet people today as ever before.

THE GREAT RUSSIAN COMPOSER

ACADEMICIAN BORIS ASSAFYEV
(IGOR GLEBOV)

THE SECRET of the vital power of Tchaikovsky's music lies in the fact that there is virtually not a single province of his music—from the gems of Russian chamber music that issued from his pen to his greatest operas or symphonic poems—in which the appeal and effect of the music was less than in any other field. The convincing nature of Tchaikovsky's melody is not dependent on the scale of the composition and its form, although the quality and character of the melodic material determines the form to a great extent. This is what makes any of the piano pieces from the famous "Four Seasons" cycle just as striking and titanic in scope as the First Piano Concerto.

If Tchaikovsky is to be studied as an outstanding master whose creative personality manifested itself in every musical "genre," we must never lose sight of the unity and wholeness of his music, expressed alike in the laconic "Skylark," in the passionate flights of the "Romeo and Juliet" overture, in the plaint of "Francesca," in the tense triumphal finale of the "1812" overture and the lyrical chorus legend about the childhood of Christ. In this consistent lyricism, one comparable in depth and penetration to that of Schubert—lies the appeal of Tchaikovsky's music and its vitality.

6

Indeed, if we discount the unsuccessful attempts of musical snobs to belittle the importance of Tchaikovsky's music, to label it "vulgar" and "in poor taste," we will find that it has won a permanent place in the musical life of the entire world as an artistic phenomenon of classical perfection and of permanent value.

We now know that one can already speak of different epochs of interpretation, *i.e.*, changes in the traditional interpretation of Tchaikovsky's music in the concert halls and theatres not only of Russia but of the world as a whole. This means that each generation has found in his music elements in harmony with the given epoch and has interpreted it accordingly. In Russia the prevailing style of performance of Tchaikovsky's works was determined by the conducting of Edward Napravnik, which was sober, harmonious and emotionally restrained yet preserving withal that charming informality peculiar to Tchaikovsky. A disciplined musician, Napravnik, a Czech by nationality, was the chief conductor of the former Imperial Mariinsky Theater of St. Petersburg. A contemporary of Tchaikovsky and one who was deeply sensitive to the Slavic nature of his music, he understood and conveyed to his audiences Tchaikovsky's classical form and melodic traces. The expressiveness of the composer's personality and what might be called the expressionist nature of his music was brought out by Mahler. Last but not least we are indebted to Arthur Nikisch for discovering fully the spiritual structure of Tchaikovsky's symphonic music with all its untold wealth and abundance of exquisite nuances and shades of feeling. Under Nikisch's baton Psyche was born anew; the soul of this music and its amazing contrasts of feeling acquired classic contours, utterly delightful and enchanting in harmonious development, and an unforgettable experience for all who had the good fortune to hear it.

There is no need to cite any further examples. I do not intend within the confines of this brief article to trace the history of the changes in the style of performance of Tchaikovsky's music. Suffice it to point out that the unflagging interest of outstanding orchestra conductors (not to speak of instrumentalists and vocalists) in the interpretation of Tchaikovsky is a striking indication of the inexhaustible vitality of his music. Thus arises an absorbing problem for every student endeavouring to analyze the source of the popular appeal of one or another work of art: does the musical mastery of Tchaikovsky transcend the boundaries of professional technique? In other words, did Tchaikovsky perhaps possess the gift of inducing the listener to follow the train of the thoughts and ideas he seeks to convey through the medium of his music? Orators possess this gift, we know; nevertheless the oratorical spirit can scarcely be applied to the Russian school of music, especially to Glinka and Tchaikovsky. The latter depended for effect rather on emotional suggestion, the concentrated effect of his chosen melodic idiom. This idiom, which had its roots in traditional intonations, dominates the emotions of the hearers, evoking harmonious nerve responses in our consciousness, like the voices of dear ones on whose love and compassion we can always depend.

Indeed, it would by no means be paradoxical to state that Tchaikovsky's music abounds in lyrical qualities that may be said to constitute something in the nature of a "dictionary" of sound, a dictionary of intonations designating caresses, compassion, sympathy, maternal or conjugal affection, and spiritual support. This voluminous dictionary of intonation is at the same time subtly woven into and generalized in the melody. Pushkin has given a brilliant definition of his attitude to this form of human intercourse through poetic intonation in his "The Stone Guest": "but love too is melody." * It is not by chance that Tchaikovsky too succeeded so eminently with the intonational sphere of the "cradle song" (not in the narrow berceuse sense but as the multifarious manifestation of human tenderness and compassion). In this sense Tchaikovsky, the most impressionable of men, showed himself to be a penetrating realistic psychologist. Tchaikovsky's lyricism emanates from a profound insight into the spiritual life of the men and women of an epoch of heightening nervous sensibility and tends toward feelings of sympathy and compassion evoked by ties of kinship and love. These basic qualities are especially palpable in Tchaikovsky's melodiousness and give rise to that peculiar flavour of his lyricism which seems to caress the soul. In a word, there is nothing of passionate abandon or emotional anarchy in Tchaikovsky's music. It comes closer to the aesthetic qualities peculiar to such Russian writers as Pushkin, Tolstoi, Chekhov and Gorky. Take, for example, the scene of Tatyana's letter in "Eugene Onegin." In this superb musical portrayal of the conflict in the soul of a young girl prey to the emotions of her first love, Tchaikovsky contrives to make compassion and tenderness the basic intonations even in passages expressing passion and spiritual ardour. And the sharper the conflict in the maiden's breast the more tender and compassionate the passages that follow. This is true, for example, of the first movement of the Sixth Symphony with its tempestuous outbursts of feeling alternating with lyrical "lullaby"

* Scene II.

themes, themes of profound compassion, maternal tenderness evoking images of Madonna paintings by famous old masters. There is the same noble simplicity about Tchaikovsky's lyricism.

The above qualities in turn give rise to their contrasts: the stormy and tense portrayal of human anguish in the spirit of the images of Dante, and Shakespeare, Pushkin and Ostrovsky transported into the turbulent atmosphere of the latter 19th century. In Tchaikovsky's music these contrasts found expression in the struggle between cantilene melodies and their opposites. Such for the most part is the content and the purpose of the so-called "development" in Tchaikovsky's music, such is its dramatic essence. Each of these conflicts has its culmination to a greater or lesser degree, after which comes a gradual building up and concentration (long organ-points!) followed as a rule by a vivid melodic assertion of tragic or triumphant feeling. The symmetry may be reversed. In "Francesca," for example, the elegiac expression of feeling by measured alternating melodic ebb and flow is the basic structure, the "centre," so to speak, while the stormy aggressive "movement" is concentrated on the flanks.

An extremely complex emotional drama is "The Tempest" (a symphonic poem few conductors can master owing to their inability to grasp the compositional structure). In this work images of the sea (both calm and stormy) are interwoven in a complex pattern with the gradual unfoldment of the love emotion and intermezzo expositions representing the genie servants of Prospero the magician, while the whole is the embodiment of the great Renaissance ideal in which the human intellect and imagination dominates the cosmos. In "The Tempest" Tchaikovsky like Shakespeare uses the character of Prospero as a vehicle for his ideas. No wonder Vladimir Stasov, an ardent admirer of Shakespeare and an art scholar with a deep feeling for Russian music, appreciated "The Tempest," apart from its musical qualities, for its dramatic treatment of the powerful fantasy of Prospero.

The symphonic poem "Tempest" may serve as a model and a point of departure for an understanding of the basic principles of Tchaikovsky's mastery as a "dramatist of the emotions," with a gift for directing the attention of his hearers to the action of the sound images as effectively as the great classical dramatists, and primarily Shakespeare. Tchaikovsky is nearer to the Shakespearean treatment of emotional conflict than to the method of emotional contrast used by Corneille, Racine or the Spanish dramatists.* I have been speaking throughout of Tchaikovsky as a dramatist, not only in the *operatic* works but in his music as a whole, for it is this quality that determines and explains the principal elements of his skill as a composer who invariably draws the listener into the action of his music and never leaves him a passive observer.

Hence the purely musical and structural principles of Tchaikovsky's craftsmanship have nothing of the aristocratic aloofness or ivory-tower detachment about them, as,

* Having interested his audience in the plot, Shakespeare literally focused the spectator's imagination on the development of the intrigue. It is worth while comparing this to the skill with which Tchaikovsky's overture to "Romeo and Juliet" is written. It is when the tempestuous mood predominates in Shakespeare, *i.e.*, the expression of emotion through conflict without resorting to calm lyrical exposition, that Tchaikovsky's music bears the greatest affinity to the great English dramatist. Through the agitated music the ear catches the dramatic ebb and flow (*e.g.* in musical "microcosm" this can, let us say, be found in the popular ballad "Is It Day" and in a more swift and elaborate form in the third movement of the Sixth Symphony).

for example, the symphonic compositions of Glazunov, which, in spite of their superficial resemblance to the Tchaikovsky intonation, no more than skim the surface of the emotions. The development of the musical ideas in the non-dramatic type of symphony is not aimed at winning the sympathies (attention) of the listener. That is why Tchaikovsky stands apart also among the great melodist composers; he was not a melodist of the wistful contemplative type as Schubert, for example, although the two composers are akin in penetration and emotional, narrative qualities of melodic fabric. Schubert, however, if we take his work as a whole, rarely succeeded in compelling the listener to follow the inner emotional path of his musical conception. With Tchaikovsky, on the other hand, this was the invariable rule in all of his compositions whatever their structure or form. The exceptions—if we take the complete catalogue of his music—are extremely few. Indeed, they are the natural consequence of spiritual weariness and creative inertia (to which Schubert was also so often prey!) the dangerous enemy of the composers of the "instinctive" melody variety.

For Tchaikovsky to have turned toward the masters of the Italian school of sensuous melody—Rossini and Verdi—would have been useless. Their element was opera as an effective vehicle of external (in the best sense) drama. Of course, Tchaikovsky also has timely "oases" of pure melody and broadly developed pauses in the action at culminating points in the emotional development (arias, ariosos, duets and static ensembles), but they spring from entirely different sources than with the Italians. They are never inserted for the sake of external dramatic effect, but arise from the inner development of the psychological drama,

This quality, most strikingly and laconically expressed in Tchaikovsky's last opera "Yolanthe" makes his operatic dramaturgy a forerunner of the lyrical dramaturgy of Chekhov and laid the foundation for the psychological realism upon which Stanislavsky's productions were built. In "Yolanthe" we find the finest qualities of Tchaikovsky's lyrical mastery while dramatically it is a synthesis of the whole of the composer's experience as a dramatic symphonist. In his lifetime the opera was accorded a cold and condescending reception. Today it has been revived in the Moscow Bolshoi Theatre and is performed under the direction of Alexander Melik-Pashayev with much sensitivity and a profound grasp of the emotional undercurrent of the symphonic action.

Tchaikovsky's operatic dramaturgy does not strive for effective dramatic conflict. I would go so far as to compare the dramatic quality of his music with the composition of Balzac's novel "Le Peau Chagrin" in which the role of the talisman increases rather than reduces the psychological and realistic development of phenomena. With Tchaikovsky too the "talisman of external operatic effect" is not an aim in itself but the means toward revealing the inner action of the opera.

It is most natural to compare Tchaikovsky's skill as a dramatist in music possessing an amazing gift for distributing the means of expression in accordance with the laws of human perception, with what Schumann did to advance music. Not one of the big composers of the middle of last century escaped the influence of Schumann in this respect. Here in Russia this influence was felt by Anton Rubinstein, and the "Big Five" * (grouped around Balakirev) as well

* Mussorgsky, Rimsky-Korsakov, Borodine, Cui and Balakirev.

as Tchaikovsky, but each in his own peculiarly Russian
manner. It was not a matter of pure imitation but of pushing
the dramatic principle in music still farther forward. For
Schumann music served not only as a medium of self-expres-
sion, it was a means of depicting spiritual conflicts in accordance with the laws of drama; in other words, it was
the artistic vehicle by whose means the emotions of the
audience could be involved in the portrayal of human
passion. The influence of the psychologically realistic
principles propounded by Schumann proved stronger and
more fruitful than the results he himself achieved. He was
incapable of applying his own magnificent lyrical qualities
to the Beethoven principles of elaborate musical thinking
in harmony with the principles of Shakespearean drama.
This was achieved by Tchaikovsky who became not only
the "regisseur of human emotion" as expressed through
opera and plays but a dramatic symphonist and thinker.

Unless this basic quality is taken into account it is impossible properly to encompass his skill as a composer, impossible to understand the psycho-realistic essence of his
operatic dramaturgy or even to evaluate fully the inexhaustible wealth of his generous melodiousness. There have
been plenty of composers in the course of the past centuries
who possessed the melody instinct, in the narrow sense of
the term, and who were masters of the Italian and European
cantilene, but very few for whom melody was a medium
for expressing ideas in dramatic form. Tchaikovsky gave
the fullest elaboration to the principles of romantic imagery
set forth by Schumann ("Carnaval," "Symphonic Etudes,"
or "Kreisleriana" in their time ushered in a new era of
symphony), but he possessed a penetrating intellect that
derived from the brilliant symphonies of Beethoven all the

lessons to be learned regarding the intensive dramatic development over broad expanses and far-reaching symphonic perspectives, while preserving the enchantment and Schubertian directness of feeling.

It is thus that we perceive the musical genius of Tchaikovsky and these are the distinctive features of his far-sighted mastery that riveted the attention of the listener and intensified the vital power of his music whose poignant intonations we love so well.

TCHAIKOVSKY THE MAN AND HIS OUTLOOK

YURI KELDYSH

Peter Ilyich Tchaikovsky was a remarkable example of an artist who was completely wedded to his art, whose whole being was dedicated to constant intensive creative work to the exclusion of everything else. His life and his art were inseparably interwoven. "I literally cannot live without working," he wrote once, "for as soon as one piece of work is finished and one would wish to relax, instead of resting, *i.e.*, abandoning oneself to the pleasures of the weary toiler who has earned the right to the alluring *dolce far niente*, one is a prey to depression and melancholy, to thoughts of the futility of earthly existence, fear for the future, fruitless regrets about the irretrievable past, the meaning of earthly existence, in a word, all that which poisons the life of a man who is not engrossed in work and inclined to hypochondria, and the result is the desire to tackle some new work without delay."

Utterances of the above nature occur frequently in Tchaikovsky's letters throughout the period of his conscious creative life. Work for him was as "indispensable as air." The only thing that paralyzed him at times and exercised an "annihilating" effect on him was the "thought of the brevity of human life," which was too short to do all that had to be done. Even when he might have wished for some temporary diversion from his work, he could not find it for "some irresistible force takes the upperhand and pins me to my desk and piano." The fear that his Muse might desert him one day and that he would lose the ability to create worried him more than anything else. Had that happened life would have become unendurable for him. "After all," he confessed, "actually my only interest in life is to write music."

This eternal indefatigable striving for productive creative work gave rise to certain specific traits in Tchaikovsky's character. For example, he constantly spoke of his "misanthropy," his "fear of people." From his early years he complained of "weariness with life"; the longing to withdraw from society and devote himself "to a quiet life of contemplation in some remote spot" became one of the principal motifs of his most intimate confessions as much as he realized the practical impossibility of its attainment.

What Tchaikovsky called his "misanthropy" had not a shade of genuine aversion or contempt for his fellow men arising from some arrogant self-adulation. Of his tendency to shun society and his fear of human contacts he himself said: "There is no element of misanthropy about this shyness. On the contrary, the more I cut myself off from society the more I love my fellow men." What Tchaikovsky admired most in his favourite writer Leo Tolstoi was "the exalted feeling of humanity" and his profound sensible interest in the spiritual world of every person however mean and insignificant.

Tchaikovsky's striving for solitude was likewise relative. He very often suffered keenly from loneliness. "Although I myself do not make friends easily," he wrote in a

letter to one of his young friends who complained of his
tendency to fits of "spleen" and malice, "I must nevertheless confess that to hold oneself altogether aloof from people with whom one must live by force of circumstances
makes for depression and despondency as well as what we
call 'spleen.' One is seized with the ungovernable desire to
see people in the most unfavourable and ridiculous light,
and to place oneself on some exalted pedestal and from
there to look down on others. And yet even the most un-
sociable people feel the need to associate with their kind.
. . . I have indulged in some idle speculation on this question just because I have suffered painfully from 'unsociability' and know by experience how pleasant it is to overcome it."

Tchaikovsky cherished a most fervent love for people
and humanity as a whole. This was by no means an "ideal"
detached emotion. In his association with various people he
was most attentive, warm and tender. His kindness and his
consideration for others were notorious. The purity and
unselfishness of Tchaikovsky's relations with his friends, of
whom, notwithstanding his "unsociability" there were always many, need hardly be stressed. Tchaikovsky was
always ready to render his friends all possible assistance
and support, both material and moral. His inexhaustible
love for his fellow men left a deep imprint on his work and
constituted the leitmotif of his music. The composer regarded his music primarily as a means of establishing contact with people.

The main reason for Tchaikovsky's persistent and unflagging interest in opera, for example, was that opera was
one of the most popular forms of art and "more direct
means of communicating with the public" than any other

form of music. "Opera and only opera brings you in close contact with people," he maintained, "it brings your music to real public, makes you accessible not only to a few exclusive sets but, given favourable circumstances, to the whole people. I think," he adds, "that there is nothing reprehensible in this striving, *i.e.*, that it was not vanity that prompted Schumann to write 'Genoveva' or Beethoven his 'Fidelio' but a natural desire to widen the circle of their audience, to *reach out to the hearts of as many people as possible.*"

Tchaikovsky loved life in its most diverse manifestations. He once described himself as "a man who passionately loved life and as passionately hated death." The pessimistic philosophy of Schopenhauer was repellent to him and he wanted "to spite Schopenhauer by loving life and nature every minute of the day." Nature as the highest and most perfect expression of the inexhaustible life force evoked in Tchaikovsky a passionate adoration, a pantheistic ecstasy. At the sight of a beautiful landscape he was capable of bursting into tears from an overflow of emotion, of falling onto the ground and kissing the earth. Only in communion with nature did Tchaikovsky find true happiness. "Even art," he said, "cannot give the moments of ecstatic delight we derive from Nature." Tchaikovsky had many deep attachments; among them the strongest and most permanent was his feeling for his native land. He had a passionate love for his country and was proud to be a Russian. During his frequent visits to other countries he was always a prey to nostalgic yearning to be home and waited impatiently for the moment when he would again set eyes on the rolling plains of Russia so dear to his heart and hear his native tongue spoken around him again. This love for his country was expressed in his sincere interest in certain concrete aspects of the native environment. Russian landscape, Russian history, Russian customs—all this evoked in Tchaikovsky feelings of warm and affectionate kinship. "I passionately love Russians, the Russian language, the Russian mind, the Russian style of beauty, Russian customs," he wrote. He was *"in love with the Russian element in general,"* he said.

Tchaikovsky's great heart manifested itself in everything: in his relations with his parents, his brothers, sisters, nephews. Having no family life of his own, Tchaikovsky was greatly attached to his relatives and considered it the height of happiness to live among people to whom he was bound by ties of kinship, in an atmosphere of mutual understanding and tender solicitude.

*   *   *

Tchaikovsky believed that music has a powerful healing influence on the human soul, not, however, through the creation of fanciful illusions, but by a profound and faithful revelation of the beauty and meaning of life. Music, in his opinion "is not a delusion, it is a revelation. And its power lies in the fact that it reveals to us elements of *beauty* that cannot be revealed in any other sphere and whose permanent contemplation will reconcile us to life forever. It enlightens and gladdens the heart."

The fervent desire to serve mankind induced Tchaikovsky to avoid relations with people that might divert him from his main path, and prevent the fulfilment of his destiny. Thanks to his exalted conception of his mission as a mentor and healer of the human soul, he invariably sought conditions that would afford the greatest opportunity for concentrating most productively on his creative work. Every day, every hour, every minute spent away from his desk and piano Tchaikovsky regarded as a criminal waste of time, and he bitterly reproached himself. "Of all the forms of waste," he maintained, "waste of time is the most senseless." However busy he might be in other fields Tchaikovsky considered himself idle when he was not composing.

In spite of what Tchaikovsky himself said of his "professional attitude to art," he actually could not have been farther from formal professionalism. His whole life was a model of genuine creative fervour and high-principled approach to art problems. Never did Tchaikovsky write coldly or indifferently, without inner fire and inspiration. Music for him was a means of expressing his innermost thoughts and emotions, his conception of life as a whole, and he invested something of himself in everything he wrote. "Whether the music I write is good or bad," he said, "one thing is certain, and that is that I write from an inner and indomitable urge. I speak in the language of music because I have always something to say. I write *sincerely*. . . ."

Music was for him the most truthful and direct expression of events and impressions gleaned from life. Tchaikovsky reproached himself for not being able to separate the literary qualities from the human element in appraising a writer. Nevertheless his own power as a composer of genius is determined precisely by the fact that the man and the artist in him constituted one harmonious entity, splendid in its spiritual beauty and perfection.

2

The beginning of Tchaikovsky's career was by no means spectacular. In his early years the public did not respond with enthusiasm to his unusual gifts. Tchaikovsky matured slowly and gradually. And even later on his works for the most part grew on the audience gradually, rarely evoking a storm of acclaim when first performed. All the more lasting, however, was its effect on the minds and hearts of people.

As is true of all artists, early childhood impressions played an important part in molding his consciousness.

The quiet, calm serenity of life in the remote corner of the Urals where he spent the first eight years of his life, surrounded by the loving care of his mother, his governess and adoring female relatives, developed that gentleness of spirit, sensitivity and dreaminess that remained characteristic of him in his maturity as well. His constant communion with nature and the simple rural environment was the source of his fervent and unalterable "love of the Russian element." If Glinka could say that it was under the influence of the folk melodies heard in early childhood that he "subsequently concentrated on Russian national music," Tchaikovsky could point to similar influences. "As regards the Russian element in my music in general," he once wrote, "*i.e.*, the affinity to the folk song method in melody and harmony, this can be traced to the fact that *I grew up in the country, from my earliest childhood I was aware of the ineffable beauty of Russian folk music, that I passionately love the Russian element in all its manifestation, that, in short, I am a Russian in the fullest sense of the word.*"

Although Tchaikovsky was the son of a landowner and

was brought up on his father's estate, he was able to appreciate the poetic aspect of life amid the beauties of nature without acquiring any of the arrogance or selfishness that were characteristic of the landed gentry. His father and all his relatives belonged to the impoverished class of the landed nobility and were modest industrious people who made their way in life by virtue of their own individual zeal and ability. The composer himself was inclined to refer with irony to his noble descent and insisted on the plebeian origin of the Tchaikovskys.

As a child Tchaikovsky's musical genius did not manifest itself. True, he made rapid progress in his piano lessons under the tutelage of some amateur music teacher and sometimes he did show signs of a heightened musical receptiveness. There was, however, not even the remotest evidence of the genius that was latent in him.

Music still played a secondary role in his life when, in 1850, at the age of 10 he left the family circle he loved so well and went to St. Petersburg to enter law school, an extremely exclusive establishment which trained court officials. The boy was not happy there. The sudden change of environment, the separation from his parents and the new adjustments that had to be made caused the gentle, impressionable boy considerable mental suffering. As time went on, however, he grew accustomed to the new life and acquired a wide circle of friends and acquaintances among the law students. True, Tchaikovsky was not cut out to be a lawyer and the brief legal career that followed his graduation from the school was by no means brilliant. His sojourn in law school, however, taught him to be a man of the world. Lively, witty and ingenious, a pianist who could give a brilliant performance of some fantasie on the theme of a popular Italian opera or an improvisation of his own, endowed moreover with no mean histrionic gifts, he was an unfailing participant in all entertainments and a great favourite with his set.

On the whole, his musical tastes in those years coincided with the tastes prevailing in the salons of the society in which he mingled. Italian opera attracted him most of all, and he had but a nodding acquaintance with classical music. True, he had his own peculiar musical attachments formed in his childhood; they included Mozart's "Don Giovianni," Weber's "Freischuetz," and Glinka's "Ivan Susanin." On the whole, however the Tchaikovsky of that period was still a dilettante in music.

This lasted until the beginning of the sixties when a radical change took place in his whole outlook and sphere of interests. "I have begun to learn to play the double bass," he wrote to his sister on October 23, 1861, "and am making remarkable progress. Who knows, in about three years you may be listening to my operas and singing my arias." Shortly before this letter was written Tchaikovsky had enrolled in music classes opened by the Russian Music Society. A year later these classes were reorganized and became the St. Petersburg Conservatory and Tchaikovsky entered as one of its first pupils. By this time his decision to dedicate himself to music had been made. "You must not think that I expect to become a great artist," he wrote to his sister. "I merely wish to follow what I believe to be my calling. Whether I will be a famous composer or a poor music-teacher my conscience will be at rest and I shall have no cause to grumble at my fate and my fellow men." These words ring with a conviction of the loftiness and importance of his destiny, combined with the modesty of a hardworking musician, a trait that was characteristic of him to the end of his days.

We cannot trace in all its details the gradual process that led to the fundamental change in the whole mode of Tchaikovsky's life and associations. There can be no doubt, however, that he was influenced by the progressive ideas of the democratic movement of enlightenment that were current during this period among the broad strata of the Russian intelligentsia. The very advent of the music societies which played such an important role in the whole creative life of Peter Tchaikovsky, the Russian Society of Music and the two Conservatories (first in St. Petersburg and several years later in Moscow), was the result of these enlightenment tendencies. Anxious to be of use to society, Tchaikovsky found application for his energies in professional musical activity.

A life of intensive labour, diverse cares and occasional hardship began for Tchaikovsky with his enrollment in the Conservatory. Having thrown up his practice, he was obliged to earn his living by giving music lessons since his father was in pecuniary straits. The once dashing, dandified government official began to assume even the outward appearance of a modest plebeian student. "There was nothing left of the young man of fashion about him," wrote his brother and biographer. "With his long hair and shabby clothes, the leftovers of his once fashionable wardrobe, he changed outwardly as radically as in every other respect. . . . By cultivating a slightly exaggerated carelessness of dress and general shabbiness he wished to emphasize the gulf between himself and his former companions, to show that henceforth he had nothing in common with them; it was a frank and brutal declaration of his unswerving resolution to cut himself off from everything that had interested him formerly."

Three years in the Conservatory made Tchaikovsky a musician with a broad cultural outlook, and gave him a firm grounding in the technique of composition. This was, naturally, achieved by dogged perseverance and hard work. His personal contact with some of his tutors and fellow-students, whose knowledge and experience was superior to his own, was extremely useful to him. Especially important was the influence of Anton Rubinstein, founder and director of the Conservatory, a distinguished pianist and a composer. Tchaikovsky studied orchestration under Rubinstein but the latter's influence extended beyond this subject. A virtuoso of world renown, an original and temperamental artist, an energetic musical organizer and popularizer, champion of the high ideals of classical music, Rubinstein was greatly admired by all who came in contact with him. Tchaikovsky was undoubtedly greatly indebted to him for the consolidation of his creative principles and his very views on art as a serious and important undertaking demanding ceaseless, untiring effort from the student.

The significance of the Conservatory period in the composer's career was best of all appraised by the famous music critic Laroche, Tchaikovsky's personal friend and fellow-student, who subsequently did much to popularize his music. In a letter written a few days after the graduation examination, in which he called Tchaikovsky the "great hope" of Russian music, Laroche wrote: ". . . All that you have done . . . I consider to be no more than the work of a schoolboy, preparatory and experimental, if I may be allowed to put it thus. Your creative work will begin perhaps five years from now, but it will be mature, classical work that will surpass everything we have had since Glinka."

3

By the seventies of last century Tchaikovsky was already an established composer, although the opinion of music critics was divided on the subject of his compositions. His music continued to win an increasing number of admirers both among the general public as well as among the outstanding representatives of the world of art and literature. Among the latter were the famous Russian authors Turgenev and Tolstoi. The composer especially valued the opinion of Leo Tolstoi who had been his favourite writer from his early youth and remained so until the end of his life. An entry in his diary ten years later recalls how the great writer wept as he listened to the Andante Cantabile of his string quartet. "I doubt whether my vanity had ever been so flattered and touched," he wrote.

Although there was no personal or intimate friendship between Tolstoi and Tchaikovsky, the occasional contacts with the writer whose greatness to Tchaikovsky was "almost divine," made a deep impression on him. "This winter," he wrote in 1877, "I had several interesting talks with the writer Count L. N. Tolstoi, which explained a great deal for me. He convinced me that an artist who works not by inner compulsion but with a subtle play for effect, the artist who prostitutes his talent in order to win the applause of the public and forces himself to pander to its taste, is not a true artist, his works will not last and his success is ephemeral. I concur fervently in that belief."

Notwithstanding his success, the increasing popularity

of his music and his association with Moscow musicians who were warmly disposed toward him, Tchaikovsky became prey to a gnawing dissatisfaction. Already in 1867, in a letter to his sister, we find him complaining of this weariness with life: "It would seem that a man who is comfortably off, who is loved and respected, who by general consent is considered to have excelled in his particular field could surely wish for nothing more. And yet in spite of all these favourable circumstances I shun society, I am incapable of maintaining any manner of acquaintance, I seek solitude and silence. The reason for all this is the abovementioned weariness with life."

What Tchaikovsky called "weariness," "misanthropy," or "fear of people," was actually the conflict between the desire to concentrate on his creative work to the exclusion of all else and the host of threads that bound him to life with its distracting fuss and pother. He felt that even his Moscow circle of friends and the Conservatory were distracting him from his main task which was to write music. Hence the duality of his attitude to Moscow and his Moscow environment. ". . . I love Moscow as something near and dear to me," he once wrote. "I feel that I am becoming more and more a part of Moscow, so that now I cannot think of living anywhere else," he admitted sometime later. "There is only one city in the world and that is Moscow." In another letter Tchaikovsky spoke of his affection for the Conservatory as for an old friend. At the same time, there was much about Moscow that was irksome to him. The disorderly Bohemian life of the Moscow art set "which indulges in the pleasures of the flesh rather than of the spirit" was repellent to him. Moreover, his duties as professor in the Conservatory wearied and bored him.

All this finally gave rise to a painful feeling of loneliness and alienation. ". . . Indeed my life in Moscow is something like that of an orphan," he complained to his brother. Early in 1875 he decided that the time had come to alter his mode of life radically. The crisis which matured two years later and which marked a sharp dividing line in his personal life as well as his creative career was gradually coming to a head.

4

The mental shock suffered by Tchaikovsky as a result of his unsuccessful marriage gave an outlet to all that had been accumulating over a period of many years. The marriage was merely the final and immediate impulse that caused the final explosion. The principal motive was dissatisfaction with the whole tempo of his existence and the need for some radical change. Only a few months of complete solitude could have cured Peter Ilyich and restored his spiritual equilibrium. At the same time, the main factor that hastened his "revival" was work, intensive, all-engrossing work. In December 1877 Tchaikovsky wrote that for the past week his "health, both spiritual and physical, had been excellent." And a few days later: "From myself alone do I derive consolation, peace of mind and happiness. A successful symphony, the feeling that I am writing something good, this is what will reconcile me tomorrow with all past and future misfortunes."

During the crisis period the composer evinced a marked interest in philosophical problems. Tchaikovsky had never adhered to any one philosophy. He was almost fifty when he declared it impossible clearly to formulate his symbol

of faith and to explain even for himself the "fateful questions" of life and death inasmuch as life with its eternal,
ceaseless bustle passed all too quickly. Tchaikovsky was
too busy living his life to waste time fruitlessly searching
for a solution of the riddle of the universe and formulating
abstract metaphysical conceptions. Nevertheless he could
not help being troubled by problems of this kind and he
searched for some philosophy that would support his own
views on the world and his aesthetic principles. In the period
we are now describing he took an interest in Schopenhauer
although a closer acquaintance with this philosopher drew
from him an indignant protest that in his writings there
was "something insulting to human dignity, something dry
and egoistic, unwarmed by love for humanity." Later on in
life Tchaikovsky was attracted by the radiant pantheism
and moral stoicism of Spinoza.

The eternal "yearning for the ideal," dissatisfaction and
striving for beauty and perfection made Tchaikovsky a
a prey to fits of scepticism with regard to existence in general. "An intelligent man cannot but be a sceptic. At any
rate, in his life there must be periods of painful scepticism,"
he wrote in 1877, the days of his inner conflict. He believed that religious faith might be the antidote to this
destructive scepticism. However, the ordinary traditional
Christian faith did not satisfy him. He spoke of the "tragedy
of a man inclined to scepticism" arising from the fact that
"having broken with the traditional faith and searching for
something to replace religion, he rushes vainly from one
philosophical theory to another in the hope of finding that
invincible force in life's struggle with which the religious
are armed." Christian methods were too rigorous, austere
and cold for Tchaikovsky, while the mystical element in all

religion clashed with man's "reasoning faculties" and the conclusions "reached by critical processes of the mind." The dogma of retribution for sins struck Tchaikovsky as "monstrously unjust and irrational." On the other hand, the conception of the hereafter as a serene untroubled existence and a state of eternal bliss he considered not only fantastic but extraordinarily flat, boring and unattractive. "I have come to the conclusion," he wrote, "that if there is indeed a life after death, it exists only in the sense that matter does not die and also in the pantheistic conception of the eternity of nature in which I constitute a microscopic phenomenon. In a word, I cannot understand individual immortality. Indeed, how can we conceive of an eternal future life of eternal pleasure? In order that there should be pleasure and bliss there must be its opposite—eternal suffering. The latter I repudiate altogether. Finally, I do not even know whether one should wish for a life after death, for the only charm that life has is the alternating joys and sorrows, the struggle between good and evil, light and darkness, in a word, the unity of opposites. How can eternity be conceived as endless bliss? According to our earthly understanding we would tire eventually of bliss too, if it were altogether unrelieved. As a result of this reasoning I have come to the conclusion that there is no eternity."

Judging by the full and direct grasp of the wealth and complexity of life in its multifarious aspects so well expressed in his quotation on life after death given above it may be said that Tchaikovsky was a realist. If he sometimes shied from the definition "realism," preferring the word "pantheism" or some other term instead, that was because he confused genuine and profound realism of the conception of the world with the then widely current cheap and vulgar physiological naturalism which he deeply abhorred. Referring to this subject in one of his letters Tchaikovsky maintained: "If by a realist one means a man who loathes all falsehood and lies in life as well as in art, then you are of course a realist." This definition might well have been applied to himself. With his violent detestation of falsehood he could find no consolation in fantastic and illusory conceptions and so he soberly accepted life as it was.

This does not mean that Tchaikovsky was always content with the life around him and did not wish to see a change for the better. On the contrary, it was precisely the sharp discord between his idealistic aspirations and the existing reality that was the cause of those insoluble contradictions in his nature of which he himself frequently said: "I am a mass of contradictions and were I to live to a ripe old age I should never make up my mind, never soothe my turbulent soul either with religion or philosophy."

His permanent and irreconcilable state of discord with his environment often compelled him to act contrary to his own innate desire and to live otherwise than as he would have wished. Although he was warmly attached to his relatives, he often spent long periods away from them, and passionately though he loved his country he was obliged to spend part of his life in strange lands. Wherever he was, he always yearned for home and yet he was forever haunted by some tormenting fateful fear of return. ". . . Russia is the only place to live in, and only by living elsewhere can one realize how deeply we love our native land, in spite of all its shortcomings," he writes. "But the trouble is," he adds, "that it is impossible for me to return to Russia." "Ah, how Russia beckons to me, my friend," he exclaimed on another occasion. "I think of her as the Jew thinks of Canaan. Yet my thoughts of her are most indefinite: how and where I shall go I am not at all sure yet."

It was not only circumstances of a personal nature that drove Tchaikovsky from his native land and aroused his fear of returning. The reason was deeper and more general. He shed some light on this question in a letter describing his arrival in Russia in the spring of 1878, after an absence of half a year. "I had thought that on entering Russia I would experience a strong sensation of joy. But no! There was nothing of the kind. On the contrary, the rude and drunken gendarme who would not allow us to pass for a long time because he could not understand whether the number of passports I had tendered corresponded to the individuals to whom they belonged; the customs official who searched our baggage and forced me to pay 14 gold rubles for dresses bought for my sister costing 70 francs, the gendarme officer who stared at me with suspicion and subjected me to a prolonged cross-examination before condescending to return my passport; the filthy cars . . . the huge hospital train filled with sick; the mass of young soldiers travelling with us, and the heart-rending scenes of parting with wives and mothers witnessed at every station* —all this spoiled my pleasure at seeing my native and dearly beloved country again."

Tchaikovsky drew a vivid picture of life in tsarist Russia in the depressing seventies when the gloom of reaction that reached its culminating point in the following decade hung like a thunder-cloud over the country. The soulless officialdom and the brutality of the established reactionary

* The scenes described had taken place during the Russo-Turkish War.

regime in Russia distressed the composer beyond words and
gave rise to that "depressing heartache" experienced during
this visit to St. Petersburg. The more he prized the poetic
aspect of his country, the beauty, the spiritual wealth and
moral integrity of the Russian, the more he suffered to see
how everything human was pitilessly crushed and disfigured
by the slavish conditions of existence. A consistent patriot,
Peter Ilyich invariably rejoiced in Russia's international
successes and was sincerely pained by her difficulties. He
had nothing but contempt for those of his countrymen who
spoke with scorn of the backwardness of their native land
and chose to live abroad. "These people are detestable to
me," he said, "they trample into the dust that which is
indescribably precious and sacred to me."

Tchaikovsky's political convictions were more conserva-
tive than radical. Nevertheless, he could not but condemn
that "form of government from which emanate all the
weakness, all the shady aspects of our political development" and yearn passionately with all the progressive people of his time for change.

The sharp and profound contradictions that permeated
the personal life of Tchaikovsky as well as his attitude to
his environment sometimes took the form of tragic conflict.
At the same time he was an utter stranger to any sort of
affectation of spiritual duality. Tchaikovsky never assumed
the effective guise of the languishing and romantic hero.
On the contrary, he invariably strove to find a way out of
his tormenting contradictions and sought a clear and positive answer to all the problems that racked his soul. This
search for an answer constituted the main element of his
music. Music had meaning for him insofar as it gave him
the opportunity to attain to the *ideal of harmonious unity*

and perfection of living which he could not find in real life. "Music alone brings enlightenment, reconciliation and peace," he said. "But it is not a straw to clutch at, it is a true friend, protector and consoler, and for it alone life is worth living."

5

Toward the eighties of last century Tchaikovsky's mode of life changed. His roving existence, the constant moving from place to place was beginning to weary him and he felt that the time had come to settle down in a home of his own. The selection of a place of residence was not a simple matter at first. The noise and bustle of Moscow and Petersburg were not conducive to fruitful work. On the other hand, a totally rustic existence did not appeal to him. ". . . I need society to a certain extent . . . Living alone in the country will not suit me. Where then shall I make my home?" Tchaikovsky wrote in the latter part of 1884. He settled finally on the outskirts of the small town of Klin, near Moscow, moving later to Klin itself.

Tchaikovsky nevertheless did not break off his diverse ties with the outside world. He frequently emerged from his retirement to visit foreign countries and cities. But these trips were no longer the aimless wanderings of a man who shunned society. Tchaikovsky now appeared before musical circles and the general public of Western Europe as a recognized and celebrated composer, a conscious representative of Russian music on the international concert stage. And he was keenly aware of the responsibility of his mission. "I have been welcomed here as a representative of all Russia," he wrote in 1888 from Prague, the capital of Czechia. "The first day was a grand triumph. Since then my visit has been a long array of all kinds of festivities, sightseeing tours, rehearsals, concerts, etc." Addressing the Czech national art society "Umelecki Beseda", which arranged an affair in his honour, Tchaikovsky said: "I must admit frankly and without undue modesty that the honours showered upon me so far exceed my services to art that they would have completely inundated and destroyed me had I not been able to separate that part that affects me personally from that which, through me, is accorded to something far higher and more important than myself."

Tchaikovsky was especially gratified by his warm and enthusiastic reception in the country of a Slavic people with whom he was bound not only by common ties of kinship and culture but also by numerous immediate associations of a personal and artistic nature. In the above speech he spoke of the outstanding role in the development of Russian musical culture of such talented Czech musicians as Napravnik, Ferdinand Laub, Grimali, Avranek and others, and stressed his intimate contact with them as fellow artists. Although he did not especially seek the favour of the West, Tchaikovsky nevertheless took great pride in the successes of Russian art abroad and noted with satisfaction the recognition accorded the great achievements of his country's art. For instance, on reading an appraisal of Leo Tolstoi by a distinguished French critic, he wrote in his diary: "I nearly wept with joy to see that our Tolstoi is so well understood by the French." And now he himself had the good fortune to contribute to the growth in the prestige and popularity of Russian art in Western Europe.

While success attended him wherever he went, Tchaikovsky's music was not equally well understood every-

where. It was in London that he found the deepest understanding and appreciation of his work notwithstanding the
fact that his visit to the British capital was extremely brief
and outwardly less spectacular than elsewhere. The reviews
in the London press, however, showed a profound and
serious interest in the work of the great Russian symphonist
and laid the foundation of a popularity that grew steadily as
time went on.

A year later Tchaikovsky made another successful concert tour abroad and in 1891 he went to America to which
country he had long been drawn. The trip and his sojourn
in the United States gave him a host of vivid impressions.
American life, the candour and sociability of the American
people pleased him immensely. ". . . The frankness, sincerity, generosity, open-hearted hospitality, the readiness to
oblige and assist are truly amazing and at the same time
touching," wrote Tchaikovsky in a special detailed diary
of his trip. "This, and the American way of living, American customs and morals in general I found very much to
my taste. . . ."

World music expressed its appreciation of Tchaikovsky's genius by conferring diverse honourary titles upon
him. Many foreign music societies had long since elected
him to their membership. At the end of 1892, he was elected
Corresponding Member of the French Institute and in the
same year was asked by Combridge University to accept
an honourary doctor's degree in music. The actual presentation ceremony took place in June 1893. Saint-Saëns, Arrigo
Boyto, Max Bruch and Eduard Grieg received the degree
at the same time.

It is difficult to reconcile the shattering tragic gloom
that pervades many of his latter compositions (e.g. "The

Queen of Spades" and the Sixth Symphony which the composer himself likened to a requiem) with the fact that Tchaikovsky at this period had attained the summits of fame and at last acquired the opportunity to follow his creative inclinations. Tchaikovsky alluded to this in a letter to Rathaus, a young poet for whom he had a warm affection. "I claim to be sincere in my music," he wrote, "nevertheless I too have a predilection like yourself for songs of wistful sadness. Yet latterly at any rate I do not suffer from want and can in general consider myself a fortunate man." This seeming contradiction arose from the fact that the destiny of humanity as a whole concerned Tchaikovsky and that personal well-being alone could not satisfy him. For the great artist and humanist genuine and unclouded happiness were impossible so long as misery and suffering existed in the world. He felt the misfortune of others as keenly as his own and the ugliness of the life he saw around him caused him much pain. Thus his personal tragedy was the tragedy of mankind as a whole.

Modeste Tchaikovsky, the composer's biographer, attributes the attacks of acute depression to which his brother was prey toward the end of his life to some new psychological crisis similar to that which he experienced in the seventies. "Death which settled the matter," he writes, "was accidental, but that it came at a turning point I have no doubt whatsoever and I cannot help feeling that during the years 1892 and 1893 Peter Ilyich stood on the shadowy threshold of a new and radiant revival."

We find a hint of this revival in some of Tchaikovsky's last works. The curiously tragic "Queen of Spades" was followed by "Yolanthe," an opera which culminates in a mighty hymn to the sun and is permeated with an all-conquering yearning for light and life. The basic idea of his two ballets "Sleeping Beauty" and "The Nutcracker" on fairytale themes is likewise the triumph of the radiant life-giving element over the forces of evil. And, finally, even the two most tragically conceived works, "The Queen of Spades", and the Sixth Symphony, ring with such a passionate reaching out for life and happiness that the hopelessness of the general mood is submerged to a considerable extent.

It is difficult to guess at the nature of this new phase in Tchaikovsky's art that might have been ushered in had he lived. One thing about which there can be no doubt whatever is that throughout his career he remained true to his principles of unequivocal sincerity, truthfulness and simplicity in giving expression to human emotions and experiences. Gentle and yielding in his personal life, Tchaikovsky was exceptionally consistent and firm in everything that concerned his artistic principles. He remained utterly untouched by the decadent tendencies, the withdrawal from reality into the realm of pure beauty, that predilection for artificiality and ultra-refinement that were current in art in the nineties and which partially affected even some of the leading and striking musical personalities of the time. Abhorring "anything false and lying either in life or in art," Tchaikovsky remained true to the end to his avowed credo of sincere and profound realism in art. His honesty both as a man and an artist, his nobility, moral integrity and the purity of his spiritual aspirations are at the root of the tremendous prestige Tchaikovsky enjoyed in his lifetime and also the beneficent influence his personality and his music exercise on the broad masses of people to this day.

OPERAS

B. YARUSTOVSKY

1. A Brief Review of Tchaikovsky's Operas

TCHAIKOVSKY FIRST CONCEIVED the idea of writing opera at the age of fourteen, when a humorous libretto entitled "Hyperbole" by one Olkhovsky, an obscure writer of the fifties of last century, captured his imagination.

The next idea for an opera, this time more fully conceived, was suggested by Ostrovsky's drama "The Tempest" which appeared in the early sixties. Like the first, this idea too was not destined to be realized, for the libretto had already been taken up by another composer (Kashperov).

Instead of "The Tempest," Ostrovsky offered the young Tchaikovsky another subject, namely, "Voyevoda," after the play "Dream on the Volga." The playwright had written only three scenes and it was left to the young composer as yet inexperienced in this field to finish it. In its final form the libretto was weak and, as the author himself admitted "devoid of dramatic interest and movement." And although the opera was written (1868) and produced, the composer considered it a failure and soon destroyed the score.* Only a few excerpts were used in his other compositions.

* Incidentally the orchestral parts of the opera "Voyevoda" have been preserved in full.

Tchaikovsky passed the same harsh judgment on his next attempt at opera, "Undine" (1869) after the poem by La Motte Fouqué, translated by Zhukovsky.

After a few persistent but fruitless attempts to write an opera on imaginative and historical themes (Alexander the Great, Mandragor, Raimon Lull and others), Tchaikovsky turned back to national themes.

The "Oprichnik" (after the tragedy by Lazhechnikov) contains many of the traits characteristic of the mature Tchaikovsky, chiefly the striving for vivid theatrical effects, and the accent on psychological drama.

The action of the opera takes place in Moscow, during the epoch of Ivan the Terrible (IV). Prince Zhemchuzhny who forges the will of his friend Morozov, so that the latter's son Andrei is left without an inheritance, tries to prevent his daughter Natasha from marrying Andrei whom she loves. Andrei resolves to take revenge. To this end he joins the tsar's *oprichniki* (a military organization mustered by Ivan the IV) but in doing so he violates the tradition of his family which is bitterly opposed to the *oprichniki*. Having earned the curses of his mother, Andrei endeavours to break with the *oprichniki*. The tsar consents to release him but on condition that he marries. At the wedding the tsar takes a fancy to Andrei's bride. In fighting to defend his wife's honour Andrei loses his life.

The central figure of this opera is Natasha, a gentle, impulsive creature. Andrei is likewise the typical Tchaikovsky hero—the passionate lover who perishes tragically in the end.

One of the most vivid episodes is the long aria of *Boyarina* Morozova and the scene in which the *oprichniki* take an oath. In broad flowing lines Tchaikovsky draws

the portrait of Andrei's mother, a woman with a strong
and sharply defined character, subtly and cleverly conveying the development and conflict of her emotions which
ends with the triumph of her will. Similarly epic in style
is the music of the scene in which the *oprichniki* take the
oath.

In the "Oprichnik" Tchaikovsky draws freely on Russian folk song both directly (choruses of girls in Act I, the
dances of the *oprichniki* in Act IV, etc.) and as material
for original melodies that are intensely national and melodious. Such, for example, is Natasha's magnificent arioso
"The Winds that Blow," which is replete with emotional
force and spiritual fervour.

At the same time "Oprichnik" is not quite mature, as is
evidenced in the somewhat mechanical utilization of certain traditional grand opera forms, and in the diversity of
the musical idiom. The composer frequently alluded to this
in later years and always intended revising the opera funda-
mentally.

In 1874, Tchaikovsky finished another opera "Vakula,
the Smith" (after the famous story by Gogol *) after the
libretto by Polonsky. The combination of the ordinary and
the fantastic, the brilliant scenes of St. Petersburg and the
poetic Ukrainian landscapes appealed tremendously to
Tchaikovsky. The opera was written in less than three
months. And again notwithstanding the rich and colourful

---

* The young blacksmith Vakula is in love with the lovely Oksana.
This wilful young girl demands as proof of Vakula's love that he get for
her the tsaritsa's slippers. Solokha, Vakula's mother, is rumoured to be
in league with the devil. And indeed the latter is one of her many admirers. One day Vakula finds the devil hidden in his sack and compels
him to carry him to St. Petersburg where the Empress Catherine presents
the handsome young blacksmith with her silver slippers. The opera ends
with the wedding of Oksana and Vakula.

plot (for example, the scene at Solokha's cottage in the second act), the composer concentrated his attention on the lyrical aspect of the story.

The opera literally brims with lyrical melodies. Its chamber forms, sharply distinct from "Oprichnik," seem to serve as the prelude to "Eugene Onegin." In 1885, Tchaikovsky again returned to "Vakula" and made a number of changes in the score altering the fabric of the plot, harmonious pattern, orchestration and especially the recitative. He even changed the name to "The Little Shoes."

"Eugene Onegin," written in 1877–88, was the immediate and effective expression of Tchaikovsky's advanced aesthetic views. The living, full-blooded characters of Pushkin's novel in verse and the realism of its situations gripped Tchaikovsky. "What a wealth of poetry there is in 'Onegin.' I am not mistaken, I know very well that there will not be much stage effect and action in this opera, but the pervading poetry, warmth and simplicity of the story combined with the brilliant text, will more than compensate for all the shortcomings," the author wrote in a letter to his brother while working on the opera.*

The composer concentrated his efforts on giving musi-

* The plot is briefly as follows: Lensky, a young poet, introduces his friend Onegin to Tatyana and Olga, the daughters of his neighbour, a country squire. The sophisticated young Onegin makes a deep impression on Tatyana. In the fullness of her pure young heart Tatyana writes him a letter confessing her love for him, but Onegin does not reciprocate. At a ball, given by the squire, Onegin, wishing to play a practical joke on his friend Lensky, flirts with Olga whom the young poet loves to distraction. In a fit of jealousy Lensky challenges Onegin to a duel and is killed. Several years pass and Onegin meets Tatyana again at a grand ball in St. Petersburg. She is married. Struck by her beauty and poise, Onegin falls madly in love with her but although she still loves him Tatyana does not want to defy the conventions. She sends him away and remains faithful to her husband.

cal expression to feelings and passions familiar to each and
every one of us. The cold, calculating Onegin in the opening scenes, the tender young love of Tatyana, the jealousy
of the love-sick poet and Onegin's subsequent infatuation
for Tatyana—the whole gamut of emotions is brilliantly
expressed in the music.

The intensely national characters, the poetic figures of
Tatyana and her old nurse, the life of the squires and the
peasants, the pictures of the Russian landscape all had a
vast attraction for the composer and offered tremendous
opportunities for drawing upon accustomed musical genres.
Such is the modest waltz at the ball in the Larin's home, the
formal Polonaise at the St. Petersburg ball, the old French
song by Beauplan used by Triquet, the French tutor, for
his birthday ode to Tatyana, Russian 19th century ballads
and love songs which influenced the quartet of the guests
in Act I, and other items. Russian peasant song intonations
formed the basis for the peasant chorus in the 1st scene, the
choruses of girls in the 3rd scene, etc. Though it would be
hard to find any direct "quotation" from musical folklore
in the arias, arioso or recitative of "Onegin," they nevertheless all bear such an affinity to folk melody, so faithfully
depict the dramatic state of the heroes that the singers have
no difficulty in memorizing the vocal pattern of large scenes.

Tchaikovsky called "Eugene Onegin" not an opera but
"Lyrical scenes." And no doubt in writing it he intended
not so much to create a musical performance with an
effective plot as to record the movement of human characters, to give musical interpretation to ideas and emotions he
himself had experienced. He often remarks that the characters in "Onegin" actually lived for him. "Tatyana and her
whole environment seems to come to life as I work. I love

Tatyana and was deeply outraged by Onegin whom I regarded as a cold, heartless fop. . . ."

There is little action in the opera. The author concentrated on the psychological scenes, on the development of the action in depth, as it were, on bringing out the spiritual world of his heroes. Such scenes as that of Tatyana's letter to Onegin, in which the soul of the young Russian girl is laid bare, the duel scene revealing the inner world of the young poet in love and the final scene showing the development of the love between Tatyana and Onegin are true masterpieces of operatic music.

Structurally these scenes form a single harmonious pattern that flows on in a continuous stream, the intonations of the recitative becoming crystallized and merging imperceptibly as a rounded arioso that develops organically into an emotional duet. As distinct from the endless Wagnerian melodies, however, the *caesura* determined by the development of the action, the vivid interweaving of the thematic pattern is easily distinguishable in Tchaikovsky's opera. A striking example are the three distinct melodic lines denoting the varying states of mind of Tatyana in the letter scene (confession of love, childhood memories and doubt).

Ever since it was first performed on December 16, 1878 on the small stage of the opera class at the Moscow Conservatory of Music, "Eugene Onegin" has been a permanent feature on the repertory of all Russian and many European opera houses. It is difficult to over-estimate the significance of this opera which not only blazed new trails in Tchaikovsky's own work but played a role of inestimable importance in the rise of Russian national opera as a whole.

A year after "Onegin" was written Tchaikovsky's interest was drawn to a libretto of an entirely different nature: "The Maid of Orleans" after Schiller. The heroic story of Jeanne D'Arc could obviously be told only in the powerful forms of grand opera. Here, too, as in all of his operas, Tchaikovsky laid the emphasis on the personal drama. The basic idea of his opera was not Jeanne's heroism but the inner conflict between her duty to society and her love for the knight Lionel.

Acts III and IV in which this love is unfolded contrast rather sharply with the first half of the opera which is rather more traditional in form. Toward the end of the opera the musical portrayal of Jeanne, warm and simple at the beginning, rises to great heights of emotional tension.

These varying stages in the development of the character are expressed in the long and moving aria in Act I "Farewell, my native hills and dales" and in the two grand duets in Acts III and IV replete with passionate feeling and romance. "The Maid of Orleans" is a musical drama that ranks with the leading grand operas of the world.

A far more important landmark in the development of Tchaikovsky's operatic works was "Mazeppa," after the poem "Poltava" by Pushkin.

The poem deals with one of the most turbulent periods in Russian and Ukrainian history in the 18th century. It juxtaposes the mighty figure of Peter I, the great transformer of Russia, and Mazeppa, an ambitious and adventurous Ukrainian hetman who strove to take advantage of the unrest in the country to seize power. To this end he did not hesitate to betray his country to his enemies.

Through the poem runs the theme of the tragic love of Maria, daughter of Kochubei, who is loyal to his sovereign, for the traitor Mazeppa.

The plot of "Poltava," the enchanting music of its verse inspired Tchaikovsky's muse. "One day I read through the libretto, read Pushkin's poem, was touched by some of the scenes and verses and began with the scene between Maria and Mazeppa. . . ." * It was this scene that became the central episode in the opera. What was of secondary importance to Pushkin took first place in Tchaikovsky's conception. The composer made many changes in Burenin's libretto to suit his purpose. In the opera Mazeppa's attitude to Peter is merely touched upon. Kochubei as a dramatic figure is also confined to the role of his daughter's avenger. The character of Maria's suitor Andrei, the tragic story of the Kochubei family, the introduction of folk scenes all merely served to bring the main dramatic line of the opera into bolder relief.

For example, the very first female chorus, pensive and sorrowful, introduces us to Maria's state of mind and gives us a presentiment of the tragic outcome of her fatal love for Mazeppa.

The drunken Cossack episode in the scene of Kochubei's execution serves the same purpose. Its somewhat coarse

* The beautiful Maria, daughter of Kochubei, is attracted to the hetman Mazeppa. Her father withholds his consent to the marriage. Maria defies her father and goes to Mazeppa's castle. Kochubei and Maria's fiancé Andrei resolve to inform Tsar Peter of Mazeppa's treason. The ambitious Mazeppa intends to betray his country and help the Swedes. When he learns that he has been betrayed, Mazeppa executes the old Kochubei. Mazeppa then flees the country together with the remains of Charles XII's army smashed by the Russians. Andrei, filled with the desire for revenge, overtakes him but dies at his hand. Maria loses her reason.

humour is deliberately set off against the tragedy of Maria whose aged father is hanged before her eyes.

Maria and Mazeppa, the leading characters in the opera, are profoundly realistic figures. With great mastery Tchaikovsky reveals the spiritual world of his heroes, the "movement" of the character from one emotional state to another. Maria passes from unconscious happiness through struggle (3rd and 4th scenes) to the tragic finale where, already bereft of her senses, she sings a lullaby over the dead body of her bridegroom.

Tchaikovsky's Mazeppa is an extremely complex character: Although a definitely negative type, he is not altogether evil. His love for Maria is both powerful and sincere. Two leitmotifs are used for his musical portrayal. The first appears in the overture; it draws Mazeppa as a warlike "aggressive" figure with a fatal power over Maria. In the 2nd scene of Act II, when Mazeppa indulges in ambitious pipe dreams, there appears the triumphant march-like second motif which is more fully elaborated in the scene of Kochubei's execution.

Besides the individual numbers (arias, choruses, etc.), the structure of the opera includes also long and elaborate dramatic scenes. These scenes constitute the backbone of the action.

Such, for instance, is the finale of Act I (the scene of Kochubei's conspiracy), the dénouement, the prison scene, Maria and Mazeppa, the execution of Kochubei and the lullaby scene. The dramatic tension rises from scene to scene, culminating in a finale of Shakespearean power.

Each scene resembles a large canvas painted in rich colours. It is this quality that induced Academician Assafyev to compare the execution scene from "Mazeppa" with

Surikov's painting entitled "The Morning of the Streletsk Execution." The masterful development of the folk elements of the theme, the pliant, severe rhythms, the gradual unfoldment of the solemn procession to the scaffold, the vivid contrasting effect of the drunken Cossack episode— all these elements woven organically one into the other to create a scene of exceptional dramatic force.

In the prison scene and in Mazeppa's castle Tchaikovsky treats the tragedy of his heroes with the poignant lyricism of which he was a great master. Kochubei's gentle arioso arouses compassion for Maria's tormented old father.

Profound realism and expressiveness of character portrayal are achieved by Tchaikovsky in Act II. Maria's love and jealousy, the despair and hatred of her mother who comes to beg Maria to save her father, the ambition of Mazeppa—all this gamut of human emotions is reflected in the music. The emotional tension soars to great heights of lyrical pathos in these arias.

In the scoring of "Mazeppa" Tchaikovsky's symphonic genius is revealed, e.g. the introduction, entr'acte to the last act ("Battle of Poltava").

The idea for his next opera was conceived by Tchaikovsky in 1834 after viewing "The Enchantress," a five-act tragedy produced with great success both in the Moscow Maly Theatre and subsequently in St. Petersburg. So taken was he with the effective dramatic situations of this play that he immediately requested the author to write an opera libretto for him.

Here is the story. Nastasya, the leading character, is the keeper of an inn of such ill repute that the prince of Novgorod determines to expose and destroy her. Instead,

however, he himself falls a victim to her charms. Mad with
jealousy, his wife, the princess, sends her son Yuri to slay
the evil creature. Apprised of his coming, Nastasya goes
out to meet him and bewitches him too. They resolve to
flee together. The opera ends tragically when the princess,
taking matters into her own hands, comes to Nastasya dis-
guised as a pilgrim and poisons her. The prince loses his
mind after slaying his son Yuri in a fit of jealousy.

Again we have the theme of tragic love combined with
a powerful and striking female character. As usual Tchaikovsky makes this the pivot of the action. As in his other
operas Nastasya's two magnificent ariosos—"To Glance
from Nijni" in Act I, and "Where art Thou, Loved One"
in the last act, outline the basic phases in the evolution of
the heroine, who represents the passionate and lyrical Russian type of womanhood. The high points of the opera are
concentrated in Act III in the scenes with the prince and
especially with Yuri, in which light is thrown on the diverse
aspects of Nastasya's spiritual world. As far as the folk
scenes are concerned this opera is perhaps the most vivid
and colourful of all Tchaikovsky has written. Act I with its
wealth of folk songs and dances and humorous dialogue
presented against the background of the inn perched on the
steep bank of the Oka is unfolded like a vast picturesque
canvas.

"The Enchantress" is the only Tchaikovsky opera built
up on the principle of the through line of action * instead
of the usual division into separate items. The composer
makes skilful use of the orchestra to cement the various
opera forms into the required sequence with the result that

* A term coined by Stanislavsky denoting the conduct of one idea
throughout from beginning to end.

the small melodious ariosos, the expressive recitative, choruses a capella, abundant ensembles, including the decimet in which each voice has an independent function—are woven into a single melodic pattern held together by the delicate symphonic thread of the orchestra. . . .

The "Queen of Spades," written in 1890 after the story by Pushkin, is correctly regarded as the pinnacle of Tchaikovsky's achievement in musical drama.

Its leading idea—that of the fatal conflict between the striving for happiness and the pitiless force of destiny —is the theme of his latter symphonies, including the Sixth.

Herman, the hero, is not merely a gambler; he is a man accursed with a restless, tormented soul, gripped by the struggle between two conflicting forces—his tender love for Lisa and a consuming desire to win at cards. The latter becomes an obsession with him and finally robs him of his reason and leads to the tragic death of Lisa. The Fatum idea is embodied in the person of the aged countess who holds the secret of the three lucky cards.

The music of "The Queen of Spades" lays bare the subtle psychological process by which Herman's mind is gradually clouded by his obsession. Most striking is the 5th scene (in the barrack-room) where Herman recalls the funeral of the countess and his befuddled brain conjures up the image of the deceased. The composer reveals the struggle between the conscious and the unconscious through the interplay of two musical images—a bugle call representing the tangible world, and a funeral chorus as a reminder of death.

Gradually against the background of the slow, solemn funereal theme rises the convulsive, nervous, distorted melody of Herman's recitative with startlingly dramatic effects.

Both in this scene as well as in the scene of the Countess' death the orchestra is an important dramatic factor. It accentuates the action as well as emotionally complementing it. Take the brilliant key episode in the third scene. At this point Herman is still wavering between his love for Lisa and his passion for gambling; the latter has not yet taken full possession of his soul. The orchestral leitmotif of the three cards leading up to his recitative remark: "Three cards to know and I am rich," changes suddenly to the gentle theme that is Lisa's and to Herman's words: "Oh to see her soon and abandon these wild fancies." This orchestral and vocal dialogue is repeated and leads up to Herman's brief remark ("What if") the meaning of which is explained by the three-card theme sounding ominously in the low registers of the clarinet and bassoon as Herman decides to take advantage of his relations with Lisa to obtain a personal audience with the Countess and force her to reveal the coveted secret.

The opera abounds in similar examples of brilliant utilization of the orchestra to obtain powerful dramatic effects.

All analogous episodes are built up on the principle of "through action," combined with the ordinary opera numbers depicting the objective world rather than subjective emotions. Such is the charming scene in which Lisa and her friends sing duets, sentimental love songs and Russian folk dance tunes.

Such also is the grand society ball in the 3rd scene with the dazzling Polonaise and the colourful pastorale intermezzo.

"The Queen of Spades" is at the same time the most symphonic of Tchaikovsky's operas. The music is exceptionally monolithic in form thanks to the straightforward development of the leading idea of the drama. The principal leitmotifs representing the two opposing forces—love and the card secret—are evolved with amazing mastery both in the vocal scores and in the orchestra.

Through the varied development of melody, harmony and timbre the leitmotifs are imperceptibly transformed depending upon the movement of the dramatic force they are intended to express. In the key scene, for example, the tender love motif acquires a note of ominous warning.

*   *   *

"Yolanthe," the one-act opera written two years before Tchaikovsky's death, is based on a comparatively little known drama by Henrick Herze, a Danish poet, entitled "The Daughter of King René." In the revised version by the composer's brother, Modeste Tchaikovsky, the libretto and opera were given the title "Yolanthe" after the name of the heroine, the blind daughter of the King of Provence. At her father's desire she grew up in solitude, unaware of her affliction. A famous physician (Ebn-Jahia, a Moor) declared that only the realization of her blindness and the passionate desire to see the light will cure her. Love comes to the maiden's assistance in the person of Count Vaudemont, the knight, who wanders by accident into the royal garden. He falls in love with Yolanthe at first sight and perceiving her affliction he tells her the truth. The king discovers Vaudemont in the garden and condemns him to death unless Yolanthe is cured of her blindness. Yolanthe is willing to suffer any ordeal to save the knight whom she loves. The Moor cures her and the king consents to the marriage of the two young people.

Here again we have Tchaikovsky's favourite theme—the birth and development of strong emotion. As in his other operas, it is ushered in gently and unostentatiously. A soft, undulating chorus and ensemble and the romantic berceuse form a delicate background for the passionate lyrical arioso of Yolanthe ("Why did I not know before . . ."). The heightened restlessness of spirit and the awakening of the unfamiliar and exquisite sensation of love are masterfully conveyed in her scene with Vaudemont. The opera ends with a hymn to light and life.

The score of this opera is a document testifying to the great professional mastery and creative maturity of the composer. The overture itself which is exclusively wind and brass, presents an enchanting picture of Yolanthe's world executed in soft pastel shades.

The opera is exceptionally melodious. Both the main scenes as well as the secondary parts constitute magnificent examples of Tchaikovsky's gift for melody (e.g., King René's sorrowful arioso "May God forgive me if I have sinned," the ornamental monologue of the Moorish physician, the passionate aria by Robert, Vaudemont's friend).

The significance of Tchaikovsky's operatic works is by no means limited to his role in the history of Russian opera. His influence made itself felt to a considerable degree in Western European musical drama of the latter 19th and early 20th centuries. His Lisa and Herman, Onegin and Mazeppa were the prototypes of a whole series of heroes of many French and Italian operas.

Like Bizet's "Carmen," Tchaikovsky's operas are a happy combination of the old traditional operatic forms and a genuinely novel approach to the portrayal of human characters, the diverse utilization and mutual complementing of recitative and arioso with orchestra and vocal parts. That is why his operas are so popular with all strata of the population in all countries of the world.

Although he wrote in all operatic genres—grand, comic and lyrical—Tchaikovsky invariably concentrated his attention mainly on the inner world of his heroes. In this sense his operas might in all justice be called lyrico-psychological. In this genre Tchaikovsky was an innovator and this is perhaps his most valuable contribution to world opera.

In the Soviet Union the popularity of Tchaikovsky's operas has grown by leaps and bounds. Performances of "Eugene Onegin" and "The Queen of Spades," the two most frequently performed operas on the Soviet stage, invariably draw capacity audiences in the large opera houses of Moscow, Leningrad and many other Soviet cities. In 1938 the Moscow Bolshoi Theatre gave its 800th performance of "Onegin." The familiar arias of Tatyana, Lisa, Onegin and Herman are now sung for the first time in the Tatar, Uzbek and Belorussian languages. Young opera singers of all the national republics of the Soviet Union consider it their primary duty to acquaint their audiences with the inspired images of "Eugene Onegin" and "The Queen of Spades" in addition to their national operas. The scores of Tchaikovsky operas are studied not only by professional Soviet opera artists but also by amateur opera circles in the clubs of textile workers and engineers, typesetters and metal workers. Tchaikovsky's operas may truly be said to belong to the people.

On the occasion of the centenary of the great composer's birth in 1940 dozens of opera houses all over the country vied with one another for the best production of his works. The Moscow Bolshoi Theatre staged a revival of "Yolanthe," his last opera. Two other productions, "The Little Shoes" in the Bolshoi Theatre and "The Enchantress" in the Leningrad Opera House were awarded the Stalin Prize, the highest award in the country. "Mazeppa" is a permanent feature on the repertory of Soviet opera houses, "The Maid of Orleans" has been revived by the Saratov Opera Company. Such outstanding Soviet opera artists as Leonid Sobinov, Davydova, Kruglikova, Shpiller, Lemeshev, Nortzov, Preobrazhenskaya, Dzerzhinskaya, Kozlovsky, Migai and Khanayev have created some unforgettable Tchaikovsky roles.

The 50th anniversary of Tchaikovsky's death saw several new productions of his operas, with Soviet opera companies exerting greater effort than ever before to do justice to the great Russian composer.

II. *How Tchaikovsky Wrote His Operas*

Tchaikovsky's attitude to opera as a musical genre was not always the same. Although he spoke favourably about opera on many occasions and was constantly working in opera scores, he sometimes felt that he could not work in what he called a "false genre." These sentiments however, were rare, the result of a nervous reaction usually following some unsuccessful premiere. As a rule, opera always interested Tchaikovsky. "Opera alone," he wrote in a letter to von Meck on September 27, 1885, "brings you in close touch with people . . . makes your music accessible not only to exclusive circles but given favourable conditions to the whole people." "But," he said in another letter to von Meck dated November 27, 1879, "on the other hand, opera has the advantage that it enables one to speak the language of the masses."

Tchaikovsky chose more than 30 literary works as subjects for operas he wrote or intended to write * in the course of his life. They include historical subjects ("Boris Godunov," "The Oprichnik," "The Maid of Orleans," "Cinq Mars"), imaginative subjects ("Mandragore," "Undine" and "Watanabe") and Russian folklore themes ("Vanka, the Steward," "Sadko"), as well as masterpieces of Shakespeare and Musset, novels by French writers (Ch. Nodier and others) and the poetry of Pushkin and Lermontov.

Tchaikovsky used only 10 ** of these as librettos for his operas and even among these 10 there were a few ("Voye-

---

* This is the number established by documents. According to other information there were undoubtedly many more.

** "Voyevoda," libretto by Ostrovsky, 1868.

"Undine," libretto by Sollogub after De La Motte Fouqué, translated by Zhukovsky, 1869 (destroyed by the author).

"Oprichnik," libretto by Tchaikovsky after Lazhechnikov (1872).

"Vakula the Smith," libretto by Polonsky after Gogol (1874).

"Eugene Onegin," libretto by Tchaikovsky with the collaboration of Shilovsky, after Pushkin (1878).

"The Maid of Orleans," libretto by Tchaikovsky after Schiller, translated by Zhukovsky, Barbier (1879).

"Mazeppa," libretto by Burenin (revised by Tchaikovsky), 1883.

"The Little Shoes," libretto by Polonsky after Gogol (new revision of "Vakula the Smith"), 1885.

"The Enchantress," libretto by Shpazhinsky, 1887.

"The Queen of Spades," libretto by Modeste Tchaikovsky, 1890.

"Yolanthe," libretto by Modeste Tchaikovsky after Hartz-Zvontsev ("The Daughter of King René"), 1891.

voda" "Oprichnik" and partly "The Enchantress") whose choice he subsequently regretted.

For an opera to be a success its subject must be intensely *emotional*. Tchaikovsky clearly understood the nature of opera, he knew that truth and realism in opera are most effectively manifested in subjects which afford opportunity for the maximum elaboration of the emotional sphere through the action, the melody, the vocal and orchestral parts.

In a letter to J. I. Shpazhinskaya (wife of the author of the "The Enchantress" libretto) Tchaikovsky spoke of his desire "to write a small opera in three acts on some subject of an intimate nature affording *wide opportunities for the flow of lyrical feeling.*" He was delighted with the moving love story of "Romeo and Juliet." In his famous letter to Stasov (April 8, 1877) Tchaikovsky wrote that he "needed a subject in which the dramatic motif would predominate, for example, love (maternal, sexual—it is immaterial), jealousy, ambition, patriotism. . . ."

While stressing the importance of emotionality for opera subjects, Tchaikovsky repeatedly pointed out that the emotions must needs be profoundly *human*. "I am searching for intimate yet powerful drama founded on a conflict of situations that I myself have experienced or witnessed and that can touch me to the quick." * In a letter to Fedotova (February 21, 1892) in reply to the offer of the imaginative story of "Watanabe," Tchaikovsky wrote: "I can be happy writing music on a subject that may not be at all effective so long as the characters inspire my sympathy, so long as I love and *feel* for them as one loves and *feels* for living people. . . ." And further "lastly, a considerable

* Letter to Sergei Taneyev, Jan. 2, 1878.

obstacle also is the fact that I avoid foreign subjects in general for it is only the Russian man, the Russian girl, the Russian woman that I really know and understand. Mediaeval dukes, knights and ladies may capture my imagination but *not my heart*, and where the heart is not touched there can be no music."

There you have Tchaikovsky's credo in the selection of subject for opera. This explains his rejection of such themes as "Raimon Lull," "Ephraim," "Cinq Mars" and others of the same nature. It explains also why he could not accept the imaginative "Nal and Damayanti" used subsequently by Arensky. "It is too far removed from life. . . ." Tchaikovsky said, explaining his rejection of the plot. . . . 'I need something like 'Cavalleria Rusticana' or 'Carmen.' "

Perhaps this explains also why Tchaikovsky was later disappointed with "The Maid of Orleans" and "Undine," subjects which captured the imagination but did not touch the heart.

This too is the reason for the composer's distaste for the subjects of Wagner's operas and to some operas by Verdi.* "Goodness, how boring, and notwithstanding the brilliant mastery, how false, how senseless is the whole absurd business," Tchaikovsky remarked to his brother Modeste, after hearing Wagner's "Parsifal" (1884). It struck him as absurd to force "some sort of mythological fantastic creatures, some fanciful beings" to sing. *"Only living flesh-and-blood people can sing,"* said the composer in one of his letters on the subject. The emotions of "real, flesh-and-blood people"

---

* "I need people, not dolls," he wrote with reference to Verdi's "Aida." "I do not know, I do not understand the feelings of an Egyptian princess, a pharaoh or some crazy Nubian."

was the second prerequisite Tchaikovsky demanded for operatic librettos.

On the other hand, these "simple people with their simple human passions and feelings" should not be primitive characters. Inner contrasts and conflicts were essential for the development of the characters.

As we shall see further on, Tchaikovsky concentrated his attention on the inner conflict of his characters in his own librettos ("Mazeppa," "Maid of Orleans," etc.).

In the light of these views on the opera subject it is not hard to understand Tchaikovsky's remarkable *constancy* of interests in this respect from the very beginning of his career and ending with the pinnacle of his operatic achievement, "The Queen of Spades." One of the first subjects for opera that attracted him when he was still a student at the St. Petersburg Conservatory was Ostrovsky's "The Tempest." The powerful story of the heroine whose passion leads her to her destruction strongly impressed the young composer and struck him as the perfect subject for an opera. Indeed, one could scarcely find anything more emotional and human than the part of Katerina.

* * *

Brevity and dynamic development of action are two principal features of subject for opera as Tchaikovsky saw it. Given these qualities it was possible to revise the story in drawing up the libretto, strip it of all extraneous dramatic lines, superfluous dialogue scenes * and create a maximum number of emotionally active situations, episodes revealing the play of passions.

* This is precisely the distinguishing feature both of the drama theatre as well as of some trends in opera (*e.g.* Meyerbeer, and others).

"After mature consideration," Tchaikovsky wrote with reference to Pushkin's "Captain's Daughter," "I have come to the conclusion that this is not a subject for opera. It is too diffuse, and requires too much talk, explanation and action unsuitable for musical portrayal." "It is impossible to present such subtly conceived detail on the stage," he observed with regard to a play by Samarin, one of his contemporaries. He also considered it quite impossible to reproduce on the opera stage the final scene of "Othello." "The whole scene following the appearance of Emilia is extraordinarily difficult to express in music," he said to Stasov on this question. "Cinq Mars" by de Vigny was rejected for similar reasons. "The subject is too gaudy, too crowded with interests, effects, altogether too complex and overwhelming. . . ."

In his correspondence with the librettist Shpazhinsky, Tchaikovsky compared the development of the subject in drama with that in opera. "In drama you have the opportunity of exciting flagging interest by inserting some popular scenes, or snatches of brilliant dialogue—in opera (where all this is only partly possible) compactness and speed of action are the main things, otherwise the composer will not have enough strength to write the music nor will the audience have the patience to listen to it." "Lack of dramatic movement and too much philosophizing" caused Tchaikovsky to reject Alfred Musset ("Lovenzaccio," "Andrea del Sarto") much as he admired this author's work.*

Thus, emotionality (lyrical emotion for the most part),

* Tchaikovsky later (on April 28, 1874) gave as the reason for his disappointment with "The Oprichnik" the following explanation: ". . . there is no movement, no style in this opera. . . ."

compactness and at the same time intensity of development, contrast of moods and inner conflict of emotion in character portrayal were the basic *factors* Tchaikovsky demanded of opera subject.

* * *

Tchaikovsky had an amazing flair for grasping the essence of the dramatic development of an opera subject. Describing the content of "Yolanthe" in a letter to Valtz in 1891, Tchaikovsky wrote: "the *principal motif* of my last opera upon which I am now working is the *absence* of light and sun." His interest in a subject and his *perception* of the idea of an opera always came to Tchaikovsky through the culminating point, the elaboration of this idea, and the clash between the two main contrasting characters (Maria and Mazeppa in "Mazeppa"; the Godmother and Yuri in "The Enchantress," the scene in the Countess' bedroom in "The Queen of Spades"; Jeanne and Lionel in "The Maid of Orleans"; Yolanthe and Vaudemont in "Yolanthe"; the garden scene in "Vanka the Steward," etc.).

The idea of a piece of work as well as its development had to be clearly worked out in his mind before he tackled a libretto for his operas. "Berg, the poet, has suggested that I write an opera on the subject of the Hussites and Taborites. When I asked him whether he had any sort of plan worked out in his mind he said he hadn't. He only fancied the hymns." This was Tchaikovsky's ironic comment on some so-called libretto writers who did not understand the basic requirements of drama.*

* It is highly indicative in this connection that up to the last day of his life Tchaikovsky did not give up the idea of revising those of his operas which did not satisfy him from the standpoint of the reflection of the dramatic idea. In 1885 he revised "Vakula." In 1878 he outlined alterations for "Undine," in 1885, for "Oprichnik," in 1893, five days before his death, "The Maid of Orleans."

The next stage of Tchaikovsky's work on the scenario and libretto of his future opera was to condense the action, concentrate the dramatic material, simplify it to the maximum and at the same time strengthen the main dramatic line, stripping the plot of all dramatic situations of secondary importance. The composer's method of work on opera is revealed to some extent by his correspondence with Stasov regarding his plan for the opera "Othello." Tchaikovsky proposed deleting the 1st scene (the street), and beginning the action directly with the scene in the Council ("Brabantio runs in and reports the disappearance of Desdemona"). Expressing his approval of the successful deletion of several of the dramatis personae (Montano and others), he suggested that the plot could be still further simplified: "Could not Bianca be dispensed with in Act IV and have the handkerchief scene without her, for instance: couldn't Iago bring the handkerchief? . . ." *

I could cite many more examples showing how Tchaikovsky sought to rid his libretto of superfluous scenes, parallel dramatic lines and secondary characters.

At the same time, the composer concentrated his attention on bringing out and developing the principal dramatic line, which, since it expressed the leading idea of the opera, had to be brought out into the boldest relief. In the same correspondence with Stasov regarding "Othello," Tchaikovsky asked him to revise the development of the handkerchief intrigue ("the handkerchief incident must be made to stand out much more"), and to introduce the action more vividly. "It seems to me that the relations of the characters to one another must be explained to the audience in every detail in Act I, in Venice; the drama should begin later on in Cyprus, developing rapidly from there until it

* This is precisely what Verdi did (see his letter to A. Boyto).

culminates in Venice." This striving for clarity of dramatic
line led Tchaikovsky to rewrite the 6th scene of his
brother's libretto for the opera "The Queen of Spades." *

*   *   *

The development of the intrigue to the culmination
point is usually built up on the principle of "repetitive complexes," *i.e.*, a repetition of the dramatic element, but each
time in a new situation and on a higher emotional plane.
This principle, combined with the through line of action
is widely employed in Tchaikovsky's operas both as regards the composition of the opera as a whole, as well as
for separate scenes and episodes. Take scene 2 of "The
Queen of Spades," for example. The "through" action of
this scene is the affirmation of Lisa's love for Herman. The
method is a triple recurrence of the stage and emotional
situations: after the "main episode" (the love song, duet
and dance) Lisa remains alone, her emotional state gradually
changes and the dramatic tension notably increases; the
culminating point is reached with the entrance of Herman.
A second emotional wave ensues, rising to another culmination with the entrance of the Countess, and, finally, the
third "wave" and culmination complete the scene. Each
of these waves proceeds on a higher emotional plane than
the preceding one. The same structural principle is to be
found in the letter scene in "Onegin," in the scene of the
Godmother and the Prince, the scene of the conspiracy in
"Mazeppa," in all *principal* scenes. This principle, moreover,

* "I think that the 6th scene is better now. I am very glad that it is
there because it rounds out the opera," "it gives a pretext for introducing
Lisa's aria and later on explains Herman's madness. . . ." (to brother
Modeste February 26, 1890).

has two important advantages: 1) it rounds out a scene (or an act) and gives it a greater finish, and 2) it bears a remarkable affinity to the individual traits of Tchaikovsky's *symphonic* music, especially to the guiding principle of his symphonic development which is also based on the alternation of several successively developing emotional waves.

The same principle of scene structure Tchaikovsky applied also when working on librettos for his operas.

Tchaikovsky frequently wrote much of his librettos himself discarding the *ready-made* scenes. The libretto of "Mazeppa," for example, was written by Burenin for K. Davydov who gave it to Peter Ilyich. The composer, however, felt that the more important scenes required revision to conform with his *own* method, for he had already conceived the plan for the music. It was not until he had made these changes that he finally decided, after long hesitation, to write the opera.

* * *

Finales (likewise built up on the principle of repetitive complexes) play an extremely important role in Tchaikovsky's operas. In all, except "The Queen of Spades," no less than two acts end in a finale. In such a "major" opera as "The Maid of Orleans" the importance of finales is obvious. In other operas only the "mixed" acts (scenes), built up on alternating dramatic episodes, with "neutral material," end in finales (*e.g.* in "Onegin, only the 4th scene). Instead of finales most of the *"major"* scenes (acts), where the main conflicts are concentrated, have concluding scenes which, though extremely intensive as to the action, are nevertheless confined to "chamber" execution and are conducted on a single plane. Herein lies the difference in the use of finale as a dramatic form in Tchaikovsky's opera and in classical opera.

Nevertheless, the finales in Tchaikovsky's operas (as also in comic opera) often serve as the most important culmination in the development of scenes and dramatic conflict. In "The Little Shoes," for example, the finale of Act II is the summary of the action up to this point; put out by Oksana's coldness, Vakula departs, resolving to do away with himself. At the same time, the finale here includes both the summary and an auxiliary comic line—the scene of the opening of the sacks. In the finale of Act IV of the same opera, yearning for Vakula is followed by general rejoicing at his return.

Thus, every finale is a concentration of the dramatic action with the affirmation at the end of the triumph of one of the conflicting ideas. In this sense the finale always marks a high point in the development of the action.

This triumph in the finale is very often set forth in the conflict by *alternating* the contrasting mood of the dramatic situations. For instance, in the finale of "Vakula" the action develops from despondency to rejoicing, while in the finale of Act III of "The Maid of Orleans" the order is reversed.

All the texts of the finales provide for the participation of ensembles and choruses * but, as distinct from classical opera, the treatment of the chorus is not active. The undifferentiated choral mass is usually not a subject of the action as, for example, in Meyerbeer operas, but serves either merely to add to the tension, or as a contrasting background for the personal drama.

In Tchaikovsky's operas the composition of the dramatic

* An exception is the finale to the last act of "Mazeppa," although the original version included a chorus scene.

episodes in the big finale scenes is nearly always presented in chamber form with the participation of the two leading characters. Large complex mass scenes such as occur in operas by Meyerbeer or Mussorgsky are totally absent in Tchaikovsky opera. On the contrary, all the action in the dramatic culmination episodes in his operas is concentrated *exclusively* on the leading characters; in these scenes it is unfolded in depth, so to speak, confining the movement to the *inner* psychological world of the dramatis personae.

* * *

The placing of the arias and other complete numbers was one of the composer's primary concerns in working on the libretto.

In each case his method was the same: having established the emotional "curve" of development of a given character, and chosen some high point in the curve as the suitable place for the aria he would look for a rhymed text of a correspondingly lyrical and emotional nature. Writing to Shpazhinsky on the subject of a text, Tchaikovsky said: "You will have to write 12 or 16 lines of text if possible in rhyme and purely lyrical in quality. . . ." (letter to Shpazhinsky January 2, 1886).

As often as not the place and the nature of the ensemble was also indicated in the scenario. Almost invariably this would follow some event marking a *turning point* in the development of the action and calculated to evoke a general emotional reaction on the part of the characters, and frequently changing their relationships. In the scenario of "The Maid of Orleans," for example, we find the following remark to Act I: "Everyone believed in Jeanne. Ensemble";

in Act II after the proclamation of victory: "all are moved and weep, then begins the rejoicing—loud and melodious ensemble"; in Act IV, after the "sign" from above: "peals of thunder—ensemble."

The ensemble thus becomes an important means of treating *different* characters *simultaneously* under the influence of a *single* event; this is a great advantage of drama in opera.

Extremely characteristic, especially of Tchaikovsky's later operas, is the importance of the dramatic duets as vehicles of the main dramatic line. In lyrical scenes the duet is indispensable as a means of demonstrating the *communion* of spirit uniting the emotions of the hero and heroine. When it is necessary to show the *contrasting* states of the two leading characters, the text of the duet often consists of a dramatic juxtaposition of the different attitudes of the two characters to the *same* object. The two duets in "The Queen of Spades," for example, included in the scenario at the insistence of the composer (Yeletsky and Herman in the 1st scene and Herman and Lisa in the 6th scene) bring out the contrast in the state of mind of the characters by conveying a different reaction in the first instance to the events of a single day ("Happy day"), and in the second instance to the realization of the truth (Lisa—"So it is true that I have linked my destiny to a scoundrel. . . ." Herman—"Yes, it is true, I know the three cards"). This makes it possible, firstly, to justify uniting two characters having different emotional states in *one* ensemble, and secondly, to give a more vivid portrayal of these emotional states by means of contrasts.

*   *   *

Before receiving the finished libretto Tchaikovsky gave much thought to the subject and the characters of the future opera, allowing the idea gradually to take possession of him. It was at this stage that the leitmotif of the opera would be born. This is what happened in the case of "The Queen of Spades." It was the central dramatic episode that captured his creative imagination first. "At first I scoffed at the idea of writing an opera on the subject of 'The Queen of Spades'" he wrote, "then it occurred to me that the scene in the Countess's bedroom was magnificent, and that started it. . . ."

The very day he arrived in Florence Tchaikovsky bought a notebook to jot down the draft score (on the first page is the date of purchase—Jan. 18, 1890). Inasmuch as the order in which the entries are made in this book * coincides with the order of the creative process, we are justified in assuming that the first entries in this notebook were indeed the *first musical images* of the future opera. All of the notes relate to the 4th scene. They are as follows:

First comes the outline of an intense, ostinato background for the introduction.

Next come two laconic images of sharply contrasted structure: the first (beside it Tchaikovsky wrote: *"the beginning"*) is jerky, with the accent on the rhythm; it is static inasmuch as it contains no hint of inner movement, its structure has much in common with all the motifs associated with the image of the Countess (rhythmic pattern, general secundo intonation, etc.) The second motif, on the other hand, is deeply emotional and triste in mood.

* The order is as follows: main themes of the 4th scene, chorus theme for 1st scene, song theme for 2nd scene, theme of Lisa's aria in 2nd scene, duet for 2nd scene, Herman's arioso for 4th scene, Lisa's arioso for 6th scene, duet for 6th scene, Herman's arioso for 7th scene.

"Somewhat plaintive," * is the composer's note in the margin.

In intonation this motif has very much in common with the main theme of the third movement of the Second Quartet, with the themes of the "Chanson d'Automne" from the "Four Seasons," and partly with the theme of the finale of the Sixth Symphony.

The second motif has an element of activity and aspiration, which is immediately followed by elements paralyzing activity. These intonations are closely associated with the melodic pattern of the characters representing the "living" human element in the opera as opposed to the Fatum idea.

The third motif, outlined independently from the rest of the opera, is the theme of the card secret. Its most characteristic exposition is to be found in the final episode of the 4th scene, *i.e.*, the moment of the fatal clash of the two main characters (lower register, augmented scale, etc.).

In these laconic themes is contained the tragedy of a strong nature, a nature that loves life but is helpless in the face of "destiny." The introduction to the fourth scene of the opera is actually the generalization in symphonic imagery of the *whole* of the action of "The Queen of Spades." In this sense it is *actually* the "overture" to the opera and that is why Tchaikovsky planned it before anything else.

Tchaikovsky's other operas were written by approximately the same process. The composer criticized some of his contemporaries for neglecting what he considered to be one of the most important stages in writing opera. "(With them) the musical idea is relegated to the background," he wrote in a letter to von Meck dated July 18, 1880, "it

* In the rough draft of the manuscript of the libretto this theme is marked also as a "chronic ache."

becomes not the end but the means to the end, an excuse for one or another combination of sounds. . . ."

While pondering the general idea, Tchaikovsky at the same time worked out the principal contours of its development. The first musical sketches jotted down on the margin of the libretto manuscript afford, rich material for illustrating this point. The two surviving manuscripts of the text for "The Queen of Spades" will serve as an example.

A study of these two MSS shows that the episodes that evoke the first musical reactions in the composer are the dramatic climax in the development of the leading characters, the basic, decisive elements in the action. In the libretto for "The Queen of Spades" we find the themes of two ariosos for Herman. They express two of the hero's most sharply defined emotional states and mark the climax of his two leading passions: love (arioso "I know not her name") and the gambling passion (arioso "What is this life of ours"). Here too we find the theme of the final duet of Lisa and Herman in the 6th scene, Lisa's theme in the 2nd scene and the theme of Herman's address to the Countess in the 4th scene.

In addition to the design of the vocal numbers we find jotted down in the margin of the libretto MSS also the themes of orchestral episodes. These too are written with an eye to dramatic development of character portrayal. In "The Queen of Spades," for example, we find the outline of the three card theme, the theme carried by the cello solo expressing Herman's depressed state of mind in the 2nd scene.

Sometimes we find in the libretto MSS (or notebook) sketches not only of some more elaborate number but separate remarks as well (usually very significant from the

standpoint of drama). For example, the cue of the princess
in "The Enchantress," "Drink, my dove," and in the last
Act of "Mazeppa," Maria's cues "The old man has gone"
and "But where wert thou?"

Not all the notes are identical. Some of them (*e.g.*,
"What is this life of ours") are recorded almost in full and
in their final tonality; in other cases only the beginning or
the climax is jotted down. The remarks of the characters
are usually given in the corresponding melodic intonations.
The lyrically emotional ariosos of the Godmother ("Tarry
awhile") is designated merely by the tempo (Allegro) and
the tonality (E-minor). Sometimes in working on the piano
score the original notes would be changed here and there:
the measure (You, Sire), the tonality ("Her name I do not
know"), some of the intonations (Lisa's theme, the pastorale), but the *general* trend of the melodic design was
nearly always unerringly conceived by Tchaikovsky in the
original version and subsequently remained unchanged.

Not always were the planned culminations realized in
the final version. Some episodes were discarded altogether,
others were given in two and sometimes three versions.
There are, for instance, two versions of the duet in Act IV
of "The Enchantress," three of the arioso "What is this life
of ours," etc. The composer was particularly thorough with
the themes and leitmotifs of the basic motive forces of the
opera.*

Tchaikovsky rarely sat down to write a consecutive
musical text of a scene or episode until he clearly visualized
the main course of its development. His diary relating to

* There is evidence that Tchaikovsky worked hard on his first notes
before transferring them to the MSS folio. He returned to them again
and again, revising and altering.

the period of "The Queen of Spades" includes the following entry concerning the 5th scene of that opera: "I started to write the beginning of the 5th scene, I thought out the end yesterday. . . ."

Before beginning to compose any of the scenes in "The Queen of Spades" Tchaikovsky already had (in libretto and notebooks) all the principal motifs of the situations (theme of the arioso, aria or theme of accompaniment) prepared.

Most of the scenes for his other operas were composed in the same order. In the evening, usually during his walk, he would map out in his notebook the "musical outline" of some scene and the principal phases in the dramatic development and the following day would be spent working on the piano score.

In December 1882, when he was writing "Mazeppa," the composer wrote the following letter to L. V. Davydov: "Ask Stepan to find my little yellow notebook, the one I took with me on my walks. It contains *almost the whole of my opera* and I need it. Without it my opera is lost." *
This notebook bears diverse traces of work in the open air (water stains, shaky handwriting of notes evidently jotted down while the composer was strolling along, marginal notes such as "on the road to Trostyanki," "Vysokaya Mogila," etc.). In it we find some seventeen leitmotifs grouped approximately in the order of the scenes.

As in the case of his other operas, the notes are abbreviated to the maximum and vary considerably as to method of recording (in most cases the composer jotted down only the most *vivid* ideas as they occurred to him, sometimes it was the orchestration, sometimes only the

* The italics are mine—Yarustovsky.

tonality, etc.). It is characteristic, however, that, as in the two cases above described, all the notes relate to the culminating points of the action, the principal *emotional states* in the development of the characters; some of the entries clearly indicate that when outlining the keypoints in the development of a given scene, the author invariably did so with an eye to the development of the opera *as a whole*.

This same determining principle of "through" or sustained action can be traced also in the subsequent stages of the composer's work on the piano score of his operas.

As we already know, this process usually began with the culminating point of the "through" action, the basic episode depicting the clash of the contrasting elements, the maximum revelation of the inner world of the leading characters: in "Eugene Onegin" Tatyana's scene; in "The Maid of Orleans" the scene in the Chillon Palace; in "Mazeppa" the scene between Maria and Mazeppa; in "The Enchantress" the Godmother and the Princess; in "Yolanthe" between Vaudemont and Yolanthe, etc. These, as the author himself points out, were always *"capital"* scenes.

Rarely did Tchaikovsky write his operas in the consecutive order of scenes. Here, for instance, is the process by which "The Maid of Orleans" was composed. On December 10, 1878 the opera was started with one of the culminating moments—the advent of Jeanne in the Palace of Chillon, *i.e.*, the middle of the *2nd* Act. On January 3 he finished the second half of the *1st* Act, started also from the middle with the moment when the people fly in terror from the English. On January 9, the whole of the *1st* Act was completed, the first half being added after the second half was done. On January 14, the first half of the 2nd Act was finished. On January 23 the *first* half of the *3rd* Act was written, beginning from the battle scene and the first encounter between Lionel and Jeanne. The following day, Tchaikovsky switched over to the love scene between Lionel and Jeanne, the beginning of the 4th Act, leaving the 3rd Act undone. On January 21 the rest of the 3rd Act was completed and by February 22 the opera was ready.

With "The Queen of Spades" Tchaikovsky was hampered by the lack of a complete text for the libretto. When he left for Florence he was able to take with him only two scenes of the finished text which his brother had written some time before for the composer Klenovsky. Before his departure, the composer asked the author of the libretto to write the text of the 4th scene first, upon receipt of which Tchaikovsky at once began to work on it. Only later did he compose the 3rd scene. In the case of "Mazeppa" he began with the 3rd scene (Maria and Mazeppa) and later on judging by numerous data * the composer turned his attention to the last act. Act 1 was written last.

The scenes also began in most cases with the culminating point of the "through" action, as we have seen in the case of "The Maid of Orleans." The 5th scene of "The Queen of Spades" began with the appearance of the ghost ("the tapping at the window"—the culmination and tectonic centre of the 5th scene). In composing the 4th scene of the same opera the composer shifted from the first section ("Herman alone") to the death scene and only later did he turn back to the preceding section ("the countess alone"). The intermezzo to the 3rd scene was written before the rest of the text of that scene. "Yolanthe" was started from the middle with the love scene between Vaude-

* The order of the notes in his notebook and letters to Modeste Ilyich in 1882.

mont and Yolanthe. Similar examples can be found in nearly all Tchaikovsky operas, especially in the "post-Onegin period."

It is not difficult to draw the conclusion that this process was the basic principle followed by Tchaikovsky in composing opera. *Once he had perceived and grasped the leading idea that was to run through the whole of the opera, he set about embodying the idea in music and only then did he proceed to work out the development by episodes.*

The through line of action in a drama does not preclude but rather presupposes the inclusion of "neutral" episodes. These are necessary for various reasons. In the first place, as a temporary distraction from the main dramatic intrigue. Secondly, as a relaxation for the spectator. Thirdly, as a background for the development of the main intrigue and fourthly to offset the main dramatic line, etc.

In opera the significance of these qualities (especially the first two) is greater than in *other forms*, inasmuch as the power of emotional influence, the "synthetic" nature of operatic art demand a greater amount of "relief" for the audience.

In lyrico-psychological opera "neutral" material of this kind is furnished mainly by nature scenes, comic episodes, dances and folk scenes.* The development of the intrigue against the background of scenes of everyday life in "Eugene Onegin." ** (4th and 6th scenes), "The Queen of Spades" (1st, 3rd and 7th scenes), "Mazeppa" (1st scene),

---

* Whereas in "sociological" opera the leading idea is carried usually by the individual social groups, in psychological opera folk scenes are nearly always inserted for effect.

** In the first sketch of the scenario Tchaikovsky pointed out frankly that he had deliberately borrowed situations from Gounod's "Faust" for the 1st and 3rd scenes of "Onegin."

etc., the use of genre and folk scenes as contrasting background (chorus of girls in 3rd scene of "Onegin," the finale of "The Enchantress," "The Queen of Spades" and others)—all this is undoubtedly the result of the influence of French lyrical opera.

Tchaikovsky also made extensive use of the method of "distracting" attention from the dramatic intrigue for a time. He applied two versions of this method: episodes in the development of the main dramatic intrigue alternate with "neutral" genre scenes. This method is usually encountered in the beginning of the action, in the first and less often in the second scenes ("The Enchantress," "The Queen of Spades," etc.). In subsequent scenes the development of the dramatic intrigue necessitates too much concentration and intensity of action for such diffusion of material. The influence of the dramatic episodes on the audience becomes stronger and stronger and hence the neutral "distracting" material occurs *before* and not during these scenes. The more significant the dramatic scene the greater the "distracting" material. Such, for example, is the intermezzo and the whole 3rd scene of "The Queen of Spades" (immediately preceding the 4th and 5th scenes), the scene of Lisa and her friends before the close of the second scene and the card game just before the tragic finale.

The musical material of these episodes is not always "neutral." Quite often these genre episodes serve to bring out some characteristic feature of the action, as for instance, the modest valse or mazurka in the Larin home and the dazzling Polonaise in the St. Petersburg palace, written in the style of early 19th-century romances, the duet of Paulina and Lisa in "The Queen of Spades."

The intermezzo in "The Queen of Spades" was written

on the same principle. From the music library of the opera house Tchaikovsky took seven 18th-century scores: Salieri's "Venetian Holiday," Gretry's "Richard the Lion Heart" and "Two Misers," Puccini's "Didon," Monsigny's "Deserter," Astaritta's "Rinaldo," and Martin-y-Soler's "The Clodhopper." Of these, there is evidence that he perused the operas of Salieri, Gretry and Astaritta and only in the case of the countess' love song in the 4th scene did the composer borrow anything from these operas. There can be no doubt, however, that his perusal of these old scores was largely responsible for the inclusion of the intermezzos.

The theme of the duet and several other themes in the intermezzo are similar in melodic design and other respects to some of the themes from the above scores (e.g., from Salieri's "Venetian Holiday," and Gretry's "Two Misers").

The *prime* factor in opera, in Tchaikovsky's opinion, was to convey the given mood in the simplest musical forms, *to build up a chain of episodes harmonizing in mood and spirit with the given dramatic situation.* ". . . The most important thing in vocal music," he wrote, "is the faithful reproduction of feelings and moods, yet they (the critics) are always on the lookout for misplaced accents, discrepancies in diction, and other such trifling oversights. . . ." It was from this standpoint that Tchaikovsky evaluated the operas of other composers. On looking over the piano score of Astaritta's "Rinaldo d'Aste" among the other seven scores borrowed from the library of the Imperial theatres for his work on "The Queen of Spades" he made the following characteristic remarks: "A charming ballad and the mood is faithfully conveyed," "in No. 4 the despondent mood is very well sustained," "in No. 5—excellently held."

It is thus clear that in building up his theme the composer evidently ascertained for himself the *dominant mood* to be reflected in the melody.

The most striking examples of consistency in the succession of motifs in accordance with the mood of the heroes are to be found in the letter scene from "Eugene Onegin" or the Godmother and the Princess scene in "The Enchantress"; in the latter instance, at the time the libretto was being written the composer had already decided that this scene was to be a succession of nine different motifs, reflecting an equal number of situations.

The situation motifs usually differ from the themes of vocal numbers (ariosos, arias, etc.), in that they are not only vocal melodies but also a means of orchestral characterization. As a rule, the motif of a situation appears first in the orchestra to create the requisite "atmosphere," and only later is it taken up by the voice. Most of the situation motif is confined to the orchestra. This is especially significant for the recitative in Tchaikovsky opera inasmuch as the orchestra forms a colourful background for the relatively pallid recitative. Take, for example, the motif of Vaudemont's enchantment by Yolanthe. This small tender motif is repeated five times in the course of the scene, and inasmuch as it is intended to convey the spirit of contemplation, its development is purely "static."

The motif depicting a situation (whether the theme of an aria, arioso, outline of recitative or motifs elaborated in the orchestra) is the principal means of conveying an image. It is the connection between these motifs that has been the determining factor in the musical development of opera. Thanks to this, opera, especially of the latter period, is in great measure symphonic. Tchaikovsky never attempted self-deception by seeking artificially to blend the

words and the music as Wagner did. Tchaikovsky never
attempted to make the verbal fabric of opera the dominat-
ing, determining factor. That was precisely why he had
such a horror of verbosity, that is why the canvas of
Tchaikovsky's opera contains the minimum of dialogue,
especially brief remarks, and a maximum of solos and ensembles. He used words only to indicate and explain the
object of the emotions. Words of such significance were
usually found in the opening bars of the aria or at the
culminating point, and the music in the score was marked
in *italics*. Most of the words (texts of arias, ariosos, etc.)
play an insignificant role from the standpoint of the meaning and are frequently repeated.

Tchaikovsky's notebooks give a clear picture of the
process by which the arias, ariosos, duets and other finished
forms were written. They shed light also on the relation
between the words and the music.

Tchaikovsky's views on the relation between the words
and the music led to some interesting innovations in operatic
dramaturgy. For example, the dialogue between the Godmother and Yuri in "The Enchantress" at the moment
when Yuri is "succumbing" to the charms of the Godmother and they are both united by the *same* sentiments is
expressed by the *same* melody regardless of the fact that
the text calls for dialogue. The composer jotted down this
melody in his notebook, adding the text only in the opening bars. In the subsequent stages and in the piano score
he divided the *single* melodic line into *three* separate cues
(the Godmother, Yuri and the Godmother once more).

When the emotional state of one character was akin to
that of another character Tchaikovsky frequently used the
same melody for both notwithstanding the difference, how-

ever great, of the verbal text. Examples are Tatyana (2nd scene) and Onegin (6th scene), the Godmother and Yuri (3rd scene), Lyubov and Maria (6th scene of "Mazeppa"), etc.

Tchaikovsky's operas are frequently called "arioso" operas as distinct from the declamatory-dialogue operas of Mussorgsky. Indeed, although the declamatory element does play an important role, the melody is nevertheless the principal vehicle of expression in the vocal scores of Tchaikovsky's operas.

No less than five different types of recitative, beginning with Lecco and ending with extremely melodious arioso forms, occur in Tchaikovsky opera. Perhaps the most prevalent is the arioso, one that was quite new for 19th century opera, a cross between two contrasting forms of vocal execution—the aria and the declamatory recitative—and hence the most flexible of all vocal forms.

Arias in Tchaikovsky opera were reduced to a minimum; the form of the aria as well as its dramatic function was considerably changed as the "through line" form began to play the dominant role. This process is extremely indicative of Tchaikovsky's striving to overcome the "conventionality" of opera. The sharper the dividing line between purely musical forms (aria, etc.) and the dramatic forms (dialogue, recitative), the greater the contradiction between the singing and the dramatic action. Without entirely eschewing classical opera forms Tchaikovsky endeavoured to modify as much as possible the distinction between these two contradictory tendencies without eliminating it completely by introducing a large number of *different varieties* of the traditional form. This enabled him, firstly, to find the most appropriate musical form for the given emotional state of his character and for the given dramatic episode, and secondly, made the transition from one form to another more natural, especially in the "through line" scenes, and thirdly, made it possible to employ truly musical means of reflecting the dynamics of the development of the leading characters.

*   *   *

Recitative in Tchaikovsky opera does not play as important a role as in operas by Mussorgsky, Dargomyzhsky or Wagner. The brief dialogue cues in Tchaikovsky's librettos were, as I have already said, cut down to the minimum. Nevertheless in "through line" scenes, especially in the last operas, the importance of the recitative is manifest, its role increasing with the heightening of the role of the orchestra as an independent factor in opera dramaturgy. Interesting in this respect are the changes the composer made to the score of "Vakula" when this opera was revised as "The Little Shoes." On the margin of the draft score of many of the scenes, especially during the dramatic dialogue between Vakula and Oksana, we find in Tchaikovsky's handwriting: *"this should be recitative."*

Thus already in 1885 Tchaikovsky had realized the boundless possibilities of recitative and made some interesting experiments with this form in the score of "Vakula."

In "Onegin," too, which was written before "The Little Shoes" the composer realized the need for expressive recitative. The finished opera forms, however flexible, were clearly inadequate for carrying such complex scenes as the Letter Scene and Finale in which the author strove to reveal the struggle of the inner emotions of his characters. It was here that the problem of evolving his own style of recitative first presented itself to Tchaikovsky. And indeed the melodious quality of the recitative in "Onegin" is one of the opera's distinctive features. He applied the form to other operas as well. The recitative remarks which carry such scenes as that of Herman and the Countess, Herman in the 5th scene ("The Queen of Spades"), Maria and Lyubov ("Mazeppa") and the Godmother and the Princess ("The Enchantress") are masterpieces of expression. In these cases Tchaikovsky took great pains to accentuate the *meaning* of the words spoken whether they rhymed or not.

In the operas written in the latter decade of his life (beginning with 1883) the dramatic significance of these cues and interjections grew still greater. Characteristic of this period is the clarity of the composer's perception of the melodic design (intonation), the tonality and the rhythm in addition to the leading motifs of the given situations and the various cues in their dramatic culmination.

Already in the early stages of his work on an opera Tchaikovsky was able to create the atmosphere and mood he required by means of one-bar *response*. In his rough draft of Shpazhinsky's libretto for "The Enchantress" we find the musical outline of that dramatically significant cue given by the Princess in the last act: "Drink, my dove."

The purpose of this cue is to alter the dramatic situation. After a long, ominous-sounding monologue the Princess turns to the Godmother and offers her the poison cup. The tender intonation of this cue is in sharp contrast to the passionate agitation of the preceding phrase in the Princess's part. I could cite any number of such examples.

* * *

Character development in Tchaikovsky opera, as we have seen, is primarily the movement from one emotional state to another, the "assertion" and development of the hero's principal passions. To create the musical image that would convey the successive "qualitative" states of the hero constituted the first and most important stage in Tchaikovsky's work on opera.

This musical image was the principal means of depicting character, the main factor in the musico-dramatic development. It sums up the emotional state and is integrated with the action. Moreover, it serves as the thematic nucleus of the finished parts (arias, etc.), as material for orchestral development and as the "contours" for recitative cues.

The fact that the development of the action in Tchaikovsky opera is invariably determined by the logical development of the musical material is proof of the importance of these principles, and we know how doggedly and persistently the composer worked to accomplish this difficult task. He created a maximum variety of musical forms— from the static, traditional da capo to the most flexible "through" scenes. This is one of Tchaikovsky's greatest contributions to opera.

In his letters on "The Barber of Seville" Beaumarchais deplored the formality of the musical principles as applied to opera. "Are there reprises or rondos in drama?" he demanded. It is the opera composer's chief task, however, to combine the principles of drama with the principles of music. Tchaikovsky employed the reprise, rondo and other elements of musical form because he consciously strove to create a dramatic work through the medium of music which has its own laws and principles. The architectonics of an art like music demanded reprise, and rounded forms, especially at the end of the acts and scenes. And it is not by chance that even in the "through" line of Wagner's musical dramas we find such rounded episodes as the "Death of Isolde" and the "Invocation of Fire" at the end of acts. The action in Tchaikovsky opera moves primarily on the principle of sharp leaps from one emotional state to another expressed in more or less rounded musical forms.

* * *

The dramaturgy of Tchaikovsky opera offers inexhaustible material for a study of opera in general and Soviet opera in particular, for nowhere is the theory of musical drama elaborated to such an extent as in Tchaikovsky drama. No one has succeeded in bringing out the "dialectics" of the movement, the ideas and emotions of human character as has Tchaikovsky. And all these complex processes were embodied in simple, natural and substantially *reformed* opera forms.

Through the medium of his operas Tchaikovsky revealed the spiritual world, the psychological make-up of Russian men and women.

And it is not by chance that in reply to a letter from Pogochiev who observed that "especially valuable was Tchaikovsky's ability to create with his music the mood that best harmonized with the drama and the action," the composer wrote: "It seems to me that I am indeed gifted with the ability to give faithful, sincere and simple expression to the thoughts and emotions and images suggested by the text. In this sense I am a realist and a Russian to the core. . . ."

SYMPHONIES

DANIEL ZHITOMIRSKY

I. *Introduction*

"I ABSOLUTELY DISAGREE WITH YOU," wrote
Tchaikovsky in one of his letters to von Meck, "that music
cannot express the universal attributes of love. I believe
quite the contrary that music *alone can do it.* You say that
words are necessary for this. Oh no! This is precisely where
words are unnecessary, and when words are powerless one
has recourse to a more eloquent language, *i.e.,* music."
Tchaikovsky touches here upon one of the most important
and fundamental principles of his art, namely, the conviction that the highest sphere of musical expression is the
realm of human emotion, the spiritual life of man.

This explains Tchaikovsky's partiality for pure instrumental music. Of his Fourth Symphony he writes: "My
symphony is, of course, a programme work, but it is a
programme that is impossible to put into words, for it would
excite ridicule and sound comical. But what is a symphony
after all if not the *most lyrical* of musical forms? Should
a symphony not express all that cannot be put in words,
but which fills the soul to overflowing and yearns for
expression?" Tchaikovsky's symphonies, however, were not
limited to lyricism, however profound. Through the
medium of lyricism his art reached out toward the solution
of major ethical and philosophical problems.

86

THOUGHTS ABOUT TCHAIKOVSKY

It should not be thought that Tchaikovsky eschewed the more external forms of musical expression. Such compositions as "The Tempest," "Francesca da Rimini" and "Manfred" offer sufficient evidence of the composer's mastery of form, colour and line in symphony writing. The scores of his ballets and suites are full of rich and original tone colour. In symphony Tchaikovsky is every bit as versatile as in opera and chamber music. At the same time the lyrical and dramatic aspects were as dominant in this, as in other genres. Symptomatic in this respect is the composer's hesitancy when commencing to work on "Manfred." The abundance of figurative detail in the programme of this symphony compiled by Balakirev, worried him. "I do not know how it will turn out in the end," he wrote, "but in the meantime I am dissatisfied. No. It is a thousand times pleasanter to write non-programme music. Whenever I compose a programme symphony I invariably experience the sensation of hoodwinking the public; it is as though I were handing out worthless banknotes instead of hard cash."

Tchaikovsky's art is extraordinarily dynamic and dramatic. The element of conflict and the purposeful dynamic development may be said to constitute what we call the soul of Tchaikovsky's symphony music. Another outstanding characteristic is its power of generalization. At the same time, Tchaikovsky did not indulge in artistic abstractions. His leading ideas are unfolded through a series of concrete, full-blooded images of universal meaning.

These features of Tchaikovsky's music are determined among other things by its affinity to the popular genres of music. Song and dance themes figure in every one of his symphonies. When Taneyev reproached Tchaikovsky for

having included some "ballet" music in each movement of
his Fourth Symphony, the composer replied: "I quite fail
to see anything at all reprehensible in the term 'ballet
music.' " Indeed the lyrical generalization of simple popular genres, songs, dances and ditties is a common Tchaikovsky device.

This is perhaps what makes his symphonies preem-
inently suitable for concert performance. Their sensual
beauty, the "decorative" * melodic design, their comprehensiveness and attractiveness are an unending source of delight. It is this that makes for their tremendous popular appeal despite their philosophical depth.

The national roots of Tchaikovsky's symphonies reach
deep down into the soil of Russian folk music. They
stemmed directly from Russian classical music of the first
half of the 19th century and primarily from Glinka.

Glinka gave the first perfect examples of symphonic
development of Russian folk music. In this sense one can
trace a direct line from Glinka to the early Tchaikovsky—
not only the latter's operas and romances but also his early
symphonies which continued Glinka's experiments in sym-
phonizing simple folk genres. We find eloquent proof of
this in practically all the finales of his symphonies. The
"Kamarinskaya," the Spanish overtures, the music to
"Prince Kholmsky," the overture and dances from "Russlan"
were the ABC, as it were, of Russian classical music, for
Tchaikovsky as much as for the Big Five. No less important
is it to stress the affinity between the lyricism of Tchaikovsky and that of Glinka. While this is most strongly felt in

* As Tchiakovsky understood it when he wrote about his ideal opera
style: "I did not know how to give the listener a rest, I gave him too
much rich musical food at once. Opera style must be distinguished by
breadth, simplicity and a certain decorativeness."

the vocal compositions of both composers, as striking an example of *lyrical symphony writing* as the "Valse Fantasie" directly anticipates much of the later Tchaikovsky. The influence of Glinka was thus one of the principal factors in the development of Tchaikovsky as a national composer and as a lyrical symphonist.

When speaking of the national essence of Tchaikovsky we have in view not only the subject, the musical metaphor and material of his work. There is something else about Tchaikovsky as a symphonist that is perhaps even more important, namely, those general attributes of Russian art which Romain Rolland sensed so strongly in Leo Tolstoi ("The Life of Tolstoi"): no showy "artiness," no romantic declamation or rhetoric, instead, an utter artlessness combined with the modesty of a personal diary or confession but withal what strength of feeling, what a sweep of ideas, what a powerful play of human passions! This applies to Tchaikovsky, to Tolstoi, to Dostoyevsky, to Chekhov; it is Russian psychological realism expressing its abhorrence of oppression and slavery, its championship of life and man as opposed to Fatalism.

Examining Tchaikovsky's symphonies against the background of the development of European music as a whole, we must point primarily to its direct connection with Beethoven. Indeed the philosophy and dynamic quality of Tchaikovsky's symphonies can *only* be compared to that of Beethoven. It would be a mistake to regard Tchaikovsky's employment of the Beethoven principles of instrumental music merely as a fondness for tradition, as did some of Tchaikovsky's contemporaries. Rather was it dictated by the profound ideological essence of his music. Only the Beethoven type of symphony could embody the powerful dramatism of Tchaikovsky's own conceptions.

It was from Beethoven primarily that Tchaikovsky derived his wide range of *thematic development*, e.g., the consistent concentration of the expressive elements of the theme (for example, "compression"), and the method of lengthy progressions. From Beethoven also comes the *dynamic treatment of the form as a whole*, particularly in the sonata allegros. This influence is at work also in Tchaikovsky's method of *elaboration*, built up on the principle of a succession of "waves"; the treatment of the coda which takes the form of a second elaboration and contains the highest climax of the development (*e.g.*, in "Romeo and Juliet," in the first movements of the Fourth and Fifth Symphonies, etc.).

In some respects Tchaikovsky's symphonic music bore an even greater affinity to the romantic symphony composers of the West than to Beethoven. As has been established by modern musicologists the combination of philosophical generalization with concreteness of musical metaphor characteristic of Tchaikovsky is an important feature in the style of the Romantic composers. Like Liszt and Wagner, Tchaikovsky tended to broad and uninterrupted development, to the embodiment of major and complete philosophical conceptions. Striving to coordinate the elements of the cycle he resorted to romantic methods of leitmotif (*e.g.*, in his Fourth and Fifth symphonies, and in "Manfred"). This explains his interest in the symphonic poem.

At the same time, the various thematic groups within the larger media (poem or parts of a cycle) are usually *independent and structurally complete*. Not infrequently, these are relatively independent three-part song or dance episodes.

While deeply conscious of the particular, Tchaikovsky strove to encompass the general, the *process* of inner conflict. Hence his distaste for what was incomplete, spasmodic and unfinished, hence his strict adherence to some of the classical canons.

What has been said above determined also to a great extent Tchaikovsky's attitude to the *programme symphony* as a genre. His programme music is nearer to that created by Beethoven ("Leonora," "Coriolanus," the Fifth and Ninth symphonies), developed to its highest point by Liszt, than to the subject-programme principles of Berlioz. Sheer decorativeness or external effectiveness had no attraction for Tchaikovsky. He valued a literary programme only in so far as it contained the lyric-psychological motifs that appealed to him. His main attention was concentrated on bringing out the emotional "core" of the programme.

In his famous paper "The Symphony from Beethoven to Mahler," Paul Becker shows convincingly that in the course of the 19th century western symphonism lost the lofty ideals and social impact achieved by Beethoven. He tells us how the range of feeling and interests expressed in the symphonies of Mendelssohn and Schumann relatively diminished, how depths of content in the neo-romantic programme symphonies, beginning with Liszt and ending with Richard Strauss, was sacrificed to external effects. Against the background of this picture, faithfully drawn in many respects, Tchaikovsky as a symphonist stands out as a phenomenon of especial significance. He was the *first after Beethoven* to write symphonies that were monumental from the standpoint of idea and influence on society. Tchaikovsky posed and attempted to solve *eternal human problems*: man and his fate, life and the forces shackling it. It is this depth and, at the same time, simplicity of content expressing the innermost thoughts of millions of people, that gives Tchaikovsky's symphonies such a powerful appeal.

II. *Early Symphonies.*

In Tchaikovsky's earliest symphonies the individuality and national traits of the composer were manifested. In the first place, the *subject*, the *genre* and intonation were closely associated with Russian life and Russian folk music. Secondly, in the treatment of simple, informal genres Tchaikovsky betrayed in his earliest works a tendency to stress the *emotional factors* more than the outward characterization and tonality. The form of symphonic development he subsequently adopted in all his music, a form in which the main role is played by *dynamic treatment of the leading musical idea,* is quite clearly evident, although on a modest scale, in his early works.

The *First Symphony* (G-Minor, 1866), "Winter Reveries," is one of the most complete of his early compositions, in the sense that it embodies more fully than his other works of those years the traits peculiar to his style. Conceived as a lyrical programme cycle it consisted of several "mood pictures" and develops a favorite Russian literary motif— the poetry of winter-clad roads.

The thematic design of the first movement ("Reveries on a Winter Road") is a simple melody, a sort of echo of some melancholy folk air. As the emotional tension gradually increases in the characteristic Tchaikovsky manner the music acquires elements of the dramatic. The second move-

ment "Gloomy land, misty land" is a lyrical Russian Andante built up on a broad flowing song melody. The individuality of the composer makes itself felt here too in the
dramatic intensification of the theme (see reprise, where
the melody runs against the background of an agitated
string tremolo). The Scherzo, with its whimsical movement
and faint touch of mystery in the tonality, is written in the
romantic tradition. This type of movement which began
with the First Symphony was individualized by Tchaikovsky and became typical of his thematic material (see the
Scherzos of the Third, Fourth and Sixth symphonies). Incidentally, in the Scherzo of the First Symphony that specific nuance (grotesque, with an element of "horror") that
was subsequently to be introduced, does not figure. Note-
worthy also is the middle part of this movement—Tchaikovsky's first symphonic Waltz—one of the earliest links
in the long chain of his instrumental and vocal morceaux,
episodes and musical themes associated with this genre.

The cycle ends in a ceremonial finale consisting of two
Russian themes; one of them a Russian folk song, "The
Gardens Bloomed," used in the introduction and the second
theme. This is one of the first samples of the *Russian Festive
Finale* which can be traced back to Glinka (primarily his
overtures to "Russlan and Ludmilla" and "The Kamarin-
skaya"). Tchaikovsky consistently returned to this type of
Finale in all his symphonies excepting the Sixth.

The predomination of a single line of lyrical feeling
makes the First Symphony extremely monolithic, and in
this sense it anticipates some of the features of the mature
Tchaikovsky.

In the *Second Symphony* (C-Minor 1872) the treatment is more in the nature of a suite. There is more variety

and character in the movements. Here the composer has borrowed generously from folk material, both as regards genuine melodies as well as those associated with folk music.

The long introduction in the first movement is a variation on the theme of a plaintive Ukrainian melody.* The Allegro is written in the laconic manner of Beethoven's appassionata movement.** The second movement (Andantino marciale) is a theatricalized march with elements of the grotesque.*** The central episode of the Andantino is built up on a lyrical folk song ("My Spinning-wheel"), worked out in the form of variations. The opening and closing movements of the Scherzo are sustained in the European romantic spirit and the effect is that of swift, elusive movement. The variation on the folk theme, this time in a humorous vein, reappears in the central episode

The brilliant Festive Finale is based on the theme of the Ukrainian dance tune "The Crane." † It is written in the sonata form with a variation development. In thematic ma-

---

* In the opinion of Tchaikovsky's friend, Professor N. Kashkin, it is the Ukrainian version of the famous Russian song "The Volga Boatman."

** This dynamic Allegro, characteristic of the mature Tchaikovsky, was composed in 1879–1880. In the first version of the symphony (1872) it figures as soft melodious music, part of which was retained in the second theme of the final version.

*** The composer borrowed the theme for the Andantino marciale from his first unsuccessful opera "Undine" (MSS destroyed by the author in 1873). To the tune of this march, Aulbrand the knight with his bride and suite went to church for the wedding ceremony.

† Tchaikovsky wrote his Second Symphony in the Ukraine at Kanaka, the estate of his sister, A. I. Davydova. He once wrote in jest that the credit for the success of the finale should go not to him but "to the real composer of the said work—Peter Gerasimovich" (the aged butler of the Davydov home), who sang "The Crane" song to him while he was working on the symphony.

terial (characteristic juxtaposition of the "Crane" to an eastern theme), as well as in the predominant ornamental and colourful variation, the finale resembles the instrumental style of the Balakirev school.

The five-part Third Symphony (D-Major, 1875) has a similar colourful juxtaposition of movement and episodes and the same "suite-like" quality as the Second.

The first Allegro, preceded by an austere introduction in the style of a marche funebre, develops three themes gay and festive (D-Major), a graceful dance theme in bolero rhythm * (B-Minor) and a spirited folk dance (A-Major). The second movement is a waltz ("Alla tedesca"). The third is a melancholy Andante with a romantic theme. The fourth is a Scherzo with an effective flowing movement in the opening and closing bars and an eccentric grotesque trio. The Finale is in the nature of a Polonaise.

In his Second and Third symphonies Tchaikovsky developed in "breadth," embracing an ever-widening range of images and genres. At the same time there was a development in *depth*. Writing about the Third Symphony Hermann Laroche, the music critic who closely followed the unfoldment of Tchaikovsky's talent, said: "Tchaikovsky is going forward all the time. In his new symphony the art of form and counterpoint development stands on a higher level than in any of his previous compositions. . . . In power and significance of content, in wealth of form and nobility of style, enhanced by an original creative personality, as well as in the rare perfection of technique, Tchaikovsky's symphony constitutes one of the major musical phenomena of the past ten years not only in this country but in all of Europe."

* Not in three, but in four-time measure.

III. *Fourth, Fifth and Sixth Symphonies*

Each of Tchaikovsky's three last symphonies is unique and original both as regards conception as well as fulfilment. Nevertheless they have a great deal in common. All three are different versions of one and the same *type* of symphony and all three have a definite message. These three symphonies, like a number of other major compositions by Tchaikovsky, treat essentially of the same theme — man's tragic struggle against an inexorable fate.

This idea is evolved most fully in the *first* movements of the symphonies. The traditional Sonata Allegro, treated from an entirely new angle, is part and parcel of the creative idea of the composer. The deepgoing *fundamental contrast between the two basic themes* of the exposition is the first paramount feature of these movements. Tragic reality is counterpoised by the dream of happiness; the human consciousness casts about interminably and hopelessly between those two planes, being powerless to reconcile the two. Antithesis is on the whole quite common for many of the romantics. The distinctive quality of its embodiment in Tchaikovsky's music is that "happiness" juxtaposed to tragedy is not the metaphysical disembodied "ideal," but life as a fully perceived *reality*. It is the clash between the two realities that gives rise to the element of conflict and the sharp thematic contrasts in Tchaikovsky's music.

The main themes are impassioned, unstable, restless. Academician Asofyev (also well-known under his nom de plume Igor Glebov) defines the main theme of the first movement of the Fifth Symphony as "a *shackled im-*

pulse in flight." This definition applies equally to many other analogous themes to be found in Tchaikovsky's music.

The first theme is usually broadly developed. It grows more and more tense and agitated. In most cases this is connected with the concentration and intensification of the most dynamic elements of the theme. In some instances, this development might be roughly described as "funnel-shaped"; in proportion as the theme grows dynamic the diapason of movement narrows down and it spends itself by its very intensity.

Similar is the type of development in the main theme of the first movement of the Fourth Symphony. It is written in dynamic three-part form. Already in the central elaborated section the theme is galvanized chromatically and is at the same time condensed. The condensing is continued and leads finally to the reiteration of one of the more intensive intonations.

The restless, throbbing main theme is counterpoised by a much more balanced, serene and placid second theme. Tchaikovsky uses two varieties of second themes for his Sonata form. The first is a broad, elegiac cantilene which might be loosely termed themes of love or a rapturous contemplation of nature. To this category belong, for example, the second themes of the Allegro from the Sixth Symphony, "Romeo and Juliet" and "The Tempest." Analogous melodies are found also in the vocal works, *e.g.*, the love themes from "The Queen of Spades," "Mazeppa," many arias and romances. These melodies are very similar in type to the romantic love themes of Schumann, Liszt and Wagner.

Another variety are the dance themes, most frequently

of the waltz type; we find them in the Third, Fourth and Fifth symphonies. The floating, soaring movement of the waltz was one of Tchaikovsky's favourite vehicle of artistic generalization. Through the waltz he constantly created images of ideal, womanly sensual beauty.

While on the whole more balanced than the main themes, the second themes are by no means inwardly static. In them one is always aware of the intensive development of the main line, the dynamic reiteration of the original conception. Comparing, for example, two versions of the second theme·in the Fifth Symphony, we find that in the second version the melody is broadened, and what is even more significant, it is chromatized almost to the point of "perpetuum mobile."

The line of demarcation between the main and second themes is determined not only by the sharply contrasting nature of thematic material but also by the fact that each theme usually constitutes an independent, widely developed and structurally complete episode. Frequently the themes are written in three-part form with an independent theme in the middle. Such, for example, are the main themes of the Fourth and Fifth symphonies and "Romeo and Juliet," the second themes in the latter overture and in the Sixth Symphony.

The demarcation line between the themes is also dependent upon the character of the connecting links. With Beethoven, as is known, the connecting links fulfill a dual function: they deepen the development of the first theme and at the same time lead up to the second theme. In the case of Tchaikovsky the treatment is somewhat different. The large section devoted to elaboration that flows immediately after the exposition of the first theme and develops it is by no means a bridge to the second theme. The transition to the latter is usually accomplished by means of a small structure, extremely limited in its function. It serves not so much to develop as to switch over from one sphere to another ("Perhaps it were better to turn away from reality and abandon ourselves to reverie" we read in the author's commentary to the Fourth Symphony). These transitions, incidentally, are amazingly smooth; it is as if the composer "switches off" the tempestuous movement of the main theme and introduces soft, serene tones to lead us gently to a new, joyous theme.

It remains to be added, that the division of the themes is usually stressed by the difference of tempos (*e.g.*, in the Sixth Symphony the main theme is carried in allegro tempo, and the second theme in tempo andante). To the same end he sometimes uses the method, common to romantics, of remote tonal juxtapositions. For example, in the Fourth Symphony the F-Minor of the main theme is juxtaposed to the A-Flat Minor and B-Major of the second theme; in "Romeo and Juliet" we have the B-Minor set off against the D-Flat Major. This method, however, is also subordinate and does not, like the colourful contrasts of Liszt, disrupt the general modal structure of the piece. More characteristic for Tchaikovsky is the use of related tonalities tending towards a single central point. It is not by chance that in the Sixth Symphony, which is stylistically the most complete of Tchaikovsky's works, the modal correlation between the themes of the cycle are simple and traditional with the B-Minor and D-Major predominating.

To the main images in the first movement an independent third image is sometimes added—the Fatum theme.

The introductions to the first movements of the Fourth and
Fifth symphonies, are quite similar in conception, and are
based on the Fatum theme. The introduction of this type
of expressive symbolic theme and its utilization in various
parts of a composition is, as we have mentioned before, a
romantic tradition. In Tchaikovsky's music, however, these
themes are far more concrete and the general significance
of the subject is much greater than, for instance, the symbolic leitmotifs of Wagner. The relentless insistence of the
ominous fanfares in the introduction to the Fourth Symphony can only be perceived as the expression of some
sinister, supernatural force. It undoubtedly traces its origin
to the traditional idea of the trumpet call on Judgment
Day. The fanfare rhythm also forms the foundation of the
"Fatum Theme" in the Fifth Symphony. The harmonic
structure and form of exposition, especially the response,
lends this theme the nature of a sinister chorale and evokes
another also quite common association—death; as a matter
of fact the actual funeral motif is introduced into the first
movement of the Sixth Symphony and almost in the same
form in the final scene of "The Queen of Spades."

The significance of the "Fatum Theme" in the Fourth
and Fifth symphonies should not be underestimated. The
whole dramatic conception of the symphony, and primarily,
of course, the theme of spiritual confusion arises from it.
This direct psychological connection is stressed by the
close kinship between the thematic material of the introduction and the main theme.

The contrasting yet closely allied Fatum and "spiritual
confusion" themes are joined in a single complex offset in
toto to the serene and placid second theme. This unity of
two tragic themes is clearly brought out, for instance, in

the development of the Fourth Symphony where at the moment of climax both designs are interwoven, thus mutually enhancing their expressiveness.

The advent of the "Fatum theme" invariably coincides with some natural structural borderline. In the Andante of the Fifth Symphony, for example, the ominous fanfares divide the central part and the Reprise, and the Reprise from the Coda. This is an indication of Tchaikovsky's general tendency toward classical logic and comprehensiveness of form.

In his elaboration Tchaikovsky usually returns to the main theme and develops it on a new and substantially augmented plane. The principles of development are on the whole the same as in the exposition: increasing concentration and intensification of the main elements of the theme. As in Beethoven's dramatic elaborations, the development proceeds in the form of successively rising waves. The last and most powerful wave leads directly to the reprise. This type of *dynamic preparation for the restatement* is exceedingly characteristic of Tchaikovsky. At the same time, in many cases the main theme of the reprise serves as the direct continuation of the development, while the introduction of the radiant second theme marks the beginning of a new and clearly defined section.

In a letter about the Fourth Symphony, Tchaikovsky gives the following formula for the content of his first movement: "And so the whole of life is a perpetual alternation of painful reality with transient dreams and longings for happiness. . . . There is no haven of refuge. . . . We needs must swim in this sea until it seizes us and submerges us in its depths." This definition reveals not only the general conception, but also to a considerable extent gives the clue to the form of the first movements of his symphonies.

Tchaikovsky tended to group his material in sonata outline in such a way that the latter became a *periodic alternation of two major contrasting thematic sections*. The first section associated with the main theme *is steadily enlivened in reiteration with the result that the very contrast of the two sections is consistently sharpened*.

In the Fourth Symphony the first long section (A) is made up of the introduction and the main theme. We have already pointed out that although thematically dissimilar and in some cases even contrasting, yet taken together as a more complex tragic image, they offset the second theme. The second large section (B), contains the second and concluding themes. This section is thematically dissimilar too, but has a single idea in apposition to the first section (see the author's comments). The elements of the main theme included here are transformed to depict serene joy. The third section (A1)—the development and the main theme of the reprise connected with it—constitutes a much more dynamic reiteration of the first section. Then follows the fourth section (B1), analogous to the second, and finally, the fifth (A2), a new and sharper variation of section A. This principle is embodied in its "purest" form in the first movement of the Sixth Symphony. Sections A and B here are much more monolithic owing to the absence (as distinct from the Fourth Symphony) of inner thematic contrasts: the introduction does not have an independent theme but from the very outset develops the main theme; in section B the independent concluding part is omitted. Moreover, the major sections of the first movement of the Sixth Symphony are more finished and complete.

This treatment of the sonata outline arises directly from the message contained in Tchaikovsky's symphonies and in this sense it is individual. At the same time it has a good deal in common with the principles on which the larger instrumental forms by Chopin, Liszt and Wagner are built. In the given instance the general romantic traits represent a certain simplification of the sonata outline, an introduction of the *alternating* principle emanating from the Rondo and variation forms; although the development of each of the alternating sections is broader than the classical Sonata. The principal difference between Tchaikovsky's sonata allegros and the major instrumental forms of the romantics (Liszt's symphonic poems, for example) is that in the case of Tchaikovsky the general development is far more purposeful and dynamic. Moreover his forms are more *integral* and their inner thematic contrasts more *real* than in the case of the romantics (with Liszt, the contrasting images are often free variations on one and the same theme).

The central parts of Tchaikovsky's symphonic cycle are analogous as to their general function to the second themes of the first allegros. They constitute a diversion, a "relaxation" from tragic torment. But what is placed here in apposition to "painful reality" is by no means a vague hankering for the unattainable, it is real, full-blooded life given in the form of tender love themes, reminiscence, contemplation of nature, or the effervescent waltz. The central parts of the mature symphonies are based usually on concrete genre forms: song, romance and dance. These forms were developed and deepened both internally and externally from one symphony to another in conformity with symphonic desiderata. In the Fourth Symphony the central parts were still rather close to their genre prototypes. Characteristic in this respect is the second movement, the *Andantino in modo di canzona*. Like the Adagio in "Winter Reveries," this is a simple, lyrical "song without words." The structure of the first and last parts is rudimentary (couplet form). The development proceeds chiefly in the form of variations. In the Scherzo a popular ditty and a march are grotesqued in a fantastic pizzicato design.

In the central parts of the Fifth and Sixth symphonies the subject and symphonic development are given a much deeper treatment. In this sense the canzona from the Fourth Symphony forms quite a contrast to the Andante from the Fifth, the most monumental, as regards melodic development of the slow movements, in Tchaikovsky's symphonies.

It is most interesting to compare the Waltz in the Fifth Symphony with the dance part in the Sixth (Allegro con grazia). The first, while a form of symphonized waltz is nevertheless relatively close to the original genre. In the second we find only the general outline of the waltz. By substituting the three-time measure by the five-time, the composer achieves a greater concentration of colour (the larger, uneven bars enhance the smooth, flowing movement of the waltz).

The finales of all of Tchaikovsky's symphonies, with the exception of the Sixth, are of one type, vivid, joyous canvases conveying the spirit of rejoicing—popular rejoicing for the most part—forming a striking contrast to the subjective lyricism of the preceding movements. Russian folk song and dance genres invariably comprise their thematic foundation. The role and treatment of this type of festive finale varies, however. Whereas in the First and

Third Symphonies the finale only formally *completes* the cycle, in the Fourth Symphony it *sums up* all that has been stated in the preceding movements. In the latter instance threads are drawn from the first movement to the finale which thereby loses its purely genre character and gains in depth and dramatic tension. In this sense the variations on the theme of the folk song "A birch stood in the meadow" in the finale of the Fourth Symphony differs in principle from the variation finale of the Second Symphony. There the music hinges on externally ingenious transformations of the melody. In the finale of the Fourth Symphony there is less external invention, and the variation is directed chiefly at one aim, namely, to bring out the lyrical quality of the song. In the final passages preceding the intrusion of the "Fatum theme" the mood becomes sorrowful in a manner similar to that of numerous analogous Tchaikovsky themes (*e.g.* in the first phrase of Lensky's aria "What has the coming day in store for me"). The folk song serves here to bring out the subjective element associated with the leading idea of the composition.

The same cannot be said of the finale of the Fifth Symphony where the composer departs from the subjective lyricism of the preceding movements. Neither, however, can this finale be regarded as a simple genre scene: the development of the transformed "Fatum theme" lends a philosophical significance to this movement and thereby links it with the idea pervading the rest of the symphony. In the Sixth Symphony Tchaikovsky came closer to the Fourth in this respect than to the Fifth. In order that the principal tragic idea might predominate throughout the composer avoided the *traditional festive finale* in the Sixth. The symphony ends in a mournful adagio, concentrated, like the first movement, exclusively on the psychological motives.

A comparative study of Tchaikovsky's three mature symphonies shows a striving for an ever deeper and philosophically profound embodiment in music of the ideas that possessed his mind. This explains, first, the desire to avoid the *empirical* method of recording impressions and to give instead a more complex and thoughtful treatment of the material; secondly, the growing scale and dramatic intensity of development, and thirdly, the deeper and more organic subordination of the movements of the symphonic cycle. All these tendencies were most fully manifested in the Sixth Symphony, which is as much the stylistic as ideological credo of Tchaikovsky.

*   *   *

The Fourth Symphony (F-Minor, 1877) is one of the peaks of Tchaikovsky's creative achievement. Written simultaneously with "Eugene Onegin," it was the reflection of a period at which the composer's creative forces had reached a point of high tension. It was at this period that his ideas and the principal features of his style asserted themselves most fully.

The composer worked on both compositions with unusual inspiration, for he felt that he was investing in them his most cherished thoughts and emotions. "That which I have written literally poured out of me," he wrote, recalling his work on "Onegin." And, of the Fourth Symphony: "There is not a single line in this symphony that I have not felt with my whole being and that has not been a true echo of the soul."

As is known, the programme of the Fourth Symphony

was outlined in detail by the author in a letter to von Meck.* Judging by the postscriptum to the abovementioned

* We give the excerpt pertaining to the symphony in full:

"The introduction is the *kernel* of the whole symphony, unquestionably the leading idea (theme of the introduction).

"This is *Fatum*. The fateful force that bars the road to happiness . . . the force that hangs over us like a Damocles sword forever poisoning the soul. It is invincible and can never be overpowered. We must needs submit and chafe in vain. (The main theme.)

"The feeling of unhappiness and hopelessness grows stronger and stronger. Perhaps it were better to turn away from reality and abandon ourselves to reverie (beginning of the second theme).

"Oh joy! A sweet and gentle dream envelops us. Some blessed bright human image flits by and beckons to us (continuation of the second theme).

"How wonderful! How remote the insistent first theme of the allegro sounds now. But the dream little by little takes possession of the soul. All gloom and melancholy is banished. This is happiness. . . .

"No! It was but a dream, and fate rudely awakens us (the Fatum theme).

"And so all the whole life is a perpetual alternation of painful reality with transient dreams and longings for happiness. . . . There is no haven of refuge. . . . We needs must swim this sea until it seizes us and submerges us in its depths. That is approximately the programme of the first movement.

"The second movement of the symphony expresses another phase of yearning. This is the wistful melancholy that visits one of an evening when, sitting alone after work, one takes up a book but lets it drop listlessly from one's hands. Memories come crowding thick and fast. And it is sad to think that so much has already *been and gone*, and it is pleasant to recall one's youth. And one regrets that the past is gone but shrinks from starting life anew. One is weary of life. How pleasant it is to rest and look back at what has been. One remembers a great deal. The moments of happiness in our youth when our pulses raced and life was good; the painful moments of irreparable loss. All this is now long since over and done with. There is pain as well as a curious pleasure in looking back into the past.

"The third movement expresses no definite sensations. It consists of the whimsical arabesques, the elusive images that flit across the mind after a sip of wine, when one is in the first phase of intoxication. One is neither gay nor sad. One thinks of nothing and gives full rein to the imagination and for some reason it commences to draw these queer patterns. . . . Musing thus, one suddenly recalls the scene of merry *mushiks* and gay singing on the streets. . . . Then somewhere in the distance a military procession passes. These are the utterly disconnected letter, Tchaikovsky was evidently aware of the inadequacy of his attempt to give verbal expression to a purely lyrical composition.*

Although, close as it is to the truth, this verbal exposition ought not be taken too literally, it is nevertheless a valuable psychological commentary to the symphony. The very fact that it is given in the form of a personal letter, a human document, and not as a romantic literary programme of the Liszt or Berlioz variety, is interesting in itself. The style of the programme to an even greater extent than the "plot" gives the key to the character of the hero of the symphony—a man of simple, unassuming aspect, but capable of great feeling.

Like "Onegin," the Fourth Symphony gives the fullest expression to what Tchaikovsky called "intimate but powerful drama." The atmosphere of familiar everyday life is

---

images that emerge from the subconscious as one is about to doze off. They have nothing whatever to do with reality; they are strange, fantastic and scattered.

"Fourth Movement. If you cannot find cause for happiness in yourself then observe others. Go forth among the people. See how they enjoy themselves, how they abandon themselves completely to merriment. Scenes of popular rejoicing. But barely have you had time to forget yourself in the spectacle of rejoicing, than inexorable Fate knocks again at your door. But those others care nothing for you. They do not even turn their heads to look at you and do not notice that you are sad and alone. Ah, how gay they are! How happy, because their emotions are natural and simple. It is your own fault and not the world's that you are sad. There are simple but powerful joys. Take pleasure in the joy of others. Life is after all worth living."

* "I was about to put this letter into the envelope when I read it over and was aghast at the vagueness and inadequacy of the programme I am sending you. This is the first time in my life that I have attempted to translate musical ideas and images into words and phrases. I have clearly failed to do this properly. I was suffering from severe hypochondria last winter when I wrote the symphony and it is a faithful echo of my mental state at the time. But it is an *echo*, I repeat. How can it be translated into clear, coherent language? I don't know, I cannot do it."

combined in ideal harmonious unity with lofty psychological lyricism. In the First Movement the vivid drama of the main theme emerges from the mournful elegiac waltz movement (the author has marked it: In movimento di valse). The simple Waltz leads to the second theme with its amazing intimacy, warmth and exquisite grace. The Andantino consists of variations on a touchingly simple and "homey" romance, elevated however—like the famous Andante cantabile from the First Quartet—to a high point of lyrical concentration. In the Scherzo the street song and military march in the middle part are as essential as the fantastic pizzicato framework of "whimsical arabesques and elusive images." In the festive and objectively formal Finale the main theme (folk dance tune "A birch stood in the meadow") acquire profound lyrical expression in the process of the development; the close connection between this movement and the message of the symphony as a whole is emphasized by the intrusion of the "Fatum theme" in the opening of the Coda.

Fifth Symphony (E-Minor, 1888). Both in idea and exposition the Fifth Symphony is a variation of the concept of the Fourth Symphony and partially reproduced in "Manfred" (1885). In the Fifth Symphony this concept is embodied with even greater unity and scope. The "Fatum theme," for example, is carried consistently through the whole of the cycle, breaking in almost invariably at moments of supreme joy and contentment, ruthlessly scattering "dreams" and bringing the hero face to face with tragic reality. It is only in the finale that this theme is differently interpreted.

The main theme of the First Movement is written in the spirit of a ballad, austere in mood and full of alarming presentiments (Tomsky's ballad from "The Queen of Spades," composed two years later, has much in common with this theme). The second theme is a charming Waltz, light and airy at first but gradually acquiring an inner intensity and breadth of ·movement. The main dramatic climax of the First Movement appears in the Coda. Having reached the highest point of its development the first theme is rapidly extinguished, its melody sounding lower and lower, until finally it disappears in the sombre voices of the deep basses.

The Second Movement (Andante) is one of the most inspired of Tchaikovsky's positive images, the embodiment of his passionate love of life. This movement unquestionably ranks among his masterpieces. The development of the two main themes is based on the principle of variation, in the process of which the stream of melody grows in breadth and dynamic intensity, while preserving an inner restraint. Twice the ominous "Fatum theme" invades the serene world of the Andante.

The Third Movement is another waltz. Its lightly flowing melody and transparent fabric offers a sharp contrast to the Andante. The Fatum image flashes past like a dim shadow in the final bars.

The Finale, like that of the Fourth Symphony, completes the entire succession of images and moods in a spirit of optimism. But whereas in the Fourth, moments of subjective tragedy are still felt, the subjective is totally dissolved in the atmosphere of festive gaiety. And even the grim "Fatum theme" has the imposing sound of a triumphant march. In wealth of theme as well as variety and brilliance of elaboration, the finale of the Fifth Symphony surpasses all Tchaikovsky's other festive finales.

Sixth Symphony (B-Minor, 1893). In 1892 Tchaikovsky wrote another symphony but was dissatisfied with it. The following year he wrote to his nephew: "You know that last autumn I destroyed my symphony of which part had been written and orchestrated. I am glad I did so, for it was a poor piece of work, a foolish play of sounds without any real inspiration. During my trip (his annual winter trip abroad in the winter of 1892–93) I conceived the idea for another symphony, this time a programme work, but one that will remain a mystery to everyone. . . . The programme is as subjective as it could possibly be and often as I composed it mentally during my wanderings I wept sorely."

The Sixth Symphony was completed in Klin in August 1893, two months before the composer's death. The leading idea was far too clearly apparent in the music to remain a mystery: it treats of the same problem as the preceding two symphonies.*

The Sixth Symphony is far more tragic than the Fourth or the Fifth. Like "The Queen of Spades," it was the direct reflection of the composer's mood in the latter years of his life as can be judged by his letters and diaries. The dramatic

---

* Among Tchaikovsky's papers was found the following sketch relating in all probability to the later years of his life and possibly reflecting the process of work on the Sixth Symphony:

"The further essence of the symphony is LIFE. The first movement is all passion, confidence, thirst for activity. Should be brief (the Finale is DEATH—the result of destruction).

"2nd Movement, love; 3rd, disillusionment; 4th ends in fade-out (also brief)."

A definite hint at the content of the Sixth Symphony is found in one of the composer's letters. In reply to a request by Konstantin Romanov that he write the music for the "Requiem," Tchaikovsky remarked that his last symphony (especially the finale) "is permeated with a mood very similar to that of a 'Requiem.' "

intensity of the expression, the profundity and consistency with which the leading idea is stated, makes the Sixth the peak of Tchaikovsky's philosophic symphonies.

In the Sixth Symphony there is none of that rather superficial symbolism in the presentation of the Fatum idea that is characteristic of the preceding symphonies. The tragic element is concentrated in a single psychological image—the main theme of the First Movement. There is no dominant leitmotif in the Sixth Symphony, nevertheless all the parts of the cycle are interconnected by profound and subtle thematic ties.

The main theme of the First Movement differs from analogous themes in the Fourth and Fifth symphonies by virtue of its peculiar concentrated and laconic quality, and the absence of direct formal connecting links. The second theme too is more generalized. The elaboration of the first movement is the quintessence of Tchaikovsky's genius as a master of the symphonic drama. The main theme is developed in the form of a series of successive progressions and climaxes. At the climax of the third and mightiest progression (two bars after N *) begins the restatement of the main theme, which is at the same time a new phase of the development, overlapping the third "wave." The theme appears in a dynamic exposition and carries the melody away to a new and higher culmination. The moment of crisis is a grand dominant organ point with the fateful voices of the trombones responding to the "pleadings" of the strings and woodwinds. This is the tragic response to the preceding storm and confusion of feeling. The recapitulation of the second theme and Coda bring appeasement with a wistful sadness.

* See the printed score (Jurgenson edition).

The treatment of the leading idea of the Sixth Symphony is equally profound throughout. The graceful second movement, though in dance time, is exceedingly remote from elementary genre music. The central episode of this movement links it directly with the main tragic line of the composition. The Scherzo combines the ceaseless playful movement common to the genre (although the very playfulness is tinged with alarm) with a triumphant march which becomes predominant in the recapitulation. The splendour and magnificence of the Scherzo and the funereal plane of the Finale Adagio is the final and most outstanding tragic antithesis of the Sixth Symphony.

IV. *Programme Compositions*

Tchaikovsky's first experiment in the domain of programme music—"The Storm" overture, after the famous drama by Alexander Ostrovsky (1864)—dates back to his student years. According to his brother, it was the young composer's cherished ambition to write an opera on this subject. It is not surprising that "The Storm" should have been his choice of a subject for the large opera overture he had to write for his examination.

As is seen from the author's sketch of the programme for the overture * it was the lyrico-psychological motives combined with the Russian folk background that aroused the composer's interest in Ostrovsky's play. This subject

* "Introduction: Adagio (childhood of Katerina and her whole life until her marriage), Allegro (hints of the storm); her striving for real happiness and love. Allegro appassionato (her spiritual conflict). Sudden transition to an evening on the banks of the Volga: again struggle with a touch of fevered happiness. Omens of storm (repetition of the motif following the Adagio and its further development). The Storm: the climax of desperate struggle and death."

that came to be so typical of the future Tchaikovsky is reflected in the music: the broad melodies of the second theme and the episode in the elaboration. On the whole, however, "The Storm" was an immature experiment in the larger media. It lacked the inner integrity and unity of development that distinguished Tchaikovsky's symphonies. "The Storm" was not performed in the composer's lifetime and was published among other works after his death.

The next programme work, the symphonic poem "Fatum" (1868) was an even more obvious failure. Laroche and Balakirev both criticized it roundly for the variegated thematic material, fragmentary form, unconvincing musical interpretation of the story. The author himself was not satisfied with the poem, and subsequently destroyed the score along with several other manuscripts relating to the early period.*

One year later Tchaikovsky scored his first brilliant victory in the domain of programme symphony by completing his Fantasia-Overture "Romeo and Juliet" (1869).

Balakirev took an active part in bringing this composition into being. He not only suggested the idea of using the Shakespeare subject but also the general plan of the composition and even the general character of the various themes.** The composer, however, was interested not so much in the character details of the different themes (as was his adviser) as in the general interpretation of the dramatic "knot" of the story.

The contrast and clash of two forces—love and enmity

* After the composer's death the score was revived according to the orchestral parts and in 1896 published by the Belyaev Publishing House.
** See Professor Igor Boelza's paper "Shakespeare and Russian Music," International Literature, 1944, No. 12.

(the feud of the Montagues and Capulets) as a barrier to happiness—is the leading idea of the overture. Here we have again the usual Tchaikovsky antithesis, tragic fatality as opposed to life and beauty. The interpretation naturally lent itself to the sonata form. The allegro giusto theme suggested by Balakirev is most suitable for the duel scene. Representation, however, is not the dominant factor here. It is subordinated to a more general psychological line. The furious and at the same time repressed movement of the Allegro embodies the spiritual confusion and tragic futility typical of Tchaikovsky's main themes. In apposition to it we have the similarly typical romantic love theme, distinguished by an unusual breadth and flow of melodic development. In accordance with Balakirev's plan the overture opens with a long introduction drawing the image of Friar Lawrence. The austere yet lucid choral movement of the introduction forms a contrast also with the main and second themes. However, Lawrence's theme is not developed as an independent contrasting image. In the development and in the first part of the Coda it becomes now mournful now threatening and is associated as to general expressive significance with the main theme. Thus, as is customary for Tchaikovsky, the poem is based on *two groups* of themes.

The programme of the symphonic fantasia "The Tempest" (1873) was suggested by V. Stasov.* The fantastic plot of Shakespeare's play did not offer material for intense dramatic conceptions. The various characters and scenes,

---

* "The Sea. The magician Prospero sends Ariel, a spirit obedient to his will, to produce a tempest which wrecks the ship bearing Fernando's vessel. A fairy island. The first timid flutterings of love in Miranda and Fernando. Ariel. Caliban. The lovers submitting to the triumphant lure of passion. Prospero casts off the magic spell and leaves the island. The sea."

the rolling ocean, the mighty Prospero, the tempest, the
love of Fernando and Miranda, the fantastic creatures who
serve Prospero—the light-footed Ariel and the monster
Caliban—are presented in a series of tableaux.

Nevertheless here too Tchaikovsky remained true to
himself. The dominant role in "The Tempest" is given
neither to the pictorial nor the fantastic element but to the
love theme. The gradual blossoming of feeling from the
first timid confessions to the passionate romantic hymn of
love and life constitute the main motif of this symphonic
poem. In the development of the main theme, in the major
tone of the climaxes that seems to be flooded with dazzling
light we see the prototype of many future love scenes,
from the letter scene in "Onegin" to Lisa's monologue and
the duet of Vaudemont and Yolanthe. One can but be
amazed at the vitality of this oft-repeated scheme of development and at the truly inexhaustible inspiration that
gave new life again and again to the composer's favourite
idea.

"Francesca da Rimini" (1876), borrowed from the
Fifth Canto of Dante's "Inferno," was first conceived by
Tchaikovsky as an opera. As N. Kashkin tells us in his
memoirs, the composer "was ready to begin writing the
opera, but the librettist laid down conditions to which the
composer could not agree. . . ."

K. I. Zvantsev was one of the most fanatical admirers
of Wagner and he wanted the composer to write his
"Francesca" in conformity with all the reformist theories
of Wagner; he even wished to reserve to himself certain
control rights in this respect and this caused the rupture.
In the summer of 1872 Tchaikovsky wrote to his brother:
"This morning in the train (en route to Bayreuth, where the

famous Wagnerian festivals were held), I read the Fifth Canto of Dante's "Inferno" and became fired with the desire to write a symphonic poem called "Francesca da Rimini." He carried out his intention in the autumn of the same year.

The form of the new symphonic poem was dictated by the structure of its programme; the latter can be found in detail in the author's manuscript of "Francesca." *

The poem consists of the following parts: I—introduction (Andante lugubre) and the first movement (Allegro vivo), depicting the journey of Dante and Virgil and scenes of the Inferno; II—(Andante non troppo)—Francesca's story; III—diminished restatement of the first movement ("Francesca in Paolo's arms is again whirled violently away").

* "Dante, accompanied by the shade of Virgil, descends to the second circle of the Inferno. The air is rent by groans, screams and cries of despair. A tempest rages amidst the sepulchral gloom. The infernal hurricane in its wild fury sweeps away the souls of men whose minds were dulled in life by sensual passions. Among the myriads of human souls swirling in the blast Dante's attention is caught by two in close embrace, the lovely shades of Francesca and Paolo. Overcome by the heartrending sight of this young couple, Dante beseeches them to tell him for what crime they have been subjected to such a horrible punishment. The shade of Francesca, weeping bitter tears, tells her sad story. She loved Paolo, but was married against her will to his brother, the repulsive, jealous tyrannical hunchback Rimini. The bonds of marriage into which she was forced could not make Francesca relinquish her tender love for Paolo. One day they were reading together the love story of Lancelot. 'We sat together and read aloud, suspecting nought,' says Francesca. 'Now and again we paled and our confused glances met. But one moment destroyed us both. When finally the happy Lancelot stole his first kiss, he from whom nothing can now tear me asunder pressed his lips to my trembling mouth and the book which had revealed to us the first secret of love fell from our hands.' At that instant Francesca's husband entered unexpectedly and stabbed both of them to death. As she recounts this Francesca in Paolo's arms is once again borne away violently by the whirlwind. Seized with an overwhelming compassion Dante loses consciousness and falls as though dead. . . ."

Notwithstanding the programmatic nature of the piece, the subject and the correlation of those thematic sections are handled in characteristic Tchaikovsky fashion: tragedy on the one hand (Inferno), and inspired love (Francesca's tale) on the other.

The descriptive element is felt in the introduction and in the first and last parts of "Francesca" even more strongly than in "Romeo and Juliet." It is known that Tchaikovsky composed "Francesca" having in mind Gustave Dore's famous drawings on the subject of Dante's "Inferno." The whirlwind in "Francesca" bears an affinity to the tempest episode in Liszt's "Preludes." As in "Romeo," however, the emotional and psychological elements dominate rather than the decorative: not the whirlwind, but the "human souls" in eternal torment. This is the image embodied in the main theme of the first and last parts consisting of separate moaning intonations that seem to rise above the infernal storm. This theme evolves gradually from the chaotic and seemingly amorphous whirlwind movement and develops from scattered intonations to a broad, coalescent melody.

Concentrated in the central part of "Francesca" are images which Tchaikovsky is fond of juxtaposing to his tragic main themes. Francesca's narrative begins as a simple, warm song with a faint Russian touch. It continues as a new and more agitated phase of recollection. The middle episode (L'istesso tempo), evidently connected with the story of the lovers reading the love story of Lancelot, is treated in waltz form. This is an idyllic moment untouched by tragedy. The whole development of the central part, in which the exposition is mainly in the form of variations, is distinguished at the same time by a steady increase in tempo. The development is climaxed characteristically by the intrusion of sinister (tutti) notes (depicting the death of the lovers) at the end of the love theme just as the Fatum image breaks into the Andante in the Fifth Symphony.

In "Francesca" as in "Romeo and Juliet," the type of subject, the musical images and drama were all admirably suited to Tchaikovsky's temperament. Not for a single moment is the lyrical flow of the music sacrificed to external illustrative element. Nowhere does the subject serve merely as the outer verbal commentary to the music. Both compositions are among Tchaikovsky's finest symphonic poems.

*   *   *

The first of the programme works written in the following decade was the "1812 Overture" (1880), in honour of the Patriotic War of 1812 against Napoleon. The broad and slow-moving introduction is built up on the theme of a prayer of thanksgiving for the victory of Russian arms (Largo) and strident militant fanfares (Andante). A battle Allegro with Marseillaise and a Russian folk song woven into it form the exposition. The development and the beginning of the recapitulation depicts the battle scene. Themes from the introduction appear in the triumphant Coda, and the Russian anthem completes the piece.

Patriotic in conception, and written with consummate mastery, the "1812 Overture" won immense popularity almost at once and figured constantly in the programme of the composer's works. To this day it is performed with unfailing success in the concert halls of Moscow, Leningrad and other cities of the Soviet Union. Another programme piece is the symphonic picture of the "Battle of Poltava"

(1883), which forms the entr'actes to the Third Act of "Mazeppa." It opens with the scene of the battle followed by a traditional "Slava" (Hail) and chorale symbolizing the victory of the Russian forces. A triumphant march gradually receding ends the piece.

The year 1885 saw the advent of "Manfred," one of the most monumental of Tchaikovsky's scores. Once again Balakirev acted as initiator and adviser. In a letter to Tchaikovsky in 1882 he wrote that he had offered the subject some time previously to Berlioz, "who refused on account of old age and sickness and inability to compose anything more. Your 'Francesca' induced me to believe that you could handle this subject in brilliant fashion." *

The first scene, profound in emotional and psychological import, was closest of all to Tchaikovsky's creative temperament. The other parts of the programme where the main line of the story is eclipsed by the external decorative elements (mountain waterfall, scenes of village life, the orgy and palace of Ariman), offered greater difficulties which were nevertheless brilliantly coped with.

* In its final version, published on the pages of the score, the programme reads as follows:
Part I. Manfred wanders in the Alps. Haunted by problems of existence, tormented by a burning sense of futility and the memory of a criminal past, he is a prey to spiritual anguish. Initiated into the secrets of black magic, Manfred communicates with the mighty powers of darkness but neither they nor anything on earth can give him the oblivion for which he is vainly seeking. Memories of the dead Astarte, whom he once loved passionately, torment his soul and there is no limit, no end to the abysmal despair of Manfred.
Part II. The Alpine spirit appears before Manfred in a rainbow formed by the sprays of a waterfall.
Part III. A scene depicting simple, poor but free life of the mountaineers.
Part IV. Underground palace of Ariman. Infernal orgy. Advent of Manfred among the bacchanalia. The shade of Astarte appears at his summons. He is forgiven. He dies.

While offering the programme of "Manfred" to Tchaikovsky, Balakirev had definite ideas as to the style in which
it ought to be written. The very genre of the symphony,
the story of the romantic hero and his wanderings, calls
to mind Berlioz, and follows a pattern similar to that contained in the works of many of the romantics. Such, for
example, is the rustic idyll with the traditional shepherd
scene and the distant tinkling of a bell (third movement)
contrasted to the spiritual suffering of Manfred; this part
has elements in common with the Meadow Scene from
Berlioz's "Symphonie Fantastique," the "March of the
Pilgrims" from his "Harold on Italie" and with the pastorale
episode from Liszt's "Les Preludes." The same applies
to the "Orgy in Ariman's Palace" in the fourth movement
of "Manfred," which is easily associated with the "Witches'
Dance" from Berlioz's "Symphonie Fantastique" and Liszt's
"Mephisto Waltz." In the finale of "Manfred" we find an
external theatricality, melodramatic pose and philosophical
rhetoric which are on the whole quite untypical of Tchaikovsky.

The idea of Byron's poem is most comprehensively expressed in the first movement of the symphony. The first
three major constructions of this movement (they may be
roughly classed as the introduction, main and connecting
themes) reveal the spiritual world of Manfred himself, his
fateful presentiments, his anguished longings and his painful memories of the past. The leitmotif here is the sombre
tragic theme of Manfred which plays a dominant role
throughout the work.

The three constructions aforementioned are counterpoised by a fourth section (of the type of a second theme
in sonata form) through which runs the serene and

womanly theme of Astarte; as well as the theme of Manfred's love pleas (Andante in F-sharp minor).

The fifth section (Andante con duolo) is a powerful
dramatic Coda built up again on the main Manfred theme.
Bursting like a grim warning into the idyllic atmosphere
of the second and third scenes, the main theme reappears
in the Finale, this time as a symbol of Manfred's power.
Then comes the episode of the summoning of Astarte's
shade (Adagio), once again hope, the faintest suggestion
this time, reappears, followed by the tragic end of Manfred,
analogous to the concluding passages of the first part of
the Coda.

Considering the various scenes of "Manfred" to be
uneven and the entire cycle too drawn out, Tchaikovsky
intended at some later date to rewrite it as a symphonic
poem, using the first movement as the foundation. But this
plan was never destined to be carried out.

In 1888 Tchaikovsky was commissioned to write the
music for the production of Shakespeare's "Hamlet" in
connection with a grand charity performance to be held in
St. Petersburg. Since the performance never came off
Tchaikovsky used the material of the overture he had begun
for a concert overture-fantasia for an extended orchestra.*

In a review of Ambroise Thomas' "Hamlet" written
long before the above score was composed, Tchaikovsky
said: ". . . the predominant aspect of Hamlet, namely,
that scourging irony that permeates all of his utterances, the
purely intellectual processes that make for his gloomy
scepticism are absolutely unsuitable for music however

* Later in 1891 Tchaikovsky did write the theatrical music for
"Hamlet" for the jubilee of the famous French actor Guitry. He undertook the task with great reluctance, borrowing most of the numbers from
his previous compositions.

powerful it might be in expressing the workings of the human soul." There is no doubt that even when he was writing his own "Hamlet" Tchaikovsky adhered to this conviction which was quite just from the standpoint of his musical asthetics. In Tchaikovsky's "Hamlet" the main emphasis is laid on the dramatic and lyrical motives of Shakespeare's play.

The overture consists of a juxtaposition of the thematic groups typical for Tchaikovsky. On the one hand, the tragic element (introduction, Lento lugubre) from which evolves the agitated impulsive Allegro (main theme); on the other hand, forming the two love themes—one pensively gentle, the other more active.

The exposition culminates in a march in a gradual crescendo. After a brief transition the whole exposition is repeated. In the last section of the overture (Allegro, Coda) the tragic pleading motif of the introduction resounds against the restless agitated movement of the strings. The rising march rhythm appears shot through by the swift first theme and the movement breaks off. A few impassioned recitative passages and then the mournful motif of the 'cellos leads to the concluding bars of the overture in the spirit of a funeral march.

The last programme work by Tchaikovsky is the symphonic ballad "Voyevoda" (1891), on the subject of the ballad of the same name by Pushkin (after Mickiewicz). The dark sinister colouring of the first movement corresponds to the spirit of the opening lines of the poem. The middle part depicts the love scene by the fountain—where the main mournful lyrical theme (E-minor) is evidently associated with the hero's sad farewell ("All is lost . . ."). There follows a brief imperious and ireful episode (Allegro

giusto) faintly reminiscent in idea to the fateful end of
Francesca's story. And finally, the restatement of the first
movement in the form of a sombre epilogue. The composer
was dissatisfied with this ballad and destroyed the score
after its first performance.

Tchaikovsky's attitude to this work may have been influenced by Taneyev who criticized it rather severely. "It
seemed to me," said Taneyev in his memoirs, "that the main
part of this piece was the central love episode; the beginning merely serves as preparation for it. Yet this middle
part is infinitely inferior musically to similar episodes in
Peter Ilyich's earlier compositions such as 'The Tempest,'
'Romeo' and 'Francesca'."

The score of "Voyevoda" was revived after the composer's death from the orchestral parts found among his
papers, and published posthumously among other works.

Tchaikovsky himself was rather sceptical about the
artistic merit of his programme works. Nevertheless he was
attracted to programme music throughout his career. He
produced a good number of symphonic poems and attained
heights of creative mastery in this as in other genres.

His search for a symphonic programme was as persistent
as for librettos for his operas. He looked for subjects that
would serve as concrete, effective and comprehensive vehicles for expressing the vital problems that interested him.
His constant striving for the concrete dramatization of
general problems was evidence of the profound realism of
his art.

Tchaikovsky never showed a tendency toward objective description of a subject. Rarely did he endeavour to
embrace the entire subject chosen. What he did was to
emphasize the motives and situations he considered im-

portant. He was partly right when he wrote that some of his programme works "do not reproduce the given subjects, they merely use it as a basis." Hence his doubts as to whether his programme symphonies were satisfactory.

Yet it is precisely because he probed beneath the surface of the programme that Tchaikovsky was able to give us immortal musical interpretation of famous subjects some of which are congenial to the literary originals. It may be confidently asserted that no other musician in the world has given such powerful and human interpretations of Dante and Shakespeare as Tchaikovsky in his "Romeo and Juliet" and "Francesca da Rimini." Nor has the active and optimistic aspect of Byron's genius been so masterfully conveyed as in Tchaikovsky's "Manfred." In this fusion of the creative element of Tchaikovsky with the great spiritual wellsprings of world art in the past, in the rebirth through his music of the immortal characters of classic literature we have one of the most important contributions of Tchaikovsky's programme symphonies.

V. Suites

Notwithstanding his predilection for the monumental and philosophic, Tchaikovsky was nevertheless irresistibly drawn to the simpler genres of instrumental music—the lyrical salon morceau, the suite and the concert rhapsody.

These diverse forms were usually closely interconnected and reflected the general attributes of his art—profundity combined with comprehensiveness and universal significance. In his symphonies and concertos to a no lesser degree than in his chamber pieces and suites we feel the same association with such familiar genres as the song, the dance,

the lyrical improvisations, all with that simple warm poetry
of everyday life so dear to the heart of the author of "The
Four Seasons." His suites are closest of all to this type of
music, yet in depth of content, scope and tension of development, as well as in expressiveness of exposition, they
frequently approach the symphony and concerto class.

For Tchaikovsky suites were not only a vessel for his
favourite lyrical images, but also a pretext for the statement
and solution of creative problems.

For example, in almost every suite we find experiments
in *stylization*. Tchaikovsky was fond of delving into old
music and had a great feeling and gift for conveying the
spirit of distant historical periods. Yet he invariably remained true to himself and brought his own peculiar *lyricism* and *pulsation* of symphonic development.

With amazing technical ease he solved a number of
highly interesting problems in *orchestral tonality, form
and thematic development* in his suites.

First Suite (op. 43, 1879) opens with an "Introduction
and Fugue" (D-Minor); the severe, virile theme is developed with tremendous inner intensity followed by a
number of lighter genre and character pieces. No. 2
"Divertimento," a sort of symphonized Waltz No. 3—a
poignant elegiac "Intermezzo"; No. 4 "Miniature March,"
one of those typical grotesque toy pieces in which the
wooden mechanical movement of toys is masterfully reproduced; the orchestration creates the appropriate "music-
box" atmosphere; No. 5—a sweeping scherzo in dance time,
with a middle section resembling the Lezghinka from
"Russlan"; No. 6—"Gavotte."

Second Suite ("Character," op. 53, 1883) consists of
five parts: 1. "Play of Sounds," 2. Waltz, 3. "Humorous

Scherzo," 4. "Child's Dreams," 5. "Savage Dance" (in the style of Dargomyzhsky). In nearly every movement we find interesting and ingenious tone novelties, but the orchestral color of the fourth piece, "Child's Dreams," is undoubtedly the best. Its fantastic lacework design seems to be woven of the finest timbre threads. The "Humorous Scherzo" is a grotesque picture of a gay street scene with an accordion and rollicking song. The "Savage Dance" that ends the suite is akin in style to the variations on the theme of the "Crane" song from the Second Symphony and is one of those pieces in which Tchaikovsky's orchestration bears a close affinity to that of the Big Five.

Third Suite (op. 55, 1884) undoubtedly surpasses the preceding two in wealth and variety of content. It begins with an "Elegy," in which the development of the main theme—a broad lyrical cantilene—is framed by a gentle pastorale introduction and conclusion. The second movement, "Melancholy Waltz," with its cold sombre tones, "austere, bleak hopelessness" (Laroche), is one of the most profoundly lyrical of all Tchaikovsky's Waltz themes. The first and last parts of the Scherzo are built up of a ceaseless, whimsical movement; a toy-like trio in march time leads us into that peculiar little world of which Tchaikovsky was perhaps the discoverer, a land of make-believe in which tin soldiers march to mock wars. The fourth part—a theme and variations—is in the nature of an independent suite in which a series of diverse pieces (scherzo, chorale, epic song, dance, elegy, etc.) ends with a grand, festive polonaise.

Fourth Suite. "Mozartiana" (op. 61, 1887), is the orchestral version of three piano pieces and one chorus by Mozart. This suite is one of the most perfect examples of stylization by Tchaikovsky. His amazing feeling for the

style of the epoch (the 18th century) he loved is equally
manifest in the pastoral intermezzo from "The Queen of
Spades," written soon after "Mozartiana."

The *Serenade for String Orchestra* (op. 68, 1880) may
also be classed in the suite category. It consists of four
parts: 1) "Pezzo in forma di sonatina"; 2) Waltz; 3)
Elegy; 4) Finale on a Russian theme. Bearing a close kinship with chamber lyricism, the Serenade is painted in idyllic
and gentle tones almost throughout.

The first part consists of a magnificently compact string
tutti of vibrant tone; the waltz is delightfully elegant and
graceful; the elegy rings with the warm lyricism of solo
instruments. The integrity of the mood, the beauty of the
harmony that flows through all the pieces in this cycle
makes the Serenade one of the finest specimens of symphonic lyricism produced by Tchaikovsky.

Similarly related to the suite genre are the few one-part
symphonic morceaux. Among these is the *"Italian Capriccio"* (1880). (Capriccio Italien.)

"We are at the very height of the carnival," Tchaikovsky began one of his letters from Rome in 1880. "The
shouting, laughter and hubbub are indescribable . . . the
evenings are given over to masquerades and fireworks. Last
night I went for a walk down the Piazza Navona which
was all decorated with magnificent garlands of flowers and
colored lamps." At the end of the letter he adds: "I have
thought out the rough outline of an Italian Fantasia on folk
themes. It should be quite effective because of the delightful themes I have picked up partly from printed music,
partly through my own ear on the streets." The "Italian
Capriccio" is one of the most vivid popular festival canvases Tchaikovsky ever painted. It is as fascinating a spec-

tacle of gay, carnival throngs as is afforded by the best of his symphonic finales. Painted with a particularly generous brush, the "Capriccio" more than any other symphonic composition by Tchaikovsky bears testimony to his brilliant mastery of concert music.

In speaking of Tchaikovsky's one-part symphonic pieces mention should be made also of the "Marche Slav" on the themes of Slav folk melodies (1876). "The boy of seven who delighted in pouring into verse his love for his native land always remained alive in Peter Ilyich," writes the composer's brother, "and throughout his life every patriotic movement invariably found in him an ardent supporter. The extraordinary and unanimous sympathy felt by Russians in 1876 for the Turkish Slavs struck a responsive chord in his soul and hence when Nikolai Rubinstein conceived the idea of arranging a concert in the riding school in aid of the Slav Charity Committee which was equipping Russian volunteers for Serbia he willingly undertook to write a piece of music corresponding to the prevailing sentiments." The "Marche Slav" was a tremendous success during the composer's lifetime, and to this day is one of his most popular pieces here.

*   *   *

Tchaikovsky's symphonies have exercised a vast influence on world music from the end of the 19th century up to the present.

This influence is felt in the early work of Gustav Mahler, the last of the 19th-century symphonists of Western Europe. The author of "Song of the Earth" was irresistibly drawn to Russian art. He once said that all of his work treats essentially of one question posed by Dostoyev-

sky: ". . . how can I be happy so long as another being is
suffering somewhere." The ethics and the lofty moral and
philosophical message of Russian art appealed to Mahler.
Hence his passion for Tchaikovsky, whose works he took
so much pleasure in conducting at the close of the 19th
and the beginning of the present century. His own symphonies are on a lofty moral and philosophical plane. Their
tense emotionalism and wealth of vocal melodies are more
than reminiscent of Tchaikovsky.

In Russia Tchaikovsky had a direct influence on his
younger contemporaries (Taneyev, Arensky, Glazunov,
Kalinnikov, Ippolitov-Ivanov and others) and on all subsequent generations of musicians. In the work of Scriabine,
the greatest Russian symphonist after Tchaikovsky, we
come across the same impassioned treatment of philosophical and psychological problems that distinguished the work
of the great 19th-century symphony writers. Rachmaninov,
Scriabine's contemporary, inherited and transmuted through
his own individuality the symphonic style of Tchaikovsky
with its sweep and stirring excessiveness of melodic line.

Soviet music is bound to the music of Tchaikovsky by
a thousand historical threads. A direct heir to Russian classical music is Nikolai Myaskovsky, one of the leading modern symphonists. His dramatic Sixth Symphony is in the
true Tchaikovsky tradition. The tragic line is developed in
his Seventh, Eleventh and Sixteenth symphonies, as well as
in his recent works, the Twenty-Second and Twenty-
Fourth symphonies, written during the Patriotic War with
fascist Germany. His splendid Fifteenth, Eighteenth and
Twenty-First symphonies continue the lyrical and melodic
stream of Tchaikovsky's music.

Notwithstanding the individuality of his musical idiom

Dmitri Shostakovich's art too stems from the Tchaikovsky tradition. Shostakovich wrote of his Fifth Symphony: "The theme of my symphony is the assertion of the individual. *Man* with all his joys and sufferings is the basic conception of this work which is lyrical from beginning to end." Compare this to Tchaikovsky's statement that the symphony "is the most lyrical of musical forms." The gift of penetration into the "dialectics of the human soul," inherited by Shostakovich from Tchaikovsky helped him to create his stirring poem dedicated to our times—his famous Leningrad Symphony.

Indeed there is not a single Soviet composer of note who has not in his own way developed some aspect of the multifarious Tchaikovsky legacy. This applies to the concertos and symphonies of Aram Khachaturyan, the cantatas of Yuri Shaporin, the ballets of Sergei Prokofiev, the operas of Dmitri Kabelevsky and numerous works by the younger Soviet composers.

The Tchaikovsky tradition can thrive only on the soil of genuine realistic art whose roots reach deep down into the soil of popular life, while the stem and branches reach out to the heights of spiritual culture. This is the ideal toward which Soviet music aspires. Soviet composers learn from Tchaikovsky as from a great realist philosopher, an artist moved by lofty humanitarian ideas, creator of a symphonic style of great power and expressiveness.

THE BALLETS OF TCHAIKOVSKY

VASILI YAKOVLEV

I

IN BALLET TOO Tchaikovsky was true to himself. It was not only an abstract attraction to dance music that made him a great ballet composer. He was spurred on also by his innate striving to write music measuring up to the urgent needs of the moment, to introduce regenerating, revivifying elements into ballet music that would elevate it to a higher plane while adding to its popularity. An integral part of this objective was the inculcation of more exacting standards of appreciation upon the public.

Hence when Tchaikovsky began writing ballet music he did so to elevate its purport, break through the narrow confines that had become established for the genre, and to make it eventually the bearer of a greater message. He wanted to win for ballet a place among the arts as a poetic, musical genre. A friend of his, Hermann Laroche, with whom he studied during his Conservatory days, has left us ample testimony to this effect, showing that Tchaikovsky expressed these views as far back as in the early 60's.

The roots of Tchaikovsky's interest in the ballet may be traced back practically to his childhood years when as a mere youngster he displayed a keen appreciation of the beauty of movement and the enchantment of the folk dance. As a young man Tchaikovsky not only danced himself, but also wrote dance music for his friends and relatives, joining with the others at youthful gatherings to enjoy his waltzes and polkas. Like Glinka and later most of the other Russian composers of his generation, Tchaikovsky could not but be struck by the beauty and expressiveness of the folk dances that kept alive the ancient Russian choreographic tradition among the rural and partly urban population. Traces of these impressions remained with Tchaikovsky all his life. It is this perhaps more than the dictates of convention that induced him to include dance episodes in all of his operas with the exception of "Yolanthe." How much importance he attached to this aspect can be seen from his work both before "Eugene Onegin" with its famous peasant dances (Act I) and after it: the Hopak in "Mazeppa," and the dances in "The Enchantress" and particularly in "The Little Shoes." Old-fashioned dances of the 18th and 19th centuries are major elements in "Eugene Onegin" and "The Queen of Spades"; here they are an integral part of the dramatic story, forming the background or providing the light-and-shadow contrasts for psychologically momentous situations.

From youthful attraction to the folk dance it was the natural course to take the ballet stage, where the fantastic element captivated the eye and the dramatic aspect greatly enhanced the impressions. In this, of course, a definite role was played by the early attempts at dramatic plots made in the romantic ballets of Tchaikovsky's youth. An important factor too in Tchaikovsky's development as a composer of ballet music was his keen interest in all forms of the theatre—opera, drama and ballet—with the exception perhaps of pantomime, which, judging by everything did not interest him very much.

Dance rhythms occupy a prominent place and acquire unquestionable artistic significance in Tchaikovsky's symphonic and suite compositions as well as his instrumental solos. Russian music scholars have long drawn attention to this predilection for dance melodies, waltzes in particular. It may be of interest to recall what Tchaikovsky himself said in advocacy of introducing "ballet" music in symphonic compositions. "I simply cannot understand," he wrote in a letter, "why the term *ballet music* should be associated with something *reprehensible*. After all, there is such a thing as good ballet music." As a matter of fact, Tchaikovsky's richly emotional compositions played their part in setting the course of Russian ballet, which in his time lacked dancers endowed with a profound feeling for the lyrical, toward the delicate poesy of inspired dance.

In the course of the century and a half since its inception the Russian ballet had its ups and downs before it achieved the unsurpassed heights it has attained today. There were the years when it prospered with the famous Frédéric Didelot, the dancer and teacher, and then with a number of able representatives of Western European choreography who did much to develop the Russian ballet, the world-famous Marius Petitpas of St. Petersburg and the less famous but talented A. Glushkovsky (Moscow) and Lev Ivanov (St. Petersburg). All of these names, well known to authorities on ballet, are landmarks in the development of this difficult and complex art. But there were intervening years of stagnation.

It was in one of these periods of decline that Tchaikovsky began working in the field of ballet in Moscow. Yet the reason for this retrogression was by no means the lack of talented dancers—danseuses, to be more exact, for the role of male dancers on the ballet stage in those days was negligible.

"In the distant future," Hermann Laroche wrote in 1869, shortly before "The Swan Lake" was written, "ballet art may perhaps be developed and revivified so that there will be greater harmony between the dancing and the principal conception of the piece. In most probability this new impetus to ballet will be given in Russia, for our people are unquestionably endowed with a remarkable talent for choreography and have latterly produced ballet dancers that have taken Western capitals by storm. When the ballet will be elevated to a higher plane, when people with original and poetic talent will take an interest in it, it may perhaps become popular with the general public. At the present time the number of people who visit the ballet regularly and zealously is extremely small and the performance of old ballets with the old casts rarely draws full houses. Only a new ballet or a new danseuse can for a short time fill the theatre. This coldness of the public is justified to a certain extent by the content of the ballet itself. The drab and prosaic plot, the wearisome routine dances and the monotony of all the details are the outstanding characteristic of all the latest ballets and compel the balletomane to sigh wistfully for the good old days when such graceful and luxurious productions as "Les Sylphides" or "Giselle" could be seen."

This comment by a critic who though young already enjoyed considerable prestige, cannot but be regarded as an echo of the opinions prevailing in the circle of advanced musicians grouped around the Moscow Conservatory to which Tchaikovsky belonged.

As for ballet music, here is what Tchaikovsky himself had to say on the matter in one of his feuilletons (1872):

"We are given a ballet orchestra which, although it may include several decent musicians, is nevertheless accustomed to pipe the vulgar effusions of Messrs. Pugni, Minkus and their ilk." The sharp irony of these words may be ascribed to the fact that at this period Tchaikovsky as well as Laroche was already convinced of the need for drastic reforms in ballet music to extricate it from the stagnant state in which it languished especially in Moscow, where ballet masters were fewer and weaker than in St. Petersburg. A few composers who wrote "potboilers" for the ballet stage Tchaikovsky nevertheless recognized as good musicians (e.g. Herbert), but he could not believe that a composer who could have turned out o many ballets (300!) as Pugni, could have written good music, in spite of the fact that Pugni began his career as a serious and talented musician.

In the early 70's Tchaikovsky was commissioned to write a ballet on the subject of "Cinderella" but the work was soon suspended and nothing is known of the music.

Let us now pass on to a discussion of Tchaikovsky's work on "Swan Lake."

2

"I have wanted to try my hand at music of this kind for a long time," wrote Tchaikovsky in the spring of 1875 to Rimsky-Korsakov upon receipt of a commission from

Moscow theatres to write a ballet. The programme of the ballet, which in all probability was compiled with the composer's assistance, shows the influence of romantic ballets of the 30's and 40's. According to the memoirs of Yuri Davydov, Tchaikovsky's nephew, the composer wrote a one-act ballet for children entitled "Swan Lake" in the summer of 1871. The ballet was performed in Kamenka, in the home of Tchaikovsky's sister and by the children of that family. The main swan theme from the children's ballet Tchaikovsky later incorporated in the ballet produced in the Bolshoi Theatre.

It may be assumed that the story of phantom unrequited love appealed to Tchaikovsky as it had in the case of "Giselle," the old ballet by Theophile Gauthier and Adan. The narrative, however, lacked imagination and the only redeeming feature of the scenario was the continuity of the line of action, which for Tchaikovsky, with his insistence on a unified, well-knit performance was a decided asset. On the other hand, the ballet master diverted the composer's attention to the most routine mise-en-scènes for the cheap divertissements that were in vogue at the time, with the result that the music, conceived as an integral whole, was radically altered: several numbers were omitted as being inconvenient for dancing, or substituted by numbers from other ballets; obedient to fashion, the ballet master insisted on introducing "Russian dances" although they were hardly in place in this ballet; the dancers themselves invented their own variations and all the performers participated in staging the dances. In a word, there was no unity in the work and the composer had less to do with the production than anyone else. Nevertheless Tchaikovsky invested a great deal of genuine warmth, sincerity and poetry in the music reflected through the prism of personal experience.

The scenario of the ballet, as compiled for the initial production, was as follows:

The young prince Siegfried is celebrating his coming of age. At his mother's command he is to choose a bride at the ball to be held to celebrate the occasion. The day before the ball, Siegfried sees a flock of wild swans fly past and he goes off to hunt them. He comes to a lake and is about to shoot at the swans as they swim toward the shore when they are magically transformed into human shape. It is the enchanted Princess Odette and her attendants. Her stepmother, a sorceress, has bewitched her and only marriage can break the evil spell. By day Odette and her maidens become swans, but at night they assume their own form. Siegfried falls in love with the beautiful Odette and promises to save her. She reminds him that at the ball the next day his fancy may be taken by some other maiden and warns him that her stepmother will do her best to prevent their happiness. Siegfried vows his loyalty to Odette. Dawn comes, the girls vanish and the swans reappear on the lake. At the ball Siegfried is fascinated by Odillia, the daughter of Rotbart, who bears a startling resemblance to Odette. At the moment when the parents join the hands of Siegfried and Odillia an owl's cry is heard. Rotbart turns into a demon and a white swan appears at the window. The horrified prince realizes his mistake and rushes down to the lake. A storm rises and the lake's waters seethe. In vain does Siegfried implore his Odette to forgive him. They must part forever. In despair Siegfried tears the wreath off Odette's head and throws it into the storm-tossed waters of the lake. The waves leap up and engulf the lovers. The storm subsides, the waters are stilled and the swans reappear swimming on the placid surface of the lake again.

The story is based on a folk legend which has many different versions. One version, no doubt, is the "Tale of the Tsar Saltan" which inspired Pushkin's superb poem. There, too, we have the bewitched swan-girl who strives to return to her human life. There is a distinct similarity between this story and that of "Undine," Tchaikovsky's first opera, which he subsequently destroyed. It was a theme that had attracted him from his childhood and it is not unlikely that some of the best passages in the new ballet were taken from "Undine." Indeed Professor Nikolai Kashkin, one of Tchaikovsky's intimates, tells us that one of the duets from that opera was used for "The Swan Lake" (in the Adagio).

In spite of the limitations of ballet coupled with the composer's lack of experience in this genre and his inability to obtain any authoritative advice on the specific technique of ballet music Tchaikovsky succeeded in elevating the dance forms, when necessary, to the level of serious drama.

In this ballet Tchaikovsky's remarkable gift for scoring unfolded itself. People said that he was the "master" of the orchestra, that he had orchestral technique at his fingertips, but the real secret of his success was that his innate talent for orchestration was combined with an incessant striving for perfection. The wealth of melody in the ballet, compensating for the absence of the human voice, conveys through the various instruments and groups of instruments the emotions of the characters in the story. Tchaikovsky is sometimes reproached with an over-fondness for brasses and especially for percussion instruments. Tchaikovsky himself was inclined to admit the justice of such criticism in certain cases. "Why must the trumpets, trombones and kettle-drums boom when the flock of swans are seen swimming at the far end of an empty stage?" asks one critic. "Surely that was the moment for soft, gentle sounds," he says. But the composer had a definite reason for doing this. The swans appear more than once and the sorrowful tender "flight" theme occurs at different times both in the oboe and the clarinet and is caught up and accentuated by the whole orchestra when necessary; but in this particular instance the composer deliberately introduced an ominous note in order to create the atmosphere of dramatic tension demanded at this point at the plot.

"Swan Lake" marks a definite step forward in ballet music, showing that development of image, individualization, and dramatic realism are quite compatible with this romantic genre.

*   *   *

Reviews of the premiere of "Swan Lake," which was held in Moscow in February 1877, testify to the poverty and drabness of the staging and the unimaginativeness of the settings. Striking only were the mechanical effects, but they too were often out of place and served only to drown out the music. The dancing, although the best Moscow ballet stars took part, was extremely monotonous and the general impression carried away by those unaccustomed to serious music in ballet was one of unrelieved dullness. The music suffered considerably by the substitution of several of the original numbers by items from different ballets which were completely unsuited to Tchaikovsky's music.

In a letter to the composer in 1880 von Meck wrote: "On Sunday we saw 'Swan Lake' (in the Bolshoi Theatre, Moscow). What divine music, but what a poor production. I had seen it before but this time the posters announced that it had been *improved and embellished* (the italics are V.M.'s), but it was all so poor, so deadly . . . everything was terrible, even choreographically it is a very poor ballet. The lovely Russian dance music is completely lost in a hodge-podge of French mixed with everything else. . . . The Hungarian dance was the best and the public clamoured for an encore. The theatre was packed although it was a benefit performance and the tickets were extremely expensive."

But although he himself criticized this ballet quite severely at times, Tchaikovsky always had a soft place in his heart for "Swan Lake" and was delighted when during a visit to Prague in February 1888 Act II of the ballet was included in a programme of the concert given in his honour. The performance was "superbly done," according to his diary, and the composer experienced "moments of supreme happiness." The ballet's success caused Tchaikovsky to revise his attitude to ballet music in general so that when at the end of 1888 he was commissioned by the St. Petersburg theatre to write the music for "Sleeping Beauty," he accepted with alacrity.

3

"Sleeping Beauty" set another landmark in the development of ballet music which had begun with "Swan Lake."

The story, taken from an old French folk tale, "La

Belle au Bois dormant", appealed to the joyous and romantic side of Tchaikovsky's nature and gave him an outlet for the expression of his childhood dreams of a "golden
age." As distinct from "Swan Lake," the new ballet was
magnificently produced by the famous ballet-master Petitpas and Vsevolozhsky, artist and author of the scenario.
And although there was actually no central idea to link
the component parts of the production the music was so
enchanting, the settings and costumes so luxurious, the
tableaux so impressive and the dancing so brilliant that this
defect was unmarked.

Tchaikovsky, on his part, while adhering to the general
atmosphere of the production nevertheless remained true
to himself, which explains the inimitable charm of his
ballet. It is claimed that one cannot be merry to order;
Tchaikovsky proved that you could, in the sense that the
"order" provided an outlet for emotions he would otherwise have been reluctant to express. In the naive fairy tale
permeated with the earnest, childlike faith in the triumph
of good over evil and spiritual beauty over moral ugliness
he was able to give expression to his profound and sincere
sympathy for the main idea of that enchanted world of
old folk legend.

The story of "Sleeping Beauty" is too well known to
require recounting here. Judging from his diary, Tchaikovsky was delighted with it and expressed the belief that it
would be one of his best compositions. "The subject is so
poetic, it lends itself so admirably to music that I enjoyed
composing it very much and worked with a zeal and eager-
ness that always makes for good results."

To begin with the conditions in which the composer
worked were the exact opposite of those obtaining when

he wrote his first ballet. At Tchaikovsky's request, Petitpas, who was extremely musical in addition to his many other artistic accomplishments, gave him a clear outline of the entire sequence of the dances, the number of measures, the type of music and the time required for the performance of each item. This considerably facilitated the composer's task while at the same time giving him plenty of freedom. Petitpas, who had the greatest respect for Tchaikovsky's talent, showed the utmost consideration and tact in collaborating with him. A careful study of the ballet score today, however, has revealed some discrepancies between the music and the staging, in some cases quite considerable. As was the case in most other genres, Tchaikovsky's music, while attuned to the epoch in some of its elements, was at the same time in advance of its time so that although the composer was impelled to write for his contemporaries he at the same time created new standards whose value was only appreciated later on. Therein lies the tremendous historic force of Tchaikovsky's great talent.

Generations have admired the scoring of "Sleeping Beauty." The composer himself observed that the orchestration of this ballet had given him more trouble than his other compositions. As a matter of fact in this period, beginning with "Mazeppa," Tchaikovsky had observed more than once that the process of work on the orchestration was slowing down and sometimes it worried him. The truth is, as we know today, that from year to year Tchaikovsky added more and richer colour to his orchestral palette, attaining to ever greater summits of perfection in this sphere.

The world of fantasy has inspired Russian composers before and after Tchaikovsky. Glinka, Mussorgsky,

Borodine and Rimsky-Korsakov have all given the
world gems of imaginative music in their operas and symphonies.

Tchaikovsky himself had ventured into the realm of
fantasy before "Sleeping Beauty"; excerpts from "Undine,"
the insects' chorus from the unfinished opera "Mandragore," the mermaids' chorus in "The Little Shoes," and
finally many episodes from "The Swan Lake," are all
executed with great poetic skill, grace and elegance. At the
same time, Tchaikovsky's fantasy is permeated with the
composer's own deep personal emotions. Scant attention
was paid formerly to this individual aspect of his imaginative works. Like the other elements (comic, topical and
even tragic) it was outshone by the disarming lyricism which
induced people to regard Tchaikovsky exclusively as the
"bard of his own sorrow." Thus in spite of the individuality
of his genius, the author of the Sixth Symphony and
"Queen of Spades" was dismissed summarily as a lyric
artist with a great gift for orchestration.

"Sleeping Beauty," when produced, was acclaimed as
the outstanding work of an experienced master, but one
who "abuses his art." "Why, for instance, did the composer have to resort to such crude colours, such massed
orchestration to depict the 'christening of Aurora.' " "Judging by the music one might think it was intended to de-
scribe Macbeth and his witches." Such opinions were by
no means exceptional. The privileged caste of "balletomanes" in St. Petersburg, where the ballet had its premiere
on January 3, 1890, stubbornly refused to recognize the
composer's innovations—choreographical prejudices are as
strong as any other. Only the "waltzes," a few of the classical pas and variations, and the character dances in the last

act were recognized as music proper and fitting for the ballet theatre of the epoch.

The famous "Peasant Waltz" with its charming melody, was an immediate success, vying in popularity only with the melodious second movement of Tchaikovsky's First Quartet. The composer's predilection for the waltz form is well known. "I could write waltzes ad infinitum," he once remarked. It was a form that lent itself most easily to the expression of emotional warmth. In the song "At the Ball," he uses it to express the wistful memory of a bright image that flitted across his vision; in "Eugene Onegin" the waltz that occurs on Tatyana's appearance at the St. Petersburg ball is used to depict a definite dramatic situation. In "Sleeping Beauty," we have a wide variety of waltzes; the one in Act I is festive in tone; developed symphonically it constitutes one of the loveliest pages in the ballet score, a point on which both professionals and laymen agree. Yet this waltz, notwithstanding its predominant optimism, is overshadowed by the sense of impending sorrow. Such contrasts and transitions are invariably sharply drawn in Tchaikovsky's music.

The character dances in the last act, cleverly conceived, fresh as to harmony, brilliant as to orchestration, are a delight to both adults and children.

As in "Swan Lake," the pantomime scenes of "Sleeping Beauty" afford wide scope for Tchaikovsky's imagination, and it is here that the dramatic action is most fully revealed. Through the two contrasting images personified by the bad and good fairies, the composer creates some striking musical characterizations almost entirely new to ballet music; the two opposing forces good and evil, warmth and cold, light and darkness, the vital force of Spring and the torpor of

Winter are expressed in the music with the concreteness demanded by ballet. Linking up the different scenes and situations thematically, Tchaikovsky evokes the necessary associations in the listener, thereby rounding out the images, giving dynamic force to the plot and meaning to the action. As I have said before, Petitpas's detailed plan provided the composer from the very outset with all the threads he needed to weave the fabric of the music. Yet Tchaikovsky rose immeasurably higher than the original conception of the author of the scenario, with the result that the simple fairy tale, like the primitive legend of "Swan Lake," was transformed by the genius of the composer into an exquisite poem.

"Sleeping Beauty" may be said to have opened the way to genuine drama in ballet through the music.

4

Tchaikovsky's theatrical successes, especially in St. Petersburg, heightened the interest of the theatres in a composer so popular with the public. After the production of "Sleeping Beauty" and "The Queen of Spades," (1890) he was given a commission. It was decided to present an opera and ballet in one evening, which meant that both works must of necessity be shorter than usual. Tchaikovsky had long been toying with the idea of an opera for the small stage, and the proposal that he use the story of "Yolanthe" appealed to him, the more so that he knew the subject well (the theory that Herz's drama "King René's Daughter," on which his new opera was based was thrust upon him against his will is incorrect; there exists sufficient proof that the original idea of writing an opera on the story of "Yolanthe" was his own). Similarly, we learn from one of his private letters that Hoffmann's fairy tale about the Nutcracker he read "with the greatest pleasure." That was in 1882. Unfortunately, the scenario of "Nutcracker," after the French version by A. Dumas, was not as well-rounded and complete as that of "Sleeping Beauty." It lacked the "through line" of action which Tchaikovsky valued so highly and which was essential to his type of musical drama.

The story, taken from a series of short stories by E. T. A. Hoffmann, confronted the composer with new musical and psychological problems, while the scenario laid emphasis chiefly on the traditional ballet libretto with the usual tinsel and glitter of of the divertissement. Tchaikovsky appears to have immediately sensed the duality and falseness of the conception which had strayed so far from the original after the literary adaptation by Dumas and the changes inserted into the stage version by Petitpas. What must have appealed to Tchaikovsky was the quaint combination of the naive childish world of make-believe with Hoffmann's sharp irony, the idyllic pictures interwoven with the numerous grotesque moments—and all this together with the participation of children in the leading roles, was an attractive innovation in ballet and promised a rich field for new musical discovery as well. The scenario, however, broke the unity of the idea, interfered with the development of the imagery and extended the static and unnatural situations with the result that the last act was no more than the standard display of "character dances." And once again Tchaikovsky, as in "Swan Lake," but with even great artistic success, overcome all the difficulties and produced a ballet of enduring value.

The programme of the "Nutcracker" ballet is briefly the following. The action takes place in a small German town. The mayor is giving a Christmas party for the children. The guests arrive and the tree is lit up. The doors are thrown open and the children enter clapping their hands with delight. During the dancing and general merriment, a new figure appears. It is Drosselmeyer, an old eccentric and friend of the children who makes them gifts of dolls that can move as though alive. To Masha, the mayor's daughter, who is his favourite, he gives besides an ordinary nutcracker. The little girl is more pleased with the nutcracker than with all her other presents. But her brother and the other boys covet the new toy and in obedience to her parents' wish, Masha gives it to them. The boys play with the nutcracker and break it; Masha is much aggrieved and she nurses the nutcracker as though it were a baby. The guests depart and the evening is over. The Christmas tree is darkened and the room deserted. But Masha cannot sleep for thinking about the nutcracker and at night, when everyone is asleep, she goes to have another look at her favourite toy. It is midnight, and in the stillness of the night she hears mice scampering about on all sides. And a curious spectacle takes place before her eyes—the tree seems to grow bigger and bigger and the toys on it come to life. Her nutcracker too comes to life. And a war begins between the dolls and the mice, the gingerbread soldiers are vanquished by the mice led by the tsar of mice; but then the tin soldiers appear on the scene led by the Nutcracker, and another battle breaks out. Just as the mice leader is overcoming the Nutcracker, Masha takes off her shoe and throws it at him. He dies, the mice are vanquished, and the Nutcracker who turns into a handsome youth, thanks his protector and leads her by the hand to an enchanted land.

The curtain rises on a fir woods in winter. It is snowing and a blizzard rises. The white snowflakes represented by 60 dancers weave a charming design, whirling and eddying until they form a huge snowball. Another strong gust of wind scatters the snow and the dancers whirl about once more.

The second and last act presents a picture of an enchanted world of sweetmeats, delicacies and toys come to life.

From this outline, brief though it is, it will be seen that for an artist of Tchaikovsky's calibre such a presentation of the subject could hardly suffice. As was the case with "Sleeping Beauty," the librettist made a fairy tale display of the ballet (in fact, the posters advertised it as a "ballet fairy tale"), and the composer was obliged to reconceive the plan in order to contrive a production that would be of musical interest as well. Added to Tchaikovsky's difficulties was the fact that the commission was originally of an urgent nature and the composer had not been furnished with a detailed plan of the scenes. However, approaching the subject in the spirit of his own musical personality, Peter Ilyich was soon able to announce to his brother: "I am working with all my might and am beginning to be reconciled to the subject," and when he subsequently obtained more time to complete the work, he gradually found himself becoming absorbed in it. He could not derive creative satisfaction from his work unless he could conceive of it as a composite whole. And we see that in the "Nutcracker" ballet Tchaikovsky surpassed the intentions of the initiators and compilers of the ballet libretto even more than was the case in "Sleeping Beauty." Before he had re-adjusted himself to the libretto, he wrote: "The Nutcracker and even 'King René's Daughter' (Yolanthe) have turned for me into an awful fevered nightmare more repulsive than I can express. . . ." And elsewhere: "I feel that it is im-possible to reproduce that *konfiturenberg* (as the final scene of the ballet was entitled in the scenario) in music." "It is possible to make it extremely effective," he wrote, "but it (Act II) requires exquisite filigree work and for that I have no time, and what is more important, I have neither the inclination nor the desire to work." When he finished the ballet Tchaikovsky expressed the opinion that the "Nutcracker" was "infinitely worse than 'Sleeping Beauty.' "

Not until some time had passed and he was able to view his work more calmly, did he appraise it differently: "It is curious that all the time I was writing the ballet I thought it was rather poor, and that when I began my opera I would really do my best. But now it seems to me that the ballet is good, and the opera is mediocre."

In this ballet Tchaikovsky showed himself to be a *colourist* of amazing originality. Preserving all the indi-viduality of his psychological approach to the music, the composer developed those aspects that were previously manifested in different episodes in his operas, suites and in "Sleeping Beauty," but in the "Nutcracker" the musical characterizations and the psychological depiction of the at-mosphere of the action was even more subtly executed (like most of the scenes in "Queen of Spades"). The melo-dies, so simple in design, are a perfect complement to the stage character, the dance rhythms and orchestral colour add variety and scope to the image and create musical and

stage effects that are unsurpassed in refreshing charm. By
means of elaborate pantomime scenes and carefully considered passages connecting one situation with another,
Tchaikovsky knits the disconnected parts of the libretto together into one comprehensive whole. Tchaikovsky does
not eschew the suite form customary in ballet; but he
weaves them into the general design so that they form part
of the through line. Act I, for example, is a striking example of a complete unity between the action and the music
and a closer study of it merely serves to heighten the delightful first impression. The score of the "Nutcracker"
ballet abounds in sections of sheer beauty which are skilfully integrated into the pattern of the ballet. The night
scene in Act I is one of the most significant symphonic
episodes in the whole of Tchaikovsky's music for the
theatre, giving as it does a picture of the spiritual life of the
child passing from daytime reality to dreamland, to the
night with its lurking horrors expressed in the battle with
the mice. And despite the originality and the studied artistry
of the music the whole of this fantastic scene is charmingly
natural. Even the magnificent final waltz of the "snowflakes," which has been played by orchestras the world over,
is actually no more than a character picture shedding new
light on the child's world and is again subordinated to the
composer's leading idea, which is to portray in musical
images the instability of the childish mind, to convey the
feeling of alarm and excitement evoked by life's mysteries
through the wintry scene. The contrast between "white"
and "dark" scenes creates the required atmosphere.

As we have already observed, Act II presented especial
difficulties for the composer, lacking the necessary continuity of action. But although Tchaikovsky was obliged

to fall in line with the producers and provide the musical background for an elaborate divertissement, we cannot agree with Laroche, the composer, who said that from the standpoint of "ethnography" the music left much to be desired. Of course, there is no "ethnography," and in that sense Laroche is right. The tonal colour of the music is executed with great brilliance and is by no means externally effective alone. Brilliance of exposition does not always preclude significance of content, as Tchaikovsky has proved time and again. His task was to assimilate the "divertissement" and present the group of dances as part of the magic world envisioned by little Masha in her dream. By means of contrasting colours, Tchaikovsky heightens the impressiveness of the scene and skilfully avoids the vulgar garishness suggested by the scenario. The romance of the vivid Spanish dance ("Chocolate"), changes to the melancholy Arabian ("Coffee") dance, which is followed by the deliberately exotic Chinese ("Tea") done in the style of 18th-century French "Chinoiserie." Speaking of "ethnography," it might be of interest to observe that the Arabian dance melody with its oriental structure is based on the theme of an old Georgian cradle song which the composer picked up during one of his visits to the Caucasus. The second group of dances—"Trepak," "Pastorale," and "Polichinelle," and the "Flower Waltz"—are not linked by a single idea either scenically or musically. This is one of the few concessions Tchaikovsky made to ballet tradition; nevertheless the artistic qualities of the music place it on a much higher plane than ordinary ballet music. The tremendous popularity of the brilliant "Flower Waltz" speaks for itself. In the long "pas de deux" that follows, Tchaikovsky gives reign to his lyrical muse and in the Adagio (or

Andante in the piano score) he leads up to an unexpected contrast, enchanting the listener with the broad flowing melodious waves full of poetry and true dramatic expression. This major poetic intermezzo is considered difficult from the standpoint of ballet, requiring perfect technique from the dancer, and Tchaikovsky might be reproached with justice for such an unorthodox treatment of traditional ballet "adagio" were it not for the fact that it was a deliberate attempt on his part to provide the correct emotional atmosphere for the second act. In his music for theatre Tchaikovsky invariably resorted to emotional contrasts of this kind and it is only to be regretted that such a significant musical episode should have such a pallid counterpart on the stage. In the final scene—the broad ballet coda with the new waltz and the "apotheosis"—Tchaikovsky introduces Masha's theme to remind us again of the little girl who, though forgotten by the librettist, is such an integral part of the world of make-believe to which one of the finest compositions by a great master is dedicated.

* * *

It is not surprising that the "Nutcracker" ballet, which was produced in December (old style) 1892 together with "Yolanthe," should have evoked conflicting opinions. The novelty of the idea and musical devices led to some confusion among the critics. While it was quite clear that as far as the orchestral colour was concerned Tchaikovsky had surpassed himself, it was said that the ballet, although masterfully executed, lacked inspiration; some even called it the work of a "craftsman" in the derogatory sense and not in the sense of the high craftsmanship that is the distinguishing quality of all great works of art.

In view of the illness of Petitpas, the ballet was produced by Lev Ivanov, who, though a talented artist, lacked the genius of his more famous colleague. Ivanov was reproached with lack of imagination in his production of the "Nutcracker," but a closer study of the performance today shows that this appraisal was unjust. At any rate that is the opinion of Yuri Slonimsky, the well-known Soviet ballet historian, and his arguments strike us as quite convincing. Ivanov had to cope with an awkward stage plan, evidently the result of a disagreement between the two authors of the scenario, on the one hand, and the failure of the latter to understand fully the composer's conception, on the other. Nevertheless, as the stage history of the production of "Nutcracker" shows, the dances staged by Lev Ivanov won the acclaim of the public and have proved of enduring value. The original underestimation of the work was due rather to the general attitude toward the new ballet on the part of the exclusive set of "balletomanes." The most successful dances were the "Waltz of the Snowflakes," the Trepak and the Chinese dance.

The premiere was, on the face of it, a great success. This was the public's tribute to its favourite composer. Tchaikovsky himself admitted that the production was "a shade too magnificent—the luxuriousness tires the eyes." But he hastened to observe that the "opera (Yolanthe) was evidently liked more than the ballet. And indeed, in spite of its magnificence, it turned out to be rather dull." But we know that this final reproach does not apply to the music. A certain perspective had to be acquired before that could be properly appreciated.

It is curious to note that it was not until many years after the premiere of his first ballet "Swan Lake" that

Tchaikovsky expressed the desire to make an orchestral suite from it for concert performance. In the case of the "Nutcracker," he compiled a suite, consisting of a few characteristic items convenient for concert programme, performing it himself, and permitted a small group of conductors to play it at concerts *before* the ballet was produced. This suite won tremendous popularity both here and abroad.

5

On February 17, 1894, several months after the death of the composer, a Tchaikovsky memorial evening was held in the Mariinsky Theatre in St. Petersburg. Among other excerpts from his work performed that evening was the second scene from Act I of "Swan Lake." This was the first performance in St. Petersburg of the ballet which had been produced in full only in Moscow, and it caused quite a sensation among St. Petersburg's exacting connoisseurs. A year later, on January 15, 1895, it was produced in full.

The famous ballerina P. Legnani, who danced the part of Odette at the memorial evening, was a tremendous success. The scene had been newly-staged by Lev Ivanov, who revised the last scene also when the ballet was produced in full in St. Petersburg a year later. Only the first scene and part of Act II were the work of Petitpas. The scenes staged by Ivanov differ in principle from the rest and the dance images (the swan and her friends), the movements, poses and tableaux he created were preserved almost intact in subsequent productions. The lyrical talent of this balletmaster, combined with his gift for music, had the most beneficent effect on the interpretation of Tchaikovsky's music in the "swan" scenes. Although many years have passed since this ballet was revived, the spectator is struck by the true harmony between the music and the plastic scenes which was evidently so sorely lacking in the earlier production. It is most regrettable that Tchaikovsky himself did not live to see the new mise-en-scenes of his "Swan Lake," so expressive of the elegiac beauty and the inner restlessness inherent in the music. Petitpas too left his mark on the ballet; the famous waltz in Act II which has survived so many productions, is purported to be the work of this great master.

The year 1895, in our opinion, was a decisive one in the history of the ballet, inasmuch as it was associated with the name of Tchaikovsky, and this association, as we know, brought with it the most fundamental and significant changes. That year marked a return to the lyricism and drama originally introduced in ballet by the famous ballerinas of the Pushkin epoch, a return to a genuine national interpretation of the characters on a plane corresponding to the music. New and promising vistas were opened to ballet. The subsequent revivals, which introduced slight changes and amendments, could at best proceed in the direction mapped out by the St. Petersburg producers of 1895. Leaving aside the question of excisions or insertions, the different interpretations of the final scene of the ballet or even the revision of the whole subjects with a view to bringing it closer to what was believed to be the basic musical idea of Tchaikovsky, we may merely observe that the best Russian ballet dancers have found Tchaikovsky's music an inexhaustible fount of inspiration and a spur to the attainment of something more than technical perfection in ballet.

"Swan Lake" is today the most popular ballet produced in the U.S.S.R., beloved as much for its music as for the dancing. It is enjoyed equally by people of all ages and professions and, with "Eugene Onegin," another permanent feature of the repertory of the Bolshoi Theatre, is an unending source of delight to the public.

* * *

The production of "Sleeping Beauty" in St. Petersburg was so successful that in less than a year and a half it had been presented 50 times, which was quite phenomenal for those times. Tchaikovsky attended the 50th performance, given on November 18, 1892, and was accorded an enthusiastic ovation by the public. The brilliance of the production, the "variations," the adagio and the performance of a new ballerina contributed to the success, and imperceptibly Tchaikovsky's music was accorded the recognition it deserved. As time went on opinions and tastes changed; the preservation of the classical dances in "Sleeping Beauty" side by side with the character and elaborate pantomime has not detracted from the interest in the story or the enjoyment of the music; nor has it interfered with the organic unity of the performance as a whole. Musical plastic characterization made its debut on the ballet stage and "the reform in ballet effected by Tchaikovsky," as it is now said, cannot be overestimated. The Moscow production of the ballet produced in 1899 differed slightly from that of St. Petersburg, but it too found a permanent place in the repertory of the Moscow Bolshoi Theatre.

Leading ballerinas of both capitals—Olga Preobrazhenskaya, Tamara Karsavine, L. Roslavleva—took leading roles in Tchaikovsky's ballets. His music is a source of unending

inspiration to the present generation of ballet stars—
Katerina Geltzer, Marina Semyonova, Galina Ulanova and
Olga Lepeshinskaya—whose performances have won the
widest acclaim from Soviet audiences.

The "Nutcracker" ballet has been less frequently produced, partly for the reasons given above and partly as a
result of new experiments—not always successful—on the
part of contemporary producers. There is no doubt, however, that the difficulties presented by this ballet will gradually be overcome and that the full success of Tchaikovsky's last composition for the stage is a question of the near
future.

The successors of Petitpas and Ivanov—Michael Fokine
(St. Petersburg) who was later to achieve world fame, and
Alexander Gorsky (Moscow)—were the founders of a new
interpretation of music not specially written for the stage.
This movement which won such rapid recognition all over
the world thanks to the celebrated Russian Ballet of Sergei
Diaghilev in Paris and to the work of Isadora Duncan, affected only two of Tchaikovsky's works: his symphonic
poem "Francesca da Rimini" and his Serenade for string
orchestra (op. 48). The latter work served as material for
the ballet "Eros." We shall not attempt to argue the merits
or demerits of such a method in principle; we shall merely
point out that the production of "Francesca" has left no
trace of itself in the history of the stage, and, judging by
reviews, was none too successful. As for "Eros," the ballet
did figure in the repertory of the St. Petersburg theatre for
some time. Both productions were staged by Fokine whose
name became a byword in ballet throughout Europe, when
in a number of magnificent productions he demonstrated
his mastery of the new forms in the art of dancing. This

movement, however, which played such an important historic role in the general development of world ballet, can also be traced back to Tchaikovsky as the true father of a great art whose force lay in the seriousness of approach to problems, the brilliant mastery of their solution, and the profoundly poetic kernel of the musical images embodied in ballet.

The progressive role of Tchaikovsky from this standpoint is indisputable. His powerful influence was manifest in subsequent ballets written by Alexander Glazunov, Nikolai Cherepnin, Igor Stravinsky, Sergei Prokofiev, Vassilenko, Reinhold, Gliere, Boris Asafiev, Alexander Krein and Aram Khachaturyan in this country and by many leading composers in Western Europe.

CHAMBER MUSIC

PROFESSOR ARNOLD ALSHVANG

CHAMBER MUSIC OCCUPIES a no less important place in Tchaikovsky's work than symphony and theatrical music. Besides his ten operas, three ballets, six symphonies, four concertos, four suites and twelve overtures and a quantity of other pieces, he wrote more than a hundred romances, as many pianoforte pieces, four string quartets, a piano trio, a string sextet and several other chamber works.

Tchaikovsky's chamber music has attracted the attention of few musicologists. Nevertheless even without the mediation of the critics it has won for itself the widest popularity among the general public. This was achieved not only by way of the concert hall but also through one of the very vital channels of Russian art life, namely, modest domestic musicales. For decades arias from Tchaikovsky's operas, his romances and instrumental music have graced the music shelf in tens of thousands of Russian homes. Yet while displaying strong partiality for one or another masterpiece, the rank and file music lover often passes by many a musical gem in a number of other compositions that for some unknown reason have been left in the shade. The author of this essay shall attempt an exhaustive survey of all of Tchaikovsky's chamber music in the hopes of arousing the reader's interest in works of this genre with which he is not yet acquainted and to enable him the better to appreciate the musical genius of the great Russian composer.

ROMANCES

Tchaikovsky's romances are small musical poems the essence of which transcends the boundaries of personal sentiment. These movingly sincere and profoundly truthful pages of the great composer's music are permeated with life's philosophy. The lyrics appeal to each and everyone, they are a message from one heart to another. The sincerity of the musical idiom, the perfection of form, the diversity and originality of the melody combined with the beauty of the accompaniments, which at times are little musical masterpieces in themselves, are all qualities which, combined, go to make up the style of Tchaikovsky's songs.

The romances and songs are distributed rather evenly over all periods of the composer's creative activity. They flowed like a sparkling stream amid the monumental crags of his symphonies, now whispering a melancholy note, now rushing like a mountain torrent, now meandering gently along to still and peaceful backwaters. The songs nurtured other genres of Tchaikovsky's music. Many opera arias and cantilenes trace their roots to the romances. Moreover, the romances have enriched some of the finest passages in his symphonies from the tender plaints of Francesca to the passionate sighs of Romeo and Juliet, from the colorful folk melodies to the mournful strains of the finale of the Sixth Symphony. One may say that the song is the very soul of Tchaikovsky's music, whatever the genre. The romances are its direct expression.

Tchaikovsky's romances offer an amazing variety of style. We find genuine dramatism side by side with pure lyricism; hymns of solemn triumph and simple ditties; folk melodies and waltzes. . . . Suffice it to recall "Corals," the dramatic ballad for voice, the jubilant spirit of the song "Is it Day?" in which the theme is developed in true symphonic style, or, the solemn majesty of the hymn "Hail to You, Forests," or to compare these vocal poems with lyrical miniatures like "At the Ball" to appreciate the vast diapason of musical imagery the artist has recorded in his songs. The composer borrowed generously for his musical material from the life around him. Now it was an Italian street song ("Pimpinella"), now Russian and Ukrainian peasant intonations ("Had I but Known") now the elements of the so-called gypsy song ("Nights of Madness").

Yet all through the borrowed and assimilated song genres runs the "personal theme" of the composer. It is customary to believe that this "personal theme" was the sense of the fate that hovers over man, and fear of death. Many of the composer's big works do indeed contain musical images of a tragic nature giving cause for such an interpretation of his music (the "Fatum theme" in the Fourth, Fifth and Sixth symphonies, in "Manfred," in "Francesca," in the operas "Oprichnik," "Eugene Onegin," "The Queen of Spades," in some of the songs, etc.). Usually these motifs are repeated in definite tragic situations arising from the opera libretto or the subject of the given symphonic work. There is, however, nothing at all mystical about this theme. The tragic images in Tchaikovsky's music are invariably overcome as a result of intense struggle, and in his romances this peculiar quality of Tchaikovsky's music is most strikingly evident.

In the romances, the "personal theme" occurs not so much in the idea of "fate" itself as in the exposition of the inner world of man weighed down by the burden of circumstance and fighting doggedly for his personal happiness, for the right to live a full life. It is this image that is expressed in Tchaikovsky's superb lyricism with its incomparable tranquillity rent suddenly by stormy passions, its poignant longing for an active life, and its indomitable striving for happiness.

All these gradations of personal feeling, warmed by a profound humanity, are expressed in Tchaikovsky's numerous songs and ballads which are musical gems of surpassing loveliness.

The cycle of romances begins with six songs (Opus 6), composed when Tchaikovsky, then aged 29, resided in Moscow and taught composition at the Conservatory of Music. The composer's youth has laid its bright stamp on these miniature love elegies. Goethe's lovely words: "None But the Lonely Heart . . ." that once charmed Beethoven* inspired Tchaikovsky to write a stirring ballad of love's sweet anguish. The remarkably expressive melody, calm and austere in structure, culminates magnificently on the words "and how I suffer" that precede the concluding episode. The sharp contrast between this passionate outburst of feeling and the softly spoken phrase "my breast is afire" that follows is powerfully expressive of suppressed emotion. The romance reveals the meaning of Goethe's poem by deftly applied psychological strokes.

Love's anguish is again masterfully brought out by the composer in his romance to the words of Heine's poem "Why has the blushful rose. . . ."

* Beethoven wrote four different songs to the words of this verse.

Youthful lyricism echoes in the song "Not a word, oh my friend," to words by A. Pleshcheyev. Enchanted by the poetry of the text, Tchaikovsky composed a sentimental elegy, the prototype of many of his popular songs, piano and other pieces (e.g., "Autumn Song," "Mournful Song," "Canzonetta" from the violin concerto).

As distinct from the other songs of Opus 6, that written to Alexey Tolstoi's words, "A Tear Trembles in Your Eyes," is dedicated not to personal emotion but to the problem of the brotherhood of man. It is accordingly conceived on a broader plane than the other songs. There is an operatic flavour about the slow declamatory style, the broad development and the powerful culmination.

The romance "So soon to forget" to words by a friend of the composer's, the poet Apukhtin (1870) differs from the other love lyrics by virtue of the restless flow of feeling and the sudden and powerful burst of passion. It falls clearly into three separate parts: mournful narrative, pleasant reminiscence and the stormy outburst of inconsolable spiritual anguish that flashes forth suddenly like a blinding streak of lightning and as instantly dies. There is deep hidden pain in the final passages of the accompaniment. This inspired romance opens a new page in the history of subjective psychological art.

The six romances of Opus 16 (1872) are among the early Tchaikovsky masterpieces. They include those lovely songs "Lullaby" and "New Greek Melody" to words by Maikov,* and "Wait" to words by Grekov. In them we have the music of the elements, the wind and the waves, borrowed from the folk tales, the soft and mournful lullaby

* To his words "The Death on the Hills" is written the wellknown ballad by Sir Edward Elgar.

melody expressing the peace that comes after the day's bustle.

The romance "Wait" is full of a profound meaning. The words by Grekov are inspired by Shakespeare and are something in the nature of a "transcription" of the night scene from "Romeo and Juliet." There is an ineffable charm in the romance with its introductory recitative, the slow "swaying" movement in the middle, and its philosophical resumé

Especially fine is the central part of the romance where the summer's night slowly unfolds its beauty before two loving hearts. The vocal melody is full of a languorous peace. In the "New Greek Melody" the composer has used the motif of the austere mediaeval "Dies irae." Both Berlioz and Liszt * used the same melody to convey gloomy fantastic visions and the realm of death. In Tchaikovsky's song the same spirit is conveyed in the words: "In the earth's dark nether regions the souls of the damned languish. . . ."

Two songs in the melodramatic "gypsy" style written in 1875 in the first, "Moscow" period of his career were followed by "Awful Moment," for which Tchaikovsky wrote the words himself (under the enigmatic nom de plume "N.N.") and in which melodrama reaches its apotheosis. By writing romances of this type Tchaikovsky was making a concession to the period in which he lived. In musical idiom they resembled the "passionate" (or so-called "cruel") romances of the 70's and 80's of last century.

During the same "Moscow" period the composer wrote some of his best romances based on folk themes: the dra-

* Later Myaskovsky and Rachmaninov.

matic ballad "Corals," "Why was I born" (to words by
Mickiewicz), and "At Eventide" (words by the famous
Ukrainian poet Taras Shevchenko).

"Corals" (op. 28, 1875) is much more than a romance.
It is a typical tragic ballad about a young girl who asks her
lover about to depart for the wars to bring her a string of
corals. The young man returns from the victorious cam-
paign with the corals, only to learn that his sweetheart is
dead. The stirring drama of the ballad, the variety of scenes
(battle, funeral and graveside episodes), the logic of the
music, the beauty of the form, the thematic unity and the
folk quality of the basic melody make this song a genuine
masterpiece.

Notable among the songs on folk themes is the lovely
lament of the Russian peasant girl "Had I but known," to
words by Alexey Tolstoi. This is dramatic music in its
highest form, the folk lament style being used with amazing effectiveness. The romance "Were I but a blade of
grass in the field" is another magnificent adaptation of a
simple folk melody. Both these songs are included in Opus
47 (1881).

Tchaikovsky always listened eagerly to the voice of
the people. In Italy he recorded the airs sung by a little
street singer and his famous "Pimpinella" (1878) was the
result; the Russian text was his own. He displayed great
interest in the work of Surikov, the folk poet (author of
the translation of Shevchenko's poem "Were I but a blade
of grass in the field"). "Have you any knowledge of the
Moscow poet Surikov who died this spring from consump-
tion?" he wrote in a letter to von Meck. "He was a self-
taught poet; he earned his living by sitting in a miserable
shop selling nails and horseshoes. This was his profession

until the end of his days, but he had a genuine gift and his verses are full of true feeling." (Letter to von Meck, June 5, 1880.)

The romance to Pushkin's poem "The Nightingale" (1886) shows that poetic folk images continued to attract him even in the latter period of his career. In purity of style the "Nightingale" is perhaps the best romance in the folk genre.

Tracing the development of the Tchaikovsky romances from year to year, we find a gradual broadening of subject matter and an addition of new genres. At the same time the poetic love and wistful sadness of the early romances were preserved in the later works. The composer's unfailing sense of proportion, perfection of form, and simplicity are the distinguishing traits of his romances and songs. The mood becomes more and more tranquil as time goes on, and lofty poetic images are elevated more and more to the plane of philosophical generalization. One of the most perfect romances of this type is "At the Ball" (to words by Alexey Tolstoi, 1878). An example of the mature Tchaikovsky, its elegant "salon" form cloaks a kernel of deep significance. The chance meeting with a woman who captures the poet's imagination is elevated to a much higher plane in the romance. It brings out the tragic loneliness of the artist in a world in which beauty flits past him, barely touching him with the hem of her garment and vanishes, leaving a yearning ache in the soul of the lonely poet. The composer achieves this generalization through the medium of a slow elegiac waltz measure which adds to the popular appeal of the romance.

Several songs written by the mature Tchaikovsky are wistful recollections of youthful love. In Opus 38 (1878) we have the charming romance " 'Twas Early Spring" to words by Alexey Tolstoi. The text of the poem is faintly reminiscent of the young Heine, while the music resembles some of the most poetical episodes from Schumann's love songs. The bravura "Don Juan's Serenade" from the same opus is distinguished by its brilliance. It is almost an operatic aria, executed with amazing skill. This effective romance is an indispensable item in the repertory of every baritone. One is naturally impelled to compare it with Robert's aria from "Yolanthe," written 14 years later. Both songs are brilliant and effective, and notwithstanding the difference of the texts, bear a definite similarity to each other.

* * *

The long song-poem "Hail to you, forests" (op. 47) deserves special mention. The words are borrowed from a poem by Alexey Tolstoi entitled "John of Damascus." * The hero of the poem is a poet whose soul is sick of the vanities of the world. Neither the honours showered on him by an eastern potentate nor the sacred vows of the priesthood satisfy him. He leaves the luxurious palace and later discards the garb of his monkhood, and as he abandons the Damascus palace, he sings a hymn of praise to Nature, to the forests, the mountains, the valleys, the heavens, to every blade of grass and every star in the sky. He calls upon his fellow men to join hands in brotherhood and love and to be at one with Nature. Tchaikovsky's music for this song has the serene majesty of a hymn.

The same opus 47 includes another brilliant composition "Is it Day?" to words by Apukhtin. After the delicate

* It was from this poem that Sergei Taneyev borrowed the text for his famous cantata "John of Damascus."

pastel tones of the early romances, this joyous hymn to love triumphant glows with a passionate fervour and the release of pent-up feeling. Its melody seems to have imbibed the vivifying warmth and light of the sun. It soars aloft like a bird, intoxicated with a glorious sense of freedom amid the world's loveliness. The broad, slow introduction changes to a swift agitated movement. The piano accompaniment weaves an intricate pattern. This magnificent piece of music ends with a long piano finale.

"The Golden Cornfields" (text by Alexey Tolstoi) expresses the pain of separation; the music reproduces a distant ringing of church bells amid twilight fields, the peaceful background of nature forming a striking contrast to the dramatic sorrowful plaint: "My soul yearns for you."

There are novel features also in the later romances of the "gypsy" genre. The famous "Gypsy Song" to words by Jacob Polonsky* (1886) is extremely intense; its leitmotif is of a "fateful" cast, something in the nature of an echo of the image of Carmen.

There is a similar deep meaning in "Mad Nights" to words by Apukhtin. It tells of the bitter aftermath of a dissipated life, the burning embers of a dying passion, a yearning for happiness and despair of its attainment.

"The gentle stars shone down upon us" to words by Polonsky and especially the last cycle of romances (op. 73, 1893) to words by Rathaus ("Together We Sat," "Night," "This Moonlight Night," "The Sun Set," "Midst Dreary Days," "Again as Before") are all superb examples of tender lyricism, psychologically true, human and full of a passionate zest for life.

* Most of the romances and choruses by Taneyev are written to his words.

While frequently a prey to mental anguish and vague
yearnings, the composer never descended to the abyss of
utter despair; the spirit of optimism is invariably the dominant note in his music.

*   *   *

In a class by themselves are Tchaikovsky's charming
songs for children (op. 54, 1881–1883). There are 16 of
them in all, and with the exception of two are written to
texts by Pleshcheyev, a contemporary of Tchaikovsky.
The simple melodies and easy accompaniments make most
of these songs accessible to children. In most cases the texts
point a moral: they teach kindness, consideration, sympathy and compassion. The best of these songs are "The
Legend of the Boy Christ," "Cradle in the Tempest," and
the amusing "Cuckoo."

Among Soviet vocalists there are several excellent performers of Tchaikovsky's songs and ballads. Apart from
the truly classic interpretations of Tchaikovsky's vocal
opera given by Leonid Sobinov, the celebrated tenor,
there are singers of the later generation who have succeeded
in conveying the true spirit of Tchaikovsky's music. The
most distinguished of these are People's Artist Nadezhda
Obukhova (mezzo) and Honoured Artists Vera Davydova
(mezzo) and Sergei Lemeshev (tenor). Several years ago
Lemeshev gave a series of concerts which included all the
songs and ballads by Tchaikovsky without exception. Few
of the leading Soviet singers fail to include Tchaikovsky
in their concert repertories.

*   *   *

Not the least significant of Tchaikovsky's chamber works are his vocal ensembles. Undoubtedly the best of these is the Romeo and Juliet duet in which the scene of the parting of the lovers of this immortal tragedy is presented with great poetry and passion. The duet was completed and orchestrated after Tchaikovsky's death by his friend and pupil Taneyev. The highly dramatic Scottish ballad and the charming duet for female voices "The Dawn" are outstanding among the six duets of Opus 46, 1880.

The profound lyricism of Tchaikovsky's vocal compositions has its roots in Russian folk music. As distinct from the Big Five—Balakirev, Mussorgsky and the others—Tchaikovsky drew not so much from the peasant songs—although they too are brilliantly represented in his work*—as from the urban romance which had become so tremendously popular in Russia in his time. This explains the gripping emotionalism of Tchaikovsky's romances and their accent on man's sufferings, his hopes, his passions and aspirations. At the same time Tchaikovsky better than anyone else in his time, was able to express the sense of plenitude, satisfaction, harmony and happiness.

CHAMBER ENSEMBLES

In order to understand and appreciate the tremendous role of Tchaikovsky's chamber ensembles it is not sufficient merely to study the few works of this genre.

Tchaikovsky commenced to write *serious* chamber music at a time when the audience for such music had not yet been won, when Russian musical literature in this genre

* *E.g.,* in his Second Symphony, First Piano Concerto, etc.

was limited to a very few compositions. Tchaikovsky
opened wide vistas for Russian chamber ensemble music.
The instrumental chamber works of previous Russian composers including some excellent compositions by Bortnian-
sky and Glinka, had won little recognition and it was not
until the quartets by Tchaikovsky and Borodine appeared
that Russian chamber ensembles really won wide popularity. Tchaikovsky evidently realized that the introduction
of this new genre—new for the Russian public—would
require a certain amount of publicity and hence he wrote
articles persuading music lovers to attend chamber concerts,
promising them "a deep and novel enjoyment" they had
never suspected.

While Tchaikovsky cannot be considered the founder
of the Russian chamber ensemble he must at any rate be
given credit for popularizing this genre in his own country
and for adding some splendid contributions to world chamber music. This applies primarily to his three quartets,
penned by a master who had learned from his youth to
build up a large musical structure with the logic, accuracy
and unity necessary for the expression of an exalted artistic
idea.

While still in school Tchaikovsky made a study of the
chamber ensemble, learning from the best world composers
in this genre. One piece by the young Tchaikovsky for
string quartet was performed in the St. Petersburg Conservatory two months before he graduated from its composition
department. This quartet Allegro in B-Flat Major served
in part as the material for Tchaikovsky's first piano composition Opus 1. The Allegro has as its main theme an Ukrainian folk song. The austere nature of the music is reminiscent
of Beethoven.

The first quartet Opus 11, D-Major (1871) marked the beginning of a short but extremely significant series of mature chamber compositions. The elegant polished form, the unity of each part, the accuracy of modulation, rhythm and intonation are combined in this superb piece of music for the expression of a whole gamut of radiant emotions touched now and again with a wistful sadness.

The first movement—D-Major—in spite of the many changes of mood and intricacy of development is amazingly unified as to structure; the syncopated rhythm that runs throughout the first movement, the frequent organ points and the sustained sounds, as well as the gradual cautious movement from one tonality to another lend an integrated quality to the structure that is fully in keeping with music of this type. There are few thematic contrasts although the sonata form is strictly adhered to throughout. Both themes in their original form are rather static and immobile; as is revealed by the limited range of the melody, by the organ points and by the characteristic chord structure. The purpose of the further development of theme is to overcome the immobility, to "unfetter" the melody. It is this tendency that is the motive force of the whole thematic development in the first movement of the quartet, giving an effect of noble virility and optimism.

The famous Andante Cantabile of the First Quartet, the music that moved Leo Tolstoi to tears and which has won tremendous popularity both in Russia and abroad* is marked by a radiant serenity, harmoniousness and calm. It is based on two melodious themes. The first is in the form of a broad folk song which the composer heard sung by a

* Tchaikovsky himself had often performed this part with a string orchestra.

Russian peasant. Simple and severe in outline, it forms a striking contrast to the "serenade" spirit of the second theme which takes up the whole central part of the piece. The elegant salon nature of the "serenade" is brought out also in the melodic structure and in the light faintly discernible touch of yearning. . . . The folk motif recurs, completing the piece. The Slavonic melodiousness of the Andante Cantabile never fails to stir its hearers.

The rhythmic scintillating Scherzo with its striking contrasts and its rich fantasy is followed by a broad finale brilliant and virile.

* * *

Tchaikovsky had the highest opinion of his Second Quartet, Opus 22, F-Major. "I considered it my best composition," he wrote. "None of my other pieces came so easily and naturally to me. I wrote it almost at one sitting." Indeed the music of the Second Quartet is excellent in all respects. The first movement is distinguished by the intensive, mobile polyphony which gives it a fullness of symphonic tonality that is peculiarly Tchaikovsky. The magnificent harmonies are truly inspired, not so much because of the two main themes as the ingenious variations of these themes and the ceaseless melodic pulsation that permeates the piece. There is a hint of sadness in the introduction and the main theme, where minor tonality and melancholy motifs predominate. The fact that the calm exposition of the theme is limited only to few bars and that each theme is developed by sequences, modulations and variations both in the development and directly following the occurrence of the theme and the reprise creates the impression of intense restlessness that reaches its climax in the development where the themes are altered and where some "fate" motifs occur.

The Scherzo with its predominant seven-time measure and its energetic accented waltz section is one of the most exquisitely well-proportioned and truly beautiful of Tchaikovsky's compositions. It is dominated by an inner harmony and the touches of sadness that occur now and again are completely dissolved in the pleasant sense of spiritual peace.

The brilliant Andante in F-Minor is a striking example of Tchaikovsky's lyricism. The main theme, restrained and noble, is among his best slow melodies. We believe we shall not be mistaken in attributing the amazing effectiveness of this theme to the great skill with which Tchaikovsky weaves ever new threads into the pattern of the melody. The effect of the combination of a motif of utter simplicity with the motifs of a more emotional and intense nature is quite startling. The accompaniment too is unusually rich. The exquisite mellifluous sounds touch a melancholy chord in the listener's soul. Only in the Coda, however, does this feeling reach its climax in a veritable requiem permeated with a sense of inevitability. The Coda, more than any other part of the quartet expresses the heavy sense of loss that was felt in the midst of the day's bustle (first movement) and which was crystallized in the form of the dominant mood in the loneliness of eventide. . . .

The powerful finale echoes other majestic classical finales and is coloured by a healthy optimism. In harmony with the profound and diverse treatment of the preceding movement, it is majestic in scale, ending a large cyclic form on a triumphant note of creative achievement.

The Second Quartet is richer and more complex than

the First, but is developed along similar lines. The Third
Quartet, written in 1876 and dedicated to the memory of
Ferdinand Laub, the celebrated violinist, stands in a class
by itself.

Unity and singleness of idea distinguish the Third Quartet more than any other of Tchaikovsky's chamber works.
It is a monument to a dead friend, a mournful poem of
painful bereavement. Of all the quartets the Third is the
most dramatic and covers the broadest range of feeling
from gloomy funereal notes to the triumph of life, from
the hopeless melancholy of the first and third movements
to the amazing vitality of the finale. The Quartet is difficult
to play but it is easy to listen to thanks to the unity of the
musical conceptions. The first movement is one of the
most profound of all Tchaikovsky's sonata forms. The
mournful lyricism and the passionate, active dramatism lend
a convincing power to the leading idea; the refusal of the
human mind to reconcile itself to the thought of Death, and
man's assertion of the force of life give rise to a dramatic
conflict which ends with man being forced to reconcile
himself to the inevitable. This, however, is only part of the
image: the subsequent three movements are closely linked
with the first and actually supplement it.

The second movement is more of a "grotesque" than a
"scherzo." The weird, "fey" music is relieved only by the
graceful light melody of the central part.

The third movement is a funeral march with the characteristic intricate rhythmic line reminiscent of that of the
funeral march in Wagner's "Götterdämmerung." It is not
funeral music in the accepted sense; it is more in the nature
of a memory of a tragic event. The unique approach to
theme is evidence of the fact that the thought of death

had taken hold of the composer's imagination for some time.

The composer, however, shrinks from a tragic ending and the finale once again breathes the spirit of all-pervading optimism and vitality. It is a scene of popular rejoicing, a forerunner of the finale of the future Fourth Symphony. Scarcely was there anything in European or Russian music at that time to compare with those mighty rhythms borrowed directly from folk dance tunes and elevated to great summits of dramatic tension. Tchaikovsky returned again and again to folk themes giving them much the same treatment in all his works. But in the finale of the quartet there is a mournful echo of the youthful Tchaikovsky.

*   *   *

Another composition for string ensemble is the Sextet for two violins, two violas and two violoncellos (Opus 70 D-Minor, 1890–1892) known as the Florentine Sextet. Here we have the mature Tchaikovsky at his best. The sextet is essentially closely bound up with the general trend of ideas that dominate the works of the latter period of his life. The dramatic music of the first movement is followed by a superb Adagio cantabile whose rich, full-blooded main theme is set off against a funeral dirge that breaks into the mainstream of the melody transporting the listener to that sphere of sombre images in which Tchaikovsky's music in the latter period abounds.

The third movement, Allegretto, is elegiac in mood and is marked by a unity of rhythm and striking dynamic contrasts. The main theme of the Allegretto is also funereal in quality.

The finale which combines the light rhythm of a tarantella, a heavy march and solid counterpoint with a culmination of mass dances, belongs to the massive and colourful finales.

The sextet is a conflict betwen sharp personal distress and a stubborn striving for popular, vigorous animated music. The heterogeneity of the elements, the spectre of death, the wild revelry and the fantastic caprices of imagination all combine to make this music, so uneven in quality, akin to the music of "The Queen of Spades." As a matter of fact, it was while working on that operatic masterpiece in Florence during the winter and early spring of 1890 that the composer conceived the idea of writing this instrumental version of "The Queen of Spades." At the same time, the sextet was one of the stepping stones to the Sixth Symphony and served as a connecting link between these two most perfected examples of Tchaikovsky's work.

*   *   *

Perhaps the most popular of Tchaikovsky's chamber works in his Trio for piano, violin and violoncello in A-Minor, Opus 50 (1862), dedicated to the memory of Nikolai Rubinstein, the great Russian pianist and musician who died in 1881.

The trio is famed chiefly for its magnificent first movement ("Elegy"). The lovely melancholy, main theme is introduced first by the 'cello and then the violin in broad melodious cantilene style; while the piano weaves a flowing, wave-like design composed of rich bass tones and clearcut rhythms; the theme then passes wholly to the piano. In contrast to the mournful passionate theme there comes an energetic major motif accompanied by a charming melody with a stirring, sensuous beauty that is Italian in flavour. Of the two contrasting themes, the main sombre theme is most elaborately developed, now dramatized, now brimming over into a storm of passionate weeping (epilogue of the first movement).

The second and final movement of the trio consists of a simple placid theme and 12 variations. Tchaikovsky has written no variations more subtly intricate than this delightful cycle where the thematical development attains such power, such freedom and perfection. Each variation is a character piece in itself. The third variation, for example, is a scherzo, the fifth is in the nature of pittoresque music, the sixth is a waltz, the eighth—a long fugue, the ninth—a mournful recitative, the tenth—a brilliant mazurka. This entire kaleidoscope of genre pieces and scenes is, as it were, evoked by the memory of the dead artist and his illustrious life.

The bravure finale, on which the variations end, is followed by a grand epilogue. The sorrowful main theme of the first movement sounds at once tragic and triumphant; it is as if after indulging in these pleasant reminiscences the pain of bereavement breaks out afresh. . . .

Tchaikovsky's chamber music is extensively performed in the U.S.S.R. The finest quartets in the country, the Moscow Beethoven Quartet, the Komitas Quartet of Armenia, the Glazunov Quartet, the Taneyev Quartet, the Villiome Quartet of the Ukraine as well as pianoforte trios (e.g., Lev Oborin, piano, David Oistrakh, violin and Knushevitsky, 'cello) frequently give programmes of Tchaikovsky.

Compositions for Piano

Piano works composed over a period of 26 years (1867–1893) comprise a by no means insignificant part of Tchaikovsky's chamber music. True, his compositions for the piano cannot claim a leading place in his musical legacy, nevertheless against the background of the post-Lisztian piano literature of Western Europe Tchaikovsky's works for the piano are distinguished by their variety and originality. Few of his contemporaries in the West—with the exception of Grieg and Brahms—can compare to him in the variety and significance of piano works. For Russian piano literature Tchaikovsky's compositions have the same historical significance as his orchestral works for Russian symphonism. Tchaikovsky broadened the sphere of piano music, mastering the most diverse genres from the sonata to the mood picture, from concertos to character miniatures, like "Troika," "Peasant playing the accordion," and the "Trepak."

Tchaikovsky was an excellent pianist from his youth. When he graduated law school in 1859 he played Liszt's extremely difficult fantasia on the theme of "Lucia," and when the Moscow Conservatory opened in 1866 he gave a brilliant performance of the overture to "Russlan and Ludmila." His personal tastes in piano music caused him to single out Schumann with the latter's queer fancies, his warm impetuosity and his infinite sincerity. Schumann's restless lyricism, the range of his ideas and even his exposition with its ingenuous rhythms exercised a tremendous influence on Tchaikovsky. Considerable too was the influence of Chopin. On the other hand, he was indifferent to Liszt's radical reforms in piano execution, subtle, dazzling virtuosity and effervescence of design, although he had the greatest respect for Liszt as a composer. It is not difficult to trace these diverse influences in Tchaikovsky's music for the piano but, as always, they were transmuted in the crucible of his genius and bore the unmistakable stamp of his creative individuality. It is this individuality that makes Tchaikovsky's piano compositions so difficult of execution: the pianist must project himself into the images expressed in the music before he can reveal the profound essence that is sometimes concealed behind some simple salon dance or elegant concert bravura. Until recently the late Sergei Rachmaninov was unsurpassed in his execution of Tchaikovsky's pianoforte compositions. Now these works are part of the repertory of nearly all Soviet pianists. Among the leading interpreters of Tchaikovsky in the U.S.S.R. are the pianists Konstantin Igumnov and his best pupil Lev Oborin.

A chronological review of Tchaikovsky's works for the piano must needs begin with the earliest of the published pieces, "Scherzo in Russian Style" (1867). It is intensely popular in quality and is, in fact, based on a Ukrainian folk song. The theme is developed gradually in the course of the incessant movement in spite of the recurrence of one and the same motif. It runs steadily from restrained vigour to bacchanalian abandon, interrupted only twice by more serene episodes. Even in this early work the characteristic features of Tchaikovsky's treatment of theme are evident: a lightness and freedom, extreme digression from theme pattern while preserving perfect unity—in the given instance, rhythmic unity.

Toward the end of the 60's and the beginning of the 70's Tchaikovsky wrote a number of pieces for the piano in the salon genre: several waltzes and capriccios, romances, small dance forms, nocturnes and variations. Many of these pieces are marked by a warm emotionalism. Most of them are in the urban or folk spirit. The famous "Romance" (Opus 5, 1868) dedicated to the French singer Desire Artot, is a masterpiece of the melancholy muse of the young Tchaikovsky. The remarkable beauty of the broad, flowing melody is not marred by the vivid contrasting dance episode. The transition from one genre to another is amazingly smooth. The passionate lyricism of the Russian urban song of the 60's is combined with a glorified folk dance motif.

In "Humoresque" (Opus 10, 1871–1872) the folk element is developed further. All the varied links in the "Humoresque" follow one another in the same continuous sequence as in a folk round dance. The numerous contrasts produce a picturesque effect; for example, the first motif—women's dance—is set off by the second, the men's dance, in which you can hear the stamping of feet, thus forming a contrast between grace and strength. Similarly effective is the constant reiteration of the same motifs. The oft-repeated theme in folk songs and instrumental dance music does not weary the listener. Take the motif of the "Kamarinskaya," for example; although repeated dozens of times it gives fresh pleasure to both listener and dancer each time it recurs. The very design of the "Humoresque" is patterned after the folk devices and some of the episodes in the accompaniment remind one of accordion music.

The same smooth transition from genre to genre is skillfully applied to another popular piano piece, "Song without Words" (Opus 2, No. 3, 1867). The ability to combine the elements of two contrasting genres in one piece, to effect a smooth, integrated passage from a light, graceful air to the powerful melody of a solemn dance procession within the space of a few bars, only to direct the stream of the music suddenly back into the former channel, is evidence of the many-faceted gift that was Tchaikovsky's.

Tchaikovsky's early pianoforte compositions reveal a definite fondness for the scherzo form. "Scherzo," Opus 2, No. 2, "Valse Capriccio," Opus 4, "Valse Scherzo," Opus 7, "Capriccio," Opus 8, the "Humoresque" aforementioned, Opus 10, notwithstanding their numerous differences are all basically the same genre which has its root in popular music, on the one hand, and in whimsical capriccioso intonations à la Liszt, on the other.

The six pieces of Opus 19 (1873) were in the nature of a summary of his early pianoforte compositions. The lively, impudent "Humorous Scherzo" is delightful; the Nocturne in C-Sharp Minor sums up, as it were, Tchaikovsky's youthful lyricism. The stirring tenderness, the combination of restraint with unabashed expression of emotion, the wealth and variety of the melody, the swift changes in harmonies are apparent even to the untrained ear. The "Leaf from an Album" is enchanting in its artlessness. The "Theme with Variations" in F-Major, which preserves traces of Schumann influences, has won considerable popularity. The variations constitute a brilliant and vivid series of pictures from life and a whole world of feeling. Extremely original is another cycle of "Six pieces on one theme," Opus 21 (1873). The "Prelude," "Fugue," "Impromptu," "Funeral March," "Mazurka" and "Scherzo"— all reveal a refinement of harmony that anticipated the devices to be used much later by the young Scriabine.

Perhaps the most popular of Tchaikovsky's piano music is the "Four Seasons," Opus 37 (1875–1876), a suite of 12 pieces, one for each month. Brief epigraphs in verse taken from the various Russian poets from Pushkin to Nekrassov set the mood for each of these charming little musical pictures. The first, "January," is prefaced by four lines of Pushkin expressing the cosy warmth and beauty of a winter evening by the fireside. The music conveys the same feeling of calm content; it is serene and placid, yet not without a touch of melancholy. The second piece, "February" depicts a folk holiday, painting the gay noisy Russian carnival throngs with vivid colours. The next pieces are lyrical in mood, "The Song of the Skylark" (March) and "The Snowdrop" (April) with their unpretentious melodies and expression of wistful sadness. One of the best pieces in the collection is "Barcarolle" (June) which possesses all the qualities that make for wide popularity; the melody is beautiful and easily memorized, the form perfect, it combines warm feeling with lively movement of melody and elementary simplicity of harmony and contour. The next piece, "Song of the Reaper" (July), breathes the spirit of the Russian countryside. The energetic virile melody accompanied by rich chords conveys the rhythm of physical labour. A Russian dance tune breaks into the motif. "Autumn Song" (October) ranks with the best lyrical, elegiac music by Tchaikovsky. "Troika" (November) is an extremely original combination of the folk song motif with musical narrative; one hears the swift motion of the troika and the tinkling of the sleighbells, and the general impression is one of lively animation. The concluding piece in the series is a magnificent waltz, in the slow, flowing manner of the period.

Another splendid volume of piano miniatures is the "Children's Album," Opus 39 (1878), consisting of 24 character pieces. By the simplest of musical devices the composer succeeded in conveying a surprising variety of phenomena in the little world familiar to the children for whom the composer wrote the pieces. Many of them were undoubtedly inspired by memories of his own childhood years. They constitute a selection of Russian, Italian, old French, German and Neapolitan folk dance themes in the various national styles. Especially charming are the Waltz, Polka and Kamarinskaya. The "Peasant Playing the Accordion" is pictorial music at its best. The pensive Adagio consists of a lovely Russian tune repeated four times over; the accordion player reiterates the sequence of dominant and tonic notes. The song ends with a repetition of one and the same chords in a quaint rhythm giving a comic effect. Another sketch from life is the "Organ-grinder Sings" in which an Italian opera air makes a perfect medium for reproducing the weary monotony of the hurdy-gurdy.

Tchaikovsky's album for children has lost none of its pedagogical value and some of the pieces distinguished by their originality and the markedly Russian flavour would not be out of place in the repertory of the concert pianist.

The later 70's saw the advent of several notable compositions for the piano. To the cycles already mentioned were added 12 pieces, Opus 40 (1878), some of which won wide popularity.

"Mournful Air" is one of the most ineffably moving of Tchaikovsky's melodies. "In the Village" is considered one of the gems of Tchaikovsky's music for the pianoforte. Like "Kamarinskaya" it falls into two parts: the first, a slow, plaintive song, and the second, a vivid dance melody with variations. Another folk song from the same collection, "Russian Dance" (introduced into the ballet "Swan Lake"), is built up in the same manner. Besides Russian folk dances, the cycle includes salon dances—two mazurka and two famous waltzes—A flat major and F sharp minor. The latter is especially beautiful.

A whole story is told in the last piece in the collection, "Interrupted Reverie," one of the most interesting of Tchaikovsky's piano works. It consists of two parts. The sombre, tense nature of the first movement conveys a sense of spiritual discontent. The second part is a slow, melodious, contemplative waltz on a theme Tchaikovsky heard in Venice. The melody has the subtle grace peculiar to some Italian folk airs and forms a pleasing contrast to the sombre mood of the first part.

The "Large Sonata" (G-Major) in four movements (1878), the only lengthy composition written by Tchaikovsky for piano solo, belongs to the same period. It is unusually rich in musical ideas. The first movement differs sharply from most other analogous movements of sonatas and symphonies. Built up of measured march rhythms and impassioned recitatives, it gives the impression of a greatly augmented introduction confined within the sonata framework. The march movement in three-time measure changes to a recitative theme. Elements of improvisation and drama merge in the solemn phrases of musical oratory. A passionate restless second theme is contrasted to the calm serenity of the concluding part. The solemn development is crowned by a tense march in three-time measure. The same march motif predominates in the brilliant Coda. The second movement—Andante—is extremely poetic. Its main theme, touched by a sorrowful lyricism, is set off by a number of whimsical episodes. The form of the second movement cannot be confined within the usual rondo framework: it bears a remote resemblance to the later quartets of Beethoven and some of Schumann's piano pieces.

The other movements—Scherzo and Finale—are less interesting. Outstanding in the finale is the choral dance tune based on Ukrainian folk melodies.

The sonata is rather uneven in quality. Some of its episodes are truly remarkable, others are rather colourless. Its chief virtue lies in its irrepressible vitality which overcomes all obstacles and directs man's will to the attainment of his purpose. It is an extremely emotional work and, though difficult of execution, is well worth the pianist's efforts to master it.

* * *

In 1882 Tchaikovsky produced another priceless cycle of pianoforte miniatures—the six waltzes of Opus 51. The composer's purpose in choosing the dance form for this cycle was evidently to show the diverse interpretations that could be given of this popular genre. The cycle includes three varieties of the waltz—salon, sentimental and brilliant; a polka, "not for dancing," a "humorous" minuet and a "Romance," i.e., a melodious piece in the nocturne style. The object in changing the form of all these genres was to make them the medium for the expression of other features, chiefly of a psychological nature.

The "Saion Waltz" is a perfect example of an elegant swinging waltz rhythm in a faultless pianoforte setting.

The "Polka" is a rare example of the stylized dance. The composer used it as a vehicle for subjective lyrical expression as Chopin did with the mazurka. The actual dance gives way to a charming lyrical two-time melody in measured rhythm.

The "Humorous Minuet" is witty and ingenious. A complicated design of dissonances alternates with the courtly cadences of the 18th century minuet giving the required effect of gentle irony.

The "Natalie Waltz" is one of the most well-known of Tchaikovsky's piano pieces. Though miniature in form this waltz, at once brilliant and appealing, may be compared to the famous waltz at the Larin Ball in the opera "Eugene Onegin." In both cases a host of ideas and emotions, images and scenes are compressed into the waltz form. The lovely melodies remind us of the impetuosity of youth, sweet anguish, sudden moods of wistful yearning and wild rapture. The waltz carries us along like "life's whirlwind."

The "Romance" with its complex psychological undercurrents and the "Sentimental Waltz," one of the most delightful pages of Tchaikovsky's works for the piano, complete the Opus.

Of the instrumental pieces on folk themes the most notable is the Russian village scene depicted in the pianoforte piece "Dumka," Opus 59 (1886). This piece differs sharply from all Tchaikovsky's other pianoforte compositions by virtue of its brilliant virtuosity, the unusual piano design and the contrasting tempos, all of which give it a rhapsodical character. Indeed "Dumka" might be called a rhapsody on national themes, a genre that was extremely popular at the time in various countries. In too many instances, however, the original folk melodies were barely recognizable in their rhapsody or fantasia setting. Nevertheless the popularization of national music through the

medium of effective concert genres had a definite significance at the time, and "Dumka" is still included in the
repertory of concert pianists. In structure the piece is quite
conventional for Russian folk music—a combination of
broad flowing song melodies with gay boisterous dancing.
"Dumka" was written at the time when the composer was
working on "The Enchantress," a musical tragedy on folk
themes. The song melody with which the piece begins and
ends is distinguished by its profound expressiveness while
the dance tunes are vigorous and dynamic. "Dumka" is an
example of the Russian rhapsody in the grand virtuoso
style. Its unity of form and logic of sequence distinguishes
it from most rhapsodies.

The last piano opus, 18 pieces for the piano, Opus 72,
was written six months before the composer's death. This
is not a cycle. Written in an amazingly short time—15 days
—the pieces are essentially arrangements of existing dance
and song melodies. The idiom is simple and clear, there are
no restless impulses, no excess of emotion.

In content this series presents nothing especially new.
The dances, for example the "Mazurka," "Waltz-Knick-
knack," "Character Dance," "Polonaise," and the brilliant
"Trepak" are "echoes" of the graceful, full-blooded dances
from "Nutcracker," while the "Elegiac Song," "Cradle
Song," "Distant Past," and "Rural Echo" are a reflection
of the many other elegiac, pastoral and idyllic genres
familiar in other compositions. Written in the five-time
measure the waltz is an elaboration of the principles of another waltz of the same measure written two months before
the Sixth Symphony in which it was incorporated. Having
mastered this unique waltz form the composer attempted to
apply the new device to the large diapason of melody. The

rest are character pieces, *e.g.*, the "Scherzo Fantasia," "Dialogue," and "Un poco di Chopin" and "Un poco di Schumann," and have their prototypes among the earlier pianoforte works.

The quality of the music in most of them is superb. The plaintive melody of the delightful mazurka entitled "Un poco di Chopin" breathes warmth and passion; the melody of "Tender Reproaches" and many others are among the most enduring of the composer's works. These last 18 piano pieces are notable for their calm objectivity and serene resignation of spirit. Written after the Sixth Symphony had been composed but before it was orchestrated, they serve as a weighty argument against the false contention that the "Pathetique" was the pessimistic summing up of Tchaikovsky's music. Opus 72 affords a new insight into the meaning of the immortal work and enables one to appreciate its life-asserting, optimistic elements.

Pieces for the Violin

In the period between 1875 and 1878 Tchaikovsky wrote five pieces for the violin with piano or orchestral accompaniment. The best known of these is the "Melancholy Serenade," Opus 26 (1875). All the three themes alternating in rondo form adhere to three different genres: the main minor melody is rich in sobbing intonations and belongs in the category of elegies, the second is an echo of the Russian dance tune and the third is a capricious waltz motif. These three elements are woven together in perfect harmonious design. The dominant emotion is a stirring intimate warmth.

The striking "Waltz Scherzo" (1877) for violin and

orchestra is more suitable for symphony concert than for chamber performance.

Then come three pieces for violin and piano, Opus 42 (1878). The lovely "Meditation" was originally intended for the central movement of a violin concerto which is reflected in its style. The stirring lyricism of the introductory melody gives place to a dramatic episode. On the whole "Meditation" is marked by a broad development, and intense feeling.

The last of the three pieces of Opus 42, "Melody," is distinguished by the flowing grace and the radiant mood of the main theme. It develops so naturally that we feel it must have been written at one sitting. Its prevailing mood is a cloudless serenity and contentment so rare for Tchaikovsky.

*   *   *

We have surveyed here the chamber compositions of Tchaikovsky in all their diverse forms, dwelling in detail only on the more outstanding works. It must be said that the chamber works of the great Russian composer are far from homogeneous for they include besides miniatures of the romance type and instrumental pieces, large forms with symphonic development. We might be reproached with formalism for having placed so many diverse compositions under a single heading, but the reproach would be unjust because as distinct from the operas, ballets, and symphonies, Tchaikovsky's chamber music constitutes the direct statement of primary creative impulses. It is here that one should look for the sources of the mighty melody gift that is the most outstanding and national quality of Tchaikovsky's music. In the lyrical impulsive melodies of Tchaikovsky's chamber music we find the elementary expression of his artistic personality. Herein lies the power of his romances and instrumental pieces which have gradually and imperceptibly penetrated into the very essence of our lives and which give an insight into the subtle and rich mind and being of their creator, and a glimpse of the Russian artistic environment whence he emerged.

THE ARCHIVES OF THE TCHAIKOVSKY MUSEUM

KSENIA DAVIDOVA

A FEW YEARS BEFORE his death Tchaikovsky planned a symphony whose general theme was "Life." Such was the author's title of esquisses found among the composer's papers.

In the records we refer to the following episodes are noted: "Youth." "Obstacle" . . . "Forward, forward." "The finales . . . death." The records relate to the period between the Fifth and Sixth symphonies. The symphony was never written.

Such autographs—scores with commentaries, diary notes, rough drafts in notebooks, proofsheets, manuscripts of librettos, remarks on the margins of books read—all this taken together constitutes material for studying the creative processes of the composer.

"I do not attach the slightest value to my manuscripts," Tchaikovsky wrote at the height of his fame to his publisher,* "and it is so pleasant for me, having turned over the manuscript, to thus express my gratitude."

This view, invariably adhered to by Peter Ilyich throughout his life indirectly affected the compilation of the posthumous archives and workers in the field of music had to show a great deal of initiative and energy in collect-

* P. Jurgenson.

ing documents and adding them to personal belongings and other relics preserved in the Tchaikovsky Museum in Klin.

The selection, classification and systematization of all these documents constitute the main tasks of the Museum's archive personnel.

In addition to the manuscript, library and copy departments the Museum includes also a substantial inconographic archive.

The Museum in Klin is not an ordinary museum. It is a simple, small house, surrounded by gardens, in which are collected relics, documents and data shedding light on the composer's personality, his life and his music.

The modest, unpretentious habits of the composer, the broad range of his intellectual interests, his work and his public activity—are all reflected in the material in the Museum.

The manuscript department of the Museum archives, though small in volume, embraces all aspects of the creative processes of the composer. Most interesting are the esquisses and notebooks where the composer's conceptions first took shape. Tchaikovsky loved this stage of his work most.

"You forget everything," he wrote in a letter to von Meck of June 24, 1878, "your heart flutters with a strange, sweet excitement, you cannot possibly follow all its urges, time flies past unnoticed. . . ." "This period devoted to the work of sketching is exceedingly pleasant and interesting, brings in its wake indescribable enjoyment; but at the same time it is accompanied by a feeling of unrest, a sort of nervous agitation."

Speaking elsewhere of scoring—another stage of his creative work—he said: "The execution of the plan is consummated very peacefully and quietly. To orchestrate what is already quite complete down to the smallest detail is a very enjoyable process."

Tchaikovsky detested the subsequent stages of his work as much as he liked the initial phase. Especially did he abhor the proofreading of galleys for he felt that his time could be more profitably used to write music. The conditions under which scores were published at that time were so bad that the printed matter that came off the press was sometimes quite unrecognizable. Unable to find satisfactory proofreaders, Tchaikovsky frequently did the proofreading himself. He even wanted to republish all his works in order to eliminate the mistakes in the first editions.

Among the exhibits are seventeen notebooks. They contain a variety of entries including the addresses of friends, business notes, accounts, remarks about books read, notes of some fleeting musical idea and the first drafts of various compositions. Two notebooks are devoted to the "Queen of Spades." These are the first rough drafts of some of the themes, the aria of Herman from Scene 2, some incidents from the scene in the Countess' bedroom, the duet at the Kanavka Canal, an outline of the text of Prince Yeletsky's aria, etc. These are not even esquisses; they are merely jottings of ideas as they occurred to the composer. Among them are sketches of different scenes and arias from the opera "Mazeppa" (there is a separate book on "Mazeppa"), the duet of the Princeling and the Godmother from the opera "The Enchantress"; some pieces from the "Nutcracker Suite," sketches of the Fifth Symphony, "Hamlet," the "Moscow" Cantata. More finished esquisses are those of "The Sleeping Beauty" (the divertissement from the last scene), of "Manfred," the song "On the Golden Fields," as well as the work on new numbers for the opera "The

Little Shoes," another version of the opera "Vakula the
Smith" (duet of Oksana and Vakula, the song of the school-
teacher and others). The draft of "Hamlet" was evidently
made in the course of some journey, for the lines, notes and
letters are written in an unsteady hand. There are also other
similar sketches testifying to the fact that Tchaikovsky
jotted down his ideas as and when they occurred to him.

Some of the entries give an idea of Tchaikovsky's work
as a conductor. One of the entries gives directions for the
conducting of Acts I and II of the opera "The Enchantress."
There are notes on the tempo, on pauses for the singer, etc.
One scene bears a note: "Pause on the first eighth"; "after
the deciment—accord and then do not conduct until the
Godmother finishes"; "Hold the baton on three-quarters
after Nenil's words: "Ah, matushka," etc.

These notebooks served Peter Ilych also as a diary.
There are notes on the day spent, memoranda for the day,
etc.

There was a time when Tchaikovsky studied English.
In one of his notebooks he wrote down the unfamiliar
words and expressions which he came across in the course
of his reading.

Particularly interesting are the esquisses to "The Queen
of Spades," "Yolanthe," "The Nutcracker" Ballet, the
"Voyevoda" and "Vakula the Smith"—Tchaikovsky's first
operas. These outlines have been fully preserved, thus giving a complete picture of all the stages of the work done.
Tchaikovsky often noted the date on which he began or
finished his composition. While he was composing "The
Queen of Spades" he noted down the beginning and end
of his work on every act.

The twenty-five years between the composer's first and

last operas, "Voyevoda" and "Yolanthe," saw the gradual and labourious evolution of his operatic style. It is therefore highly interesting to compare the "Voyevoda" with those of "The Queen of Spades" and "Yolanthe."

Similar comparisons can be made in other genres as well. Among his early compositions there is the Overture F-Major (1865), the Overture C-Minor (1866) and the one-part B-flat Major quartet written during the Conservatory years. Among his mature compositions there are the sketches for the Fifth Symphony, "Hamlet," "Manfred," the "Italian Capriccio," the piano concertos, the sextet and the Sixth Symphony.

The sketches for the Sixth Symphony (1893) consist of a large 72-page notebook revealing the various stages in the creation of this masterpiece.

Two lines, each containing a theme. There are whole pages without a single correction and pages which show signs of painstaking work. Tchaikovsky planned the scoring in the earliest stages of composition. Here and there one comes across such remarks as: "string," "wind," "bassoon," "flute," "cello." Sometimes there are more detailed notes and explanations of certain passages. Tchaikovsky thought in terms of the orchestra. While jotting down the sketch of a piece of music he was already hearing the orchestra play it. "I cannot conceive of a melody except as a harmonious whole," he wrote in a letter to von Meck.

The esquisses fully confirm this. A specialist will, of course, find much in these sketches that will enable him to follow the creative paths traversed by the composer, but even the layman will find them interesting.

Tchaikovsky once called the main idea of his composition the "embryo." Here is one such "embryo." Two meas-

ures in all with the inscription: "The motif: Why? Where-
fore? The beginning and basic thought of the entire symphony." The jottings of the symphony "Life" cover only
two pages. On one there are but a few lines with the theme
of the first part; the second contains the programme of the
symphony. Here is the programme:

"Part one: all passion, confidence, the thirst for activity.
Should be brief. The Finale is death—the result of destruction. Part two is love: three—disillusionment, four—ends
morendo (also short.)" This sketch bears another inscription: "Life. I. Youth. II. Obstacle! Forward! Forward!"

The esquisse for the "Manfred" symphony fills a bound
notebook and many large sheets of paper. They bear the
traces of stubborn work. The symphony did not come
easily to Tchaikovsky. In a letter to von Meck, he wrote:
"This symphony calls for tremendous exertion and labour
for the task is very complex and serious." The complexity
of the programme and the gloominess of the subject op-
pressed him. As he himself said, he "became for the time
being a sort of Manfred." On finishing the preliminary
sketch of the symphony, he immediately wrote in the notebook: "End of symphony—May 13, but there is still very
much to be done before the end." Continuing his work on
it, he notes further on: "Today, July 6, I have still made
little progress," and elsewhere: "Today is already July 31,
there is still—oh, so much to do to the end!" In spite of
all the difficulties Tchaikovsky continued to work stubbornly "straining every nerve as usual" as he himself put it.
And here, as in the Sixth Symphony, he outlined the orchestration as he proceeded. On finishing this work, he wrote
to E. K. Pavlovskaya, the singer: "This composition will
be, perhaps, the best of all my symphonic compositions."

The esquisse to the overture-fantasia "Hamlet" consists of eleven pages with three additional sheets. There are also many remarks, directions, etc.

Of particular interest are the sketches and rough draft of the unfinished E-flat Major Symphony, which Tchaikovsky re-arranged as the Third Piano Concerto and the "Andante e Finale" for piano and orchestra. The available material reflects both the work on the symphony as well as the version for the concerto and for the "Andante e Finale." As we know, Peter Ilyich was unable to finish this piece of work and after his death it was completed by his pupil and friend, Sergei Ivanovich Taneyev.

In addition to various operatic and symphonic compositions, the Museum archives also contain Tchaikovsky's vocal and pianoforte compositions. Not long ago the Museum acquired the manuscript of the "Natalie Valse."

The proof sheets of the opera "Eugene Onegin" (the first edition of the opera) and "The Queen of Spades," the symphonic fantasia "The Tempest" (it was proofread by N. D. Kashkin, but Peter Ilyich looked it over and made many notes), the overture-fantasia "Hamlet" (proofread against the manuscript by a copyist), and pianoforte compositions are among the proofs owned by the Museum.

While working on the stage arrangements of his operas, particularly on his earlier ones, Tchaikovsky made numerous alterations in deference to the requirements of the theatre administration, the conductors, the wishes and ideas of the musicians. Several of the piano scores in the Museum bearing Peter Ilyich's signature are examples of his work in this field. One of these is the piano score of the "Oprichnik" showing evidence of the joint work of Tchaikovsky and Ed. Napravnik, the conductor. There are two

scores of the opera "The Enchantress." One belonged to
the actress N. A. Fried, another to E. K. Pavlovskaya. Alterations and corrections were made in the roles of the
Princess and the Godmother. Tchaikovsky himself evidently rehearsed the roles with the actresses because the
necessary changes, notes, etc. were made in the process of
work. At the request of the actor N. N. Figner, Tchaikovsky transposed "Brindisi" for him; the aria of the last act
of "The Queen of Spades," and also wrote the Vaudemont
aria to be inserted in the opera "Yolanthe." The manuscript
for "Brindisi" was inserted in the piano score, proofread
by Peter Ilyich for the second edition of the opera. The
original score has been preserved in the Museum. The
sketch for the aria Vaudemont has also been preserved, as
has a page from a letter from the composer's brother,
Modeste Tchaikovsky, with the text of this aria.

We must particularly note Tchaikovsky's work on the
rearrangements of the opera "Vakula the Smith" as "The
Little Shoes." The composer loved this opera most of all.
While revising, he wrote his brother Modeste: "My work
is not progressing very fast, but how pleased I am with it!
How much satisfaction I derive from the thought that my
"Vakula" will rise from the waters of oblivion." (Letter
dated March 4, 1885.)

The Museum archives contain the sketch of the first
edition of this opera (1874) in the form of a bound notebook of large format. Tchaikovsky presented it to his
former pupil A. J. Alexandrova-Levenson, who subsequently gave it to the Museum.

Referring to the rearrangement of the opera, Tchaikovsky wrote: "I have written entirely new scenes; I have
thrown out all that was bad, left in all that was good, al-

leviated the massivity and heaviness of the harmony. In a
word, I have done all that was needed to rescue the opera
from unmerited oblivion. . . ." (Letter to E. K. Pavlovskaya of February 20, 1885). The sketches of these alterations are in the notebooks. There is also a piano score "for
reference" in which all the changes are recorded, and the
manuscript of insertions to the aria of Oksana.

It may not be amiss to mention here that this same notebook contains the sketch of the Second Quartet, Variations
for the Piano and the Nocturne in C-Sharp Minor.

Of great interest is also the collection of librettos in
manuscript form and Tchaikovsky's jottings in his library
books while using one or another book.

Among the librettos we must single out such important
ones as that for the opera "Voyevoda" (the manuscript by
A. N. Ostrovsky—Act I), for the opera "The Enchantress"
(manuscript by playwright I. Shpazhinsky) and for "The
Queen of Spades" (manuscript by Modeste Tchaikovsky).

The first of these manuscripts is of value in that it
is the autograph of the great Russian dramatist, A. N.
Ostrovsky. There is no writing by Tchaikovsky himself
on it. All the composer's work on the libretto of this opera
is contained in those very notebooks in which the esquisse
of the opera is to be found. The libretto of "The Enchantress" has various corrections, alterations, condensations
made by Tchaikovsky, as well as a record of the musical
themes and ideas for one or another scene.

The most interesting libretto, "The Queen of Spades,"
is a notebook of 46 sheets divided in two. On the right side
of the sheet is the libretto, while the other half was left
empty for the composer's remarks. Many places in the text
are crossed out, while changes and additions were made

to the ball scene (the aria of Prince Yeletsky and the finale
of this act were written by the composer himself); then
there are the two last scenes. The text of "Brindisi" belongs mainly to the pen of Tchaikovsky. The first musical
draft refers to the words of Herman in the 1st Act: "Her
name I do not know," then to the second scene. There is
also a draft of the duet of Liza and Paulina, the scene with
the governess and Liza's aria: "Whence these tears."

The note at the beginning of the 4th scene—the
Countess' bedroom—is interesting. Here Tchaikovsky outlined one of the main musical backgrounds for this picture
—a restless rustling of the strings. An inscription to the
sketch says: "(entr'acte and beginning of the scene)" and
lower down: ". . . chronic plaint." The rough draft of
"Brindisi" is also sketched on the margins of the libretto.

Mention must also be made of the work of the librettist,
Modeste Tchaikovsky who clearly gave much thought to
his work. In the scene of the Countess' bedroom he has retained Pushkin's text wherever possible (Herman's monologue).

The programme of "Manfred" is a sample of symphonic
programme composition. One of the copies is in the handwriting of Hermann Laroche. It bears no corrections or
changes in Tchaikovsky's hand. A second copy, almost
without changes, was written by the composer himself.

Inspired by the suggestion of the singer Lavrovskaya to
write an opera based on "Eugene Onegin," Tchaikovsky
bought a volume of Pushkin's works, and, with the help of
his friend, Shilovsky, composed a libretto of this novel in
verse. This book can be found in the composer's personal
library. Passages were chosen from the text for definite

scenes, duets, arias and marked in pencil in the margin. There are also changes in the text, depending on how they were used by the composer. Most valuable are the notes made by Tchaikovsky for a characterization of the *dramatis personae*, corresponding to the poet's conception.

No less interesting is the work of the opera "Mazeppa." The notes in this case relate directly to the use of the text. The changes and additions were made, and the theme of the future compositions outlined, on the book margins. It is worth while mentioning that Tchaikovsky not only utilized Pushkin's poem for this opera, but drew upon historical sources as well.

No unimportant place in Tchaikovsky's compositions is occupied by his songs inspired by the verse of Polonsky, Pleshcheyev, Tyutchev, Alexey Tolstoi and other Russian poets. Many of the volumes of poetry in his library bear corresponding remarks and annotations. In many cases the scores have been sketched in but there are also sketches not utilized by the composer.

The Museum contains a large collection of letters written by the composer to various persons, as well as many letters to him. Tchaikovsky's brother and biographer—Modeste Ilyich—was the first to collect the originals and copies of the composer's correspondence. Today the Museum has about 3,000 original letters written by Tchaikovsky and more than 700 copies of his letters taken from different archives or presented by private persons, and up to 7,000 letters sent to Tchaikovsky. Peter Ilyich maintained a voluminous correspondence all his life, but it became particularly extensive (there were days when he wrote no less than thirty letters) during the latter years of his life. He corresponded with many different people—with members of his family, with relatives, schoolmates, colleagues, musicians, composers, his pupils, writers, librettists, actors, etc.

Shortly after his death in the 90's of last century, individual letters were published in different magazines. These publications were of a purely sporadic nature and, of course, pursued no scientific aims. In his three volumes of "Life of P. I. Tchaikovsky" Modeste Ilyich Tchaikovsky extensively utilized the epistolary archives of his brother. We can say quite definitely that the second and, especially, the third volume of his biography are composed mainly of the composer's correspondence, supplemented by commentary and annotations by his biographer.

At the beginning of the 90's the publication of Tchaikovsky's letters assumed greater proportions. They made their appearance in magazines and periodicals of the time: (in *Russkaya Mysl*, his correspondence with V. V. Stasov; in *Russkaya Muzikalnaya Gazeta*, in the *Sibirski Vestnik*, in the *Russki Vestnik*) and in book form: "The Correspondence of M. A. Balakirev and P. I. Tchaikovsky" (1912) edited by S. M. Lyapunov and "The Correspondence of P. I. Tchaikovsky and S. I. Taneyev" (1916), edited by M. I. Tchaikovsky.

Interest in the published letters of Tchaikovsky grew steadily after 1920. A number of letters were prepared for the press on the occasion of the Tchaikovsky Centenary. Some of them were published, others were held up by the war.

Most extensive of all was the composer's correspondence with von Meck, with his brothers Anatole and Modeste, with P. I. Jurgenson and J. P. Shpazhinskaya. Smaller in volume, but no less interesting, is the correspondence with

P. M. Pchelnikov, with P. I. Slatin, with actor B. B. Korsov and composer M. M. Ippolitov-Ivanov.

Some of this correspondence has already been published. Tchaikovsky's correspondence with von Meck has been published in three volumes (1931–36). The correspondence with P. I. Jurgenson has been published in part —the first volume appeared in 1938; the second is being prepared for press.

The correspondence with von Meck is of quite exceptional interest. His letters touch upon such a variety of subjects that they afford a most illuminating insight into the character and personality of Tchaikovsky. Without them many of the composer's views on different phenomena, theories and people, would have remained a secret to us. This correspondence gives us the programme of the Fourth Symphony, comments on creative processes, on Tchaikovsky's opinions on poetry and poets, religion and philosophy, on Pushkin, on the "Big Five," on Wagner, and so on.

The correspondence which began in 1876 continued until 1890, i.e., almost up to the death of the composer. It comprises 771 letters penned by the composer.

Second in volume is the correspondence with P. I. Jurgenson, publisher and friend of Tchaikovsky. Covering the same period—from 1877 to the end of the composer's life—it consists for the most part of business letters, but the friendly relations between Tchaikovsky and his publisher considerably broadened the scope of the letters, furnishing rich material for a study of the musical life of Russia in those years. No little information on the history of Tchaikovsky's productions can be gleaned from this book.

The Klin Museum has originals of letters to Tchaikovsky's twin brothers Modeste and Anatole, which began in the latter 60's and early 70's and continued up to his very death. Letters to Anatole Tchaikovsky's wife, P. V. Tchaikovskaya, supplement the letters to his brothers.

The relations of the Tchaikovsky brothers—Peter, Anatole and Modeste—were of quite an unusual nature. Peter was ten years older than the twins. He had already completed his studies and begun to work when the two younger brothers had only begun to attend school. Left motherless and deprived of the care of their older sister who had married, Peter Ilyich himself undertook the care of his younger brothers. "I wanted to be to the twins what a mother is to her children," he wrote in a letter many years later, "because I knew by experience how indelible is the trace a mother's love and a mother's tenderness leaves in the heart of a child. . . ."

The above quotation will suffice to give an idea of the nature of his correspondence with his brothers. Friendship and sincerity is the keynote of these letters. His solicitude for his brothers' welfare continued to the end of his life, although the directly personal relationship changed with the years. As time went on, the letters later assumed a friendly, comradely tone. Towards the end, as the brothers matured, the difference in age diminished and Tchaikovsky not infrequently appealed to his brothers for advice, help, etc. The correspondence with Modeste Ilyich is no less instructive than that with von Meck.

Personal feelings, his music, questions of art, literature, dramaturgy, events in the political and musical life of Russia—all found their reflection in the correspondence of the Tchaikovsky brothers.

A sensitive, sincere attitude to people was one of the principal traits in the composer's character. The desire to help others was characteristic of him all through his life. In the last ten or fifteen years the unceasing stream of pleas for help, for intercession, for testimonials, etc., constanty increased. Peter Ilyich never remained deaf to such pleas. Many of the letters preserved in the Museum are recommendations. As an important public figure, he took a keen interest in the affairs of the musical or theatrical world, interceding for one person or another. In this sense his correspondence with P. M. Pchelnikov, the manager of the Moscow theatre, is characteristic. There he intercedes on behalf of the conductors Altani and Arends, recommends a singer for the chorus, an oboist for the orchestra, supports the well-known opera singer Khokhlov, etc.

Beginning with 1886, while he was working on the opera "The Enchantress," his correspondence with Julia Shpazhinskaya—the wife of the librettist I. V. Shpazhinsky —developed into an extensive and lasting correspondence between two friends. Shpazhinskaya's unusual personality, her superior intelligence and refinement attracted Tchaikovsky. In his letters to her we find interesting remarks about his work on the opera "The Enchantress," on the conducting of the opera "The Little Shoes," on the musical life of Moscow, a description of the trip through the Caucasus, comments on "Manfred," Byron, Chekhov and Tolstoi.

The archives also contain the diaries of the composer. There is a notebook for 1873, an album and general notebooks (in all six) for 1885 and 1886 (three notebooks) and for 1887 (two notebooks). The years 1889 and 1890 were noted in little diaries. A special book is devoted to notes on Tchaikovsky's stay in America. Not all the notes are complete, for Tchaikovsky did not make entries regularly.

One year he would write faithfully from day to day, while another year he wrote only sporadically. Nonetheless these are valuable documents of his life.

As a memorial to Tchaikovsky the Museum owes its existence to the composer's servant Alexei Sofronov, while for the collection of material, for the study of the life and work of the composer, it is indebted to Modeste Ilyich Tchaikovsky.

Modeste Tchaikovsky's personal archives are extremely interesting. They shed light on his versatile personality, his artistic nature, and his profound intellectual interests. The archives are in the main divided into two departments— literary (translations: "History of Philosophy" by Cuno Fischer, Shakespeare's sonnets, several plays, original compositions, the biography of P. I. Tchaikovsky in three volumes, an autobiography, etc., and the epistolary collection. The latter consists primarily of letters (more than 7,500) from writers, musicians, composers, workers in the field of music, publishers, artists and actors. Modeste Ilyich's circle of acquaintances was unusually wide, spreading far beyond the borders of his native land. Among his correspondents one can name such people as Maxim Gorky, Taneyev, Rachmaninov, Glazunov, Napravnik, Arthur Nikisch, Lucien Guitry, Yermolova, Vera Komissarzhevskaya, the ballet master Fokine, Nijinski, Michel Delin, translator of Eugene Onegin, the pianist Sofia Menter, Rosa Newmarch and others.

The fact that much of the correspondence relates to questions of the legacy of Peter Ilyich, information about the performance of the latter's works, the erection of memorials to him, etc., makes this archive a valuable supplement to that of Peter Ilyich.

The Tchaikovsky Museum in Klin is first among the

Tchaikovsky music museums in Russia. In the years following the Revolution the workers of the Museum, which was by then a state institution, carried on the work begun by Modeste Ilyich. At the same time they extended the Museum fund by acquiring the archives of other persons and different material relating to Tchaikovsky's musical life in general.

Today the Museum contains a number of archives, most valuable among which are those of Taneyev, Laroche, Findeisen, Arensky, Brandukov, Glazunov, and others.

The most complete is the archive of S. I. Taneyev.

The Laroche archive constitutes a large collection of his musical-literary articles, both in manuscript form as well as in printed editions (newspaper articles, brochures, etc.).

The musical value of the Arensky, Brandukov and Grechaninov archives lies in the fact that they consist for the most part of manuscripts and esquisses of their own compositions. Notable among them are the esquisses to Arensky's operas "Rafael," "Hal and Damayanti," "The Dream on the Volga," "The Snow Maiden" (quite unknown), his ballet "A Night in Egypt" and a number of vocal, instrumental and chamber pieces. The compositions of Grechaninov include scenes from "The Snow Maiden" (music to Ostrovsky's play) and "Elegy for a large orchestra," op. 18, dedicated to the memory of P. I. Tchaikovsky.

The archives of the famous violoncellist Brandukov, friend and pupil of Tchaikovsky, consists for the most part of his works for the violoncello (a number of concertos and others) and letters. Among the latter are the autographs of Eugene Ysaye, Vincent d'Indy, G. Faure.

Most interesting, both for the variety of its composition,

as well as for the treasures it contains, are the Findeisen archives.

An entire folder is devoted to Glinka, consisting of diverse documents and letters serving as material for work on the biography of Glinka.

A number of autographs of great composers make the Findeisen archive especially valuable: 1) rough MSS. drafts by Borodin (introduction to the aria of Konchakovna from the opera "Prince Igor," string sextet, piano quintet, unpublished songs), as well as a draft of his autobiography and a number of letters; 2) manuscript score of the entire opera "Boris Godunov" and a scene from the opera "Khovanshchina" by Mussorgsky, edited by Rimsky-Korsakov, as well as the autobiography of Rimsky-Korsakov begun on March 30, 1886; 3) the autograph of Eduard Grieg—a fragment from the Peer Gynt Suite.

In the epistolary archive of Findeisen are collected many interesting letters from Borodin, Cui, Rimsky-Korsakov, Anton Rubinstein, Balakirev, and others.

The general museum fund, composed mainly of material donated by different people contains musical MSS. of the composers Verstovsky, Borodine, Rimsky-Korsakov and Franz Liszt.

The manuscript-memoirs department of the museum is a collection of articles and researches on the history of Russian music and particularly on the life and work of Tchaikovsky, as well as a number of unpublished reminiscences of him.

In their hatred for Russian culture, Hitler's armed hordes destroyed and desecrated historical relics and art treasures encountered in their path. During their 24-day

occupation of Klin the Nazis played havoc with the Tchaikovsky House. Fortunately, the most valuable exhibits had been evacuated to safety in good time by order of the government. The collection of new data has now been resumed. Tchaikovsky's correspondence, annotated, has been prepared for the press; articles are being written and researches made on the basis of the Museum materials.

LIST OF TCHAIKOVSKY'S WORKS FOR THE STAGE

OPERAS

1868

"The Voyevoda," opera in 3 Acts (4 scenes). Op. 3. Libretto by A. N. Ostrovsky and the author, after A. N. Ostrovsky's "Dream on the Volga." Composed March 8, 1867, to summer of 1868. First performed Jan. 30, 1868, Moscow, Bolshoi Theatre. Conducted by E. N. Marten. Not published (Overture—July, 1892, Jurgenson; Entr'acte and dances of peasant girls Nov., 1873, Jurgenson). Score destroyed by author.

1869

"Undine," opera in 3 Acts. Libretto by V. A. Sologub after F. de Lamotte Fouquè and V. A. Zhukovsky. Composed Jan., 1869. Not performed (Fragments at concert March 16, 1870, Moscow, conducted by E. N. Marten). Not published. (Score destroyed by author; only few numbers preserved.)

1872

"The Oprichnik," opera in 4 Acts (5 scenes). Libretto by the author of opera after I. Lazhechnikov. Dedicated to Grand Duke Konstantin Nikolayevich. Composed Feb. 23, 1870, to March 20, 1872. First performed April 12, 1874. St. Petersburg, Mariinsky Theatre, conducted by E. F. Napravnik. Published 1896, Bessel.

1874

"Vakula, the Smith," opera in 3 Acts (8 scenes), Op: 14. Libretto by J. P Polonsky after N. V. Gogol ("Christmas Eve"). Dedicated to memory of Grand Duchess Elena Pavlovna. (See also: "The Little Shoes"—Cherevichki.) Composed June, 1874, to Aug. 21 (submitted to Russian Music Society contest). First performed Nov. 24, 1876, St. Petersburg, Mariinsky Theatre. Conducted by E. F. Napravnik. Not published

1878

"Eugene Onegin," opera (lyrical scenes) in 3 Acts (7 scenes), Op. 24. Libretto by author (with collaboration of K. S. Shilovsky) after A. S. Pushkin. Composed May, 1877, to Jan. 20, 1878 (Ecossaise, March 17, 1879). Moscow Maly Theatre, conducted by N. G. Rubinstein (performed by students of Conservatory); Feb. 1, 1881, Moscow, Bolshoi Theatre, conducted by E. M. Bevigniani. Published Dec., 1880, Jurgenson.

1879

"Maid of Orleans," opera in 4 Acts (6 scenes). Libretto by author after Schiller and V. A. Zhukovsky. Dedicated to E. F. Napravnik. Composed Dec. 5, 1878, to Aug. 21, 1879. First performed Feb. 13, 1881, St. Petersburg, Mariinsky Theatre. Conducted by E. F. Napravnik. Published July, Dec., 1902, Jurgenson.

1883

"Mazeppa," opera in 3 Acts (6 scenes). Libretto by V. P. Burenin (revised by author of opera) after Pushkin ("Poltava"). Composed Aug. 23, 1881, to April 16, 1883. First performed Feb. 3, 1884, Moscow, Bolshoi Theatre, conducted by I. K. Altani. Published Oct., 1899, Jurgenson.

1885

"The Little Shoes," opera in 4 Acts (7 scenes). Libretto by J. P. Polonsky after N. V. Gogol ("Christmas Eve"). (Second version of opera "Vakula, the Smith"). Composed Feb. 15, to March 22, 1885. First performed Jan. 19, 1887, Moscow, Bolshoi Theatre, conducted by author. Published 1898, Jurgenson.

1887

"The Enchantress," opera in 4 Acts. Libretto by J. V. Shpazhinsky. Composed Sept. 9, 1885, to May 6, 1887. First performed Oct. 20, 1887, St. Petersburg, Mariinsky Theatre. Conducted by author. Published 1901, Jurgenson.

1890

"The Queen of Spades," opera in 3 Acts (7 scenes), Op. 68. Libretto by M. I. Tchaikovsky (in collaboration with author) after A. S. Pushkin. Composed Jan. 19 to June 8, 1890 (commissioned by Imperial Theatres). First performed Dec. 7, 1890, St. Petersburg, Mariinsky Theatre, conducted by E. F. Napravnik. Published Aug., 1891, Jurgenson.

1891

"Yolanthe," opera in 1 Act, Op. 69. Libretto by M. I. Tchaikovsky after G. Hertz—K. I. Zvantsev ("King René's Daughter"). Composed July 10 to December 15, 1891 (commissioned by Imperial Theatres). First performed Dec. 6, 1892,

St. Petersburg, Mariinsky Theatre, conducted by E. F. Napravnik. Published Nov., 1892, Jurgenson.

BALLETS

1876

"Swan Lake," ballet in 4 Acts, Op. 20. Libretto by V. P. Begichev and V. F. Geltser. Composed Aug. 14, 1875, to April 10, 1876 (commissioned by Imperial Theatres). First performed Feb. 20, 1877, Moscow, Bolshoi Theatre, produced by Reisinger, conducted by S. J. Ryabov. Published July, 1895, Jurgenson.

1889

"Sleeping Beauty," ballet in 3 Acts with prologue (5 scenes), Op. 66. Libretto by M. I. Petitpas and I. A. Vsevolozhsky after Ch. Perrault. Dedicated to I. A. Vsevolozhsky. Composed Dec., 1888, to Aug. 16 (20), 1889 (commissioned by Imperial Theatres). First performed Jan. 3, 1890, St. Petersburg, Mariinsky Theatre, produced by M. I. Petitpas, conducted by R. E. Drigo. Published only the Piano Score (Jurgenson). Full score is being prepared for press.

1892

"The Nutcracker," ballet-fairy tale in 2 Acts (3 scenes), Op. 71. Libretto by M. I. Petitpas after E. T. A. Hoffman-A. Dumas. Composed Feb. 22, 1891, to March 23, 1892 (commissioned by Imperial Theatres). First performed Dec. 6, 1892, St. Petersburg, Mariinsky Theatre, produced by L. I. Ivanov, conducted by R. E. Drigo. Published Nov., 1892, Jurgenson.

INCIDENTAL MUSIC

1863–1864

"Boris Godunov," music to a scene ("Night. Garden. Fountain. The Pretender declares his love for Marina") from Pushkin's tragedy. Composed 1863–1864. Not published.

1867

"The Muddle," (Putanitsa) couplets to vaudeville by P. S. Fyodorov, composed December, 1867 (for amateur performance). First performed Dec., 1876, Moscow (in a private home). Not published.

1870

"Dmitri, the Pretender, and Vasily Shuisky," music for the drama (chronicle) by A. N. Ostrovsky (small symphony orchestra). Composed 1870 (at suggestion of A. N. Ostrovsky). Not published.

1872

"Barber of Seville," couplets by Count Almaviva to comedy by Beaumarchais (voice and two violins). Composed Nov.-Dec. 1872 (for pupils' performance at Conservatory). First performed Nov.-Dec., 1872. Moscow Conservatory. Published, 1906, Jurgenson.

1873

"Snow Maiden," music for spring fairy tale in four acts by A. N. Ostrovsky, Op. 12 (soloists, chorus, small symphony orchestra). 1. Introduction. 2. Dances and Bird Chorus ("The

birds assembled"). 3. Jack Frost's Monologue ("O'er the homes
of the wealthy"). 4. Shrove-Tide ("The cocks crowed at
dawn") chorus. 5. a) Melodrama, 2) Entr'acte. 6. Lyel's First
Song ("The wild strawberries"). 7. Lyel's Second Song ("Now
the forest murmurs"). 8. Entr'acte. 9. Chorus of Blind Min-
istrels ("Vibrant Strings"). 10. Melodrama. 11. Chorus of
Crowd and Courtiers ("Hail to thee, wise one"). 12. Chorus
of Girls ("Over the meadows"). 13. Dance of the Buffoons.
14. Lyel's Third Song ("The clouds and the thunder con-
verse"). 15. Brusila's Song ("The beaver's bath"). 16. Advent
of the Wood Goblin in the Shade of the Snow Maiden.
17. a) Entr'acte. b) Spring's Declamation. 18. March of Tsar
Berendei and Chorus ("We sowed millet"). 19. Finale ("Yarilo,
the god"), Lyel's Song with Chorus. Composed May 2, 1873,
Moscow Maly Theatre (on the stage of Bolshoi Theatre), conducted by N. G. Rubinstein. Published Dec., 1895, Jurgenson.

1879

"The Fairy," lullaby to the play by Octave Feuillet
(piano). Composed July, 1879. First performed July, 1879, at
Kamenka (in the Davydov home). Not published.

1880

"Montenegro on the Receipt of the News of Declaration of
War by Russia on Turkey," music for a tableau ("Chief reads
manifesto to Montenegrins"). (Small symphony orchestra).
Composed Jan. 27–30, 1880. (Commissioned for proposed performance at Bolshoi Theatre). Not published.

1886

"Voyevoda," music for a melodrama (Domovoy's monologue) from comedy by A. N. Ostrovsky (small symphony

orchestra). Composed Jan. 13–17, 1886, at suggestion of A. N. Ostrovsky. First performed Jan. 19, 1886. Maly Theatre. Published 1940 in collection "Tchaikovsky on the Moscow Stage," Moscow, Leningrad, "Isskustvo," 489 pp.

1891

"Hamlet," music for tragedy in five acts by William Shakespeare, Op. 67 (soloists, small symphony orchestra). Overture. 1. Melodrama. 2. Fanfares. 3. Melodrama. 4. Melodrama. 5. Entr'acte to Act II. 6. Fanfare. 7. Entr'acte to Act III. 8. Melodrama. 9. Elegy. Entr'acte to Act IV. 10. Scene ("Where is he who loves you so"), Ophelia's First Song. 11. Scene ("He lay with face uncovered"), Ophelia's Second Song. 12. Entr'acte to Act V. 13. Song of the Sexton ("What a fine fellow was I"). 14. Funeral March. 15. Fanfare. 16. Final March. Composed Jan. 2, 1891 (for benefit of L. Guitry of Mikhailov Theatre). First performed Feb. 9, 1891, St. Petersburg, Mikhailov Theatre. Published Feb., 1896, Jurgenson.

VOCAL MUSIC

Chorus

For soloists, mixed chorus and symphony orchestra

1863–1864

Oratorio. Composed 1863–1864. Not published.

1865

"Ode to Joy," cantata (music for hymn). (Soloists: soprano, alto, tenor, bass). Text by Schiller, K. S. Aksakov and others. Composed Oct. to Dec. 29, 1864. (Commissioned by St. Petersburg Conservatory.) First performed Dec. 29, 1865,

St. Petersburg Conservatory, conducted by A. G. Rubinstein (at public examinations). Not published.

1872

Cantata on occasion of opening of Polytechnical exhibition in Moscow (solo: tenor). Text by J. N. Polonsky. Composed Feb.-March, 1872 (on commission of Music Department of Polytechnical Exhibition). First performed May 31, 1872, Moscow (at opening of exhibition). Conducted by K. O. Davydov. Not published.

1875

Cantata (hymn) on the occasion of the 50th anniversary of O. A. Petrov (tenor solo). Text by N. A. Nekrassov. Composed Dec. 17, 1875. First performed April 24, 1876. St. Petersburg. Conducted by K. O. Davidov. Not published.

1883

"Moscow," cantata (soloists: mezzo soprano and baritone). Text by A. P. Maikov. 1. Chorus ("Streamlet"). 2. Arioso (" 'Tis Not A Star," mezzo soprano). 3. Chorus ("The Hour Has Struck"). 4. Monologue (baritone) and chorus ("Out of the Forest"). 5. Arioso (mezzo soprano). 6. Finale ("Through Russia"). Composed March 9 to 24, 1883 (commissioned by Coronation Committee). First performed May 15, 1883, Moscow, Kremlin. Granovitaya Chamber. Conducted by E. F. Napravnik. Published June, 1888, Jurgenson.

For Mixed and Children's Chorus and Symphony Orchestra

1870

Chorus of flowers and insects from opera "Mandragora." Text by S. A. Rachinsky. Composed Jan. 13, 1870. First performed Dec. 18, 1870, Moscow. Conducted by N. G. Rubinstein. Published June, 1902, Jurgenson.

For Mixed Chorus a Capella

1863–1864

"The Vision Beyond." Chorus. Text by N. P. Ogaryev. Composed 1863–1864. Published 1941 in Tchaikovsky's Collected Works, Vol. 43. Moscow, Leningrad, State Music Publishers.

1878

Liturgy of St. Chrysostomus, Op. 41. 1. Lord Have Mercy. 2. Glory to the Father and the Son. 3. Come Let Us Pray. 4. Hallelujah. 5. Glory to God. 6. Cherubim. 7. Lord Have Mercy. 8. I Believe. 9. Beatitude. 10. Of Thee We Sing. 11. Worthy. 12. Amen. 13. Our Father. 14. Hail. 15. Benediction. Composed May to July 29, 1878. Published Jan. 1879, Jurgenson.

1882

Vesper Mass, experiment in harmonizing sacred music. Op. 52. In 17 Parts. Composed May 21, 1881, to March 7, 1882. Published November, 1882, Jurgenson.

1885

Hymn in honour of St. Cyril and Methodius. Text by author. Composed March 6–8, 1885. (Commissioned by P. I. Jurgenson). Published March, 1885, Jurgenson.

9 pieces of sacred music. Composed Nov. 3–17, 1884 (1–3), March, April, 1885 (Nos. 4–9). Published Feb., 1885 (Nos. 1–3), Aug., 1885 (Nos. 4–9), Jurgenson.

Song of Law School Students (in honour 50th anniversary of Law School). Text by author. Dedicated to memory of Institute's founder. Composed Nov. 27, 1885. Published (lithograph) 1885 (St. Petersburg).

1887

"The Golden Cloud Went to Sleep," chorus. Text by M. J. Lermontov. Composed July 5, 1887. Published 1922, State Music Publishers.

1889

"To A. G. Rubinstein" chorus. Text by J. P. Polonsky. Composed Sept. 20–30, 1889. Published Nov., 1889, Jurgenson.
"The Nightingale," chorus. Text by author. Dedicated to chorus of Imperial Opera in St. Petersburg. Composed Dec. 15, 1889. Published 1890, Jurgenson.

1891

"Not a Cuckoo in the Forest" chorus. Text by N. G. Tsyganov. Dedicated to choir class of I. A. Melnikov. Composed Feb. 14, 1891. Published 1895 in volume "Russian Choruses for Mixed Voices" by I. A. Melnikov. First edition No. 7. Published by Jurgenson.
"Angel Wrathful" chorus. Composed (composition date unknown). Published Oct., 1906, Jurgenson.

For Male Chorus a Capella

1881

"Eventide" chorus (three voices). Text by author. Composed Dec. 13, 1881. Published Dec., 1881, Jurgenson.

1887

"Blessed Is He Who Smiles," chorus (four-voice). Text by Konstantin Romanov. Dedicated to Moscow University students' chorus. Composed Dec. 7, 1887. Published Oct., 1889, Jurgenson.

1891

"When Merry Voices Fall Silent." Chorus (four-part). Text by A. S. Pushkin. Dedicated to choir class of I. A. Melnikov. Composed Feb. 14, 1891. Published, 1894, in collection "Russian choruses for male voices" by I. A. Melnikov. No. 1. Published by Jurgenson.

For Female Chorus a Capella

1874

"Spring," Chorus. Composed Feb., 1874. Not published.

1881

Cantata, chorus (four-voice). Text by a student of the Patriotic Institute in St. Petersburg. Composed Dec., 1881. Not published.

1891

"Unmindful of Time," chorus (four-voice). Text by N. G. Tsyganov. Written for choir class of I. A. Melnikov. Composed Feb. 14, 1891. Published 1894 in collection "Russian Choruses for Female Voices" by I. A. Melnikov. No. 6, Jurgenson,

ENSEMBLES

For Four Voices and Piano

1893

"Night," Quartet (soprano, contralto, tenor and bass). Text by author (music taken from Fantasia No. 4 by Mozart). Dedicated to E. A. Lavrovskaya. Composed March 1–3, 1893. Published March, 1893, Jurgenson.

For Three Part Chorus and Piano

1870

"Nature and Love" trio (2 sopranos, contralto). Text by author. Dedicated to B. O. Balzac. Composed Dec., 1870 (for pupils of Prof. B. O. Balzac). Published Dec., 1894, Jurgenson.

For Four Voices and Piano

1880

Six Duets, Op. 46. Text by I. Z. Surikov (Nos. 1, 6), A. K. Tolstoi (Nos. 2, 5), F. I. Tyutchev (No. 3), T. G. Shevchenko —I. Z. Surikov (No. 4). Dedicated to T. L. Davydova. 1. Evening (high & med. voice). 2. Scottish Ballad (soprano and baritone). 3. Tears (high and med. voice). 4. In the Garden (high and med. voice). 5. Passion is Dead (soprano and tenor). 6. Dawn (high and med. voice). Composed 1860, June 4 to Aug. 24. Published April, 1881, Jurgenson.

1881

"Romeo and Juliet," Duet (soprano and tenor). Text by Shakespeare—A. L. Sokolovsky. Composed 1881 to Dec. 30, 1893 (finished by S. I. Taneyev). Published 1894, Jurgenson.

SOLO

For Voice and Piano

1857 to 1860

Four Youth Songs. Text by A. A. Fet (No. 1), A. S. Pushkin (No. 2), A. N. Apukhtin (No. 3), Italian (No. 4). 1. My Genius, My Angel, My Friend (med. voice). 2. Song of the Zephyr (high voice) (2 versions). 3. Who Goes There? 4. Mezza Notte (high voice). Composed 1857–1860. Published 1860, Leibrok (St. Petersburg), No. 4. Published 1940 in Complete Collection of Tchaikovsky's Works, Vol. 44, Moscow, Leningrad, State Music Publishers (Nos. 1, 2). Not published (No. 3).

1869

Romances, o. 6. Text by A. K. Tolstoi (Nos. 1, 4). M. Hartman, A. N. Pleshcheyev (No. 2), E. P. Rostopchina (No. 3), Heine—L. A. Mei (No. 5), Goethe—L. A. Mei (No. 6). Dedicated to A. G. Menshikova (No. 1), N. D. Kashkin (No. 2), A. D. Kochetova (No. 3), P. I. Jurgenson (No. 4), I. A. Klimenko (No. 5), A. A. Khvostova (No. 6). 1. Believe Not, My Friend (high voice). 2. Not a Word, Oh My Friend (high voice). 3. Sweet Anguish (med. voice). 4. A Tear Trembles (baritone). 5. Why (high voice). 6. None But the Lonely Heart (med. voice). Composed Nov. 15, to Dec. 17, 1869. Published 1870, Ja. Jurgenson.

1870

"So Soon to Forget," Romance (high voice). Text by A. N. Apukhtin. Composed Oct. 26, 1870. Published Nov., 1873. Jurgenson.

1872

Romances, op. 16. Text by A. N. Maikov (Nos. 1–6), N. P. Grekov (No. 2), A. A. Fet (No. 3), F. Hymens—A. N. Pleshcheyev (No. 4), N. N. (author), (No. 5). Dedicated to N. N. Rimskaya-Korsakova (Purgold) (No. 1), N. A. Rimsky-Korsakov (No. 2), H. A. Laroche (No. 3), N. A. Hubert (No. 4). N. G. Rubinstein (No. 5), K. K. Albrecht (No. 6). 1. Cradle Song (high voice). 2. Wait (high voice). 3. Try to Understand (low voice). 4. Oh, Sing that Song Again (high voice). 5. What Then? (high voice). 6. New Greek Melody (high voice). Composed Dec., 1872. Published Jan., 1873, Bessel.

1873

2 Romances (medium voice). Text by A. A. Fet (No. 1), Heine—M. L. Mikhailov (No. 2). 1. Carry My Heart Away. 2. Spring's Blue Eyes. Composed Sept. 29, 1873. Published 1875, Bernard (St. Petersburg, 1885).

1875

Six Romances, Op. 25. Text N. F. Shcherbina (No. 1), F. L. Tyutchev (No. 2), Goethe—F. I. Tyutchev (No. 3), L. A. Mei (Nos. 4, 5, 6), dedicated to A. P. Krutikova (No. 1), D. A. Orlov (No. 2), M. D. Damenskaya (No. 3), V. I. Raab (No. 4), I. A. Melnikova (No. 5). 1. Reconciliation (medium voice). 2. Over the Burning Embers (high voice). 3. Mignon's Song (high voice). 4. The Canary (high voice). 5. I Have Never Spoken To Her (low voice). 6. The Fool (medium voice). Composed March 29, 1875. Published April, 1875, Bessel.

Six Romances, Op. 27. Text by N. P. Ogarev (No. 1), N. P. Grekov (No. 2), A. A. Fet (No. 3), T. G. Shevchenko

—L. A. Mei (No. 5), A. Mickiewicz—L. A. Mei (Nos. 5, 6). Dedicated to Princess E. A. Tserteleva (Lavrovskaya). 1. The Vision Beyond (medium voice). 2. See Yonder Cloud (low voice). 3. Do Not Leave Me (medium voice). 4. Eventide (medium voice). 5. Why Was I Born? (medium voice). 6. My Little Scapegrace (medium voice) (two versions). Composed April 8, 1875. Published May, 1875, Jurgenson.

Six Romances, Op. 28. Text by Alfred de Musset—N. H. Grekov (No. 1), V. Syrokomli—L. A. Mei (No. 2), L. A. Mei (No. 3), unknown author (No. 4), A. N. Apukhtin (No. 5), N. N. (author) (No. 6). Dedicated to A. N. Nikolayev (No. 1), A. M. Dodonov (No. 2), Princess M. I. Dundukova-Korsakova (Ilyina) (No. 3), E. Massigny (No. 4), B. B. Korsov (No. 5), E. P. Kadmina (No. 6). 1. No, I shall Never Say (high voice). 2. The Corals (high voice). 3. Why? (high voice). 4. He Loved Me So (high voice). 5. No Sign, No Word, No Greeting (medium voice). 6. Awful Moment (high voice). Composed April 11, 1875. Published May, 1875, Jurgenson.

Two Romances. Text by Heine—L. A. Mei (No. 1), N. N. Grekov (No. 2). 1. Would That a Single Word (high voice). 2. We have Not Long to Stroll (medium voice). Composed June 28, 1875. Published 1875, Bernard (St. Petersburg). Oct., 1885, Jurgenson.

1878

Six Romances, Op. 38. Text by A. K. Tolstoi (Nos. 1, 2, 3, 4), M. J. Lermontov (No. 5), N. N. (the author) (from the Italian) (No. 6). Dedicated to A. I. Tchaikovsky. 1. Don Juan's Serenade (baritone). 2. 'Twas Early Spring (high voice). 3. At the Ball (medium voice). 4. Oh, If You Could (medium voice). 5. The Dead Man's Love (med. voice). 6. Pimpinella (Florentine song) (medium voice). Composed Feb. 11, 1878, to July 13. Published Sept., 1878, Jurgenson.

1880

Seven Romances, Op. 47. Text by A. K. Tolstoi (Nos. 1, 2, 4, 5), A. Mickiewicz—N. Berg (No. 3), A. N. Apukhtin (No. 6), I. Z. Surikov (No. 7). Dedicated to A. V. Panayeva. 1. Had I But Known (high voice). 2. The Soul Was Softly Wafted to the Skies (high voice). 3. Twilight Fell on the Earth (high voice). 4. Sleep, Sorrowful Friend (medium voice). 5. Hail to You, Forests (baritone). 6. Is It Day? (high voice). 7. Were I But A Blade of Grass in the Field (high voice). Composed July 10 to Aug. 24, 1880. Published March, 1881, Jurgenson.

1883

Sixteen Songs for Children (high voice). Op. 54. Text by A. N. Pleshcheyev (Nos. 1, 4, 6, 7, 9, 10, 12, 13, 14), A. N. Pleshcheyev (from the Polish) (Nos. 2, 3), A. N. Pleshcheyev (from the English) (No. 5), H. Gellert—A. N. Pleshcheyev (No. 8), L. Ratisbonne—A. N. Pleshcheyev (No. 11), T. Lenartovich—A. N. Pleshcheyev (No. 15), K. S. Aksakov (No. 16). 1. Grandmother and Grandson. 2. Little Birdie. 3. Spring. 4. My Garden. 5. Legend. 6. On the Seashore. 7. Winter Evening. 8. The Cuckoo. 9. Spring. 10. Cradle Song in a Storm. 11. The Flower. 12. Winter. 13. Spring Song. 14. Autumn. 15. The Swallow. 16. Child's Song (My Little Liza). Composed Oct. 16 to Nov. 3, 1883. (No. 16, Jan. 7, 1881.) Published March, 1884, Jurgenson. No. 16 separately, 1881, Jurgenson.

1884

Six Romances, Op. 57. Text by V. A. Sollogub (No. 1), A. K. Tolstoi (No. 2), Goethe—A. S. Strugovshehikov (No. 3), D. S. Merezhkovsky (Nos. 4, 5), A. Kristop—A. N. Plesh-

cheyev (No. 6). Dedicated to F. P. Komissarzhevsky (No. 1),
B. B. Korsov (No. 2), E. K. Pavlovskaya (No. 3), V. V.
Butakova (No. 4), D. A. Usatov (No. 5), A. N. Krutikova
(No. 6). 1. In the Shadow of Thy Branches (high voice).
2. The Golden Cornfields (baritone). 3. Ask Not (med. voice).
4. Sleep (med. voice). 5. Death (high voice). 6. Only You
(low voice). Composed Nov., 1884. Published Sept., 1885,
Jurgenson.

1886

Twelve Romances, Op. 60. Text A. S. Homyakov (Nos.
1, 11), A. A. Fet (No. 2), A. N. Pleshcheyev (Nos. 3, 12), V.
Stefanovich—A. S. Pushkin (No. 4), N. N. (author) (No. 5),
A. N. Apukhtin (No. 6), J. P. Polonsky (Nos. 7, 9, 10), N. A.
Nekrasov (No. 8). Dedicated to Empress Maria Fyodorovna.
1. Last Night (high voice). 2. I Said Not a Word (high voice).
3. O, Had You But Known (high voice). 4. The Nightingale
(high voice). 5. Simple Words (med. voice). 6. Mad Nights
(high voice). 7. Song of the Gypsy (high voice). 8. Forgive
(high voice). 9. Night (high voice). 10. Shadows Flit by the
Window (high voice). 11. The Exploit (baritone). 12. The
Gentle Stars Shone Down Upon Us (med. voice). Composed
Aug. 19, to Sept. 8, 1886. Published Dec., 1886, Jurgenson
(Nos. 1–6); Feb., 1887 (Nos. 7–12).

1887

Six Romances, Op. 63. Text by Konstantin Romanov. Dedicated to Grand Duke Konstantin. 1. I Did Not Love Thee at
First (high voice). 3. I Opened the Windows (med. voice).
3. You Do Not Like Me (med. voice). 4. First Rendez-vous
(high voice). 5. The Lights are Extinguished (high voice).
6. Serenade ("Oh, Child, Beneath Thy Window") (high
voice). Composed Nov. 17 to Dec. 15, 1887. Published May,
1888, Jurgenson.

1888

Six Romances, Op. 65. Text Z. Turquetti (No. 1). P. Kolen (Nos. 2, 3, 4, 6), A. M. Blankshkott (No. 5). (From the original French.) Dedicated to D. Arto-Padilla. 1. Sérénade (med. voice). 2. Déception (low voice). 3. Sérénade (med. voice). 4. Qu'importe que l'hiver (med. voice). 5. Les Larmes (med. voice). 6. Rondel (med. voice). Composed Nov. 17, to Dec. 15, 1887. Published May, 1888, Jurgenson.

1893

Six Romances (high voice). Op. 73. Text D. M. Rathaus. Dedicated to N. N. Figner. 1. Together We Sat. 2. Night. 3. This Moonlight Night. 4. The Sun Set. 5. Midst Dreary Days. 6. Again as Before. Composed April 23, to May 5, 1893. Published Sept., 1893, Jurgenson.

Musical Morceaux

"The Little Dog," entry in autograph album of M. A. Colovina. For voice and piano. Text by composer. Composed Sept. 22, 1876. Not published.
"No News from My Beloved," addressed to V. L. Davydov, for voice and piano. Text by composer. Composed 1892. Not published.

INSTRUMENTAL MUSIC

Orchestra

For Grand Symphony Orchestra

1863–1864

Allegro, for classic orchestra (without cymbals). (Composed 1863–1864) (student work). Not published.

"Romans in the Coliseum," piece for orchestra. Composed 1863–1864. Not published.

"The Storm," overture to drama by A. N. Ostrovsky. Composed summer of 1864. Published 1896, Belyaev.

1865

Character Dances. Composed 1865, winter (second version). Dances of peasant girls in opera "Voyevoda" (1868). First performed Aug., 1865. Pavlovsk. Conducted by T. Strauss. Not published.

1866

Concert overture C Minor. Composed 1865, summer to Jan. 19, 1866). First performed 1931. Saratov. Conducted by K. S. Saradjev. Not published.

Overture (5). Composed middle of Feb., 1866) second version) Commissioned by N. G. Rubinstein. First performed March 4, 1886, Moscow. Conducted by N. G. Rubinstein. Not published.

"Winter Dreams," 1st Symphony, Op. 13 (G minor). Dedicated to N. G. Rubinstein. 1. Thoughts on a Winter Road. 2. Bleak Land, Misty Land. 3. Scherzo. 4. Finale. Composed March-Aug., 1868 (first version); Nov. to Dec. 10, 1866, (second version); Sept., 1874 (third version). First performed Feb. 3, 1869, Moscow. Conducted by N. G. Rubinstein. Published Jan., 1875, Jurgenson (third version).

Triumphal Overture to Child's Hymn Op. 15. Composed Sept. to Nov. 12, 1866. (Commissioned by N. G. Rubinstein). Published Sept., 1892. Jurgenson.

1869

"Romeo and Juliet," Overture-Fantasia after William Shakespeare. Dedicated to M. A. Balakirev. Composed Sept. 25 to

Nov. 15, 1869. (first version); July 10, to middle of August, 1870, (second version); Aug. 24 to 29, 1880 (third version). At suggestion and after programme of M. A. Balakirev. First performed March 4, 1870, Moscow. Conducted by N. G. Rubinstein. Published Bothe and Bock (Berlin) 1871. (second version); 1881, same publisher (Berlin). (third version).

1870

"Romeo and Juliet," Overture-Fantasia (second version). See 1869.

1873

Second Symphony (C-minor) Op. 17. Dedicated to Moscow Branch Russian Musical Society. 1. Andante sostenuto Allegro vivo. 2. Andantino marziale. 3. Scherzo. 4. Finale. Composed beginning of June to Nov. 22, 1872 (first version); Dec. 18, 1879, to Jan. 4, 1880 (second version). First performed Jan. 26, 1873. Moscow.˙ Conducted by N. G. Rubinstein (first version); Jan. 31, 1881, St. Petersburg conducted by N. K. Zike (second version). Published 1881, Bessel (second version).

1873

"The Tempest," symphonic fantasia after William Shakespeare, Op. 18. Dedicated to V. V. Stasov. Composed Aug. 7, 8, 10, 1873. At suggestion and after programme of V. V. Stasov. First performed Dec. 7, 1873, Moscow. Conducted by N. G. Rubinstein. Published July, 1877, Jurgenson.

1874

"Winter Day Dreams," First Symphony G minor. Op. 13 (third version). See 1866.

1875

Third Symphony D-major, Op. 29. 1. Moderato assai Allegro brillante. 2. Alla tedesca. 3. Andante. 4. Scherzo. 5. Finale. Composed June 5, to Aug. 1, 1875. First performed Nov. 7, 1875, Moscow. Conducted by N. G. Rubinstein. Published Jan. 1877, Jurgenson.

1876

Slavonic March. Op. 31. Composed Sept. (? to 25), 1876 (at suggestion of N. G. Rubinstein). First performed Nov. 5, 1876, Moscow. Conducted by N. G. Rubinstein. Published Feb., 1880. Jurgenson.

"Francesca da Rimini," Symphonic Fantasia after Dante. Op. 32. Dedicated to S. I. Taneyev. Composed Sept. 25 to Nov. 5, 1876. First performed Feb. 25, 1877, Moscow. Conducted by N. G. Rubinstein. Published Feb., 1878, Jurgenson.

1877

Fourth Symphony (F-Minor), Op. 36. Dedicated "To my best friend." (N. F. von Meck.) 1. Andante sostenuto. Moderato con anima. 2. Andantino in modo di canzona. 3. Scherzo. IV. Finale. Composed May 1 to Dec. 26, 1877. First performed Feb. 10, 1878, Moscow. Conducted by N. G. Rubinstein. Published Aug., 1880, Jurgenson.

1879

First Suite, Op. 43 (dedicated unofficially to N. F. von Meck). 1. Introduction and Fugue. 2. Divertissement. 3. Intermezzo. 4. Miniature March. 5. Scherzo. 6. Gavotte. Composed Aug. 15, 1878, to April 24, 1879 (2nd part Aug. 12–21). First performed Nov. 11, 1879, Moscow. Conducted by N. G. Rubinstein. Published Nov., 1879, Jurgenson.

1880

Second Symphony C-minor, Op. 17 (second version). See 1872.
Capriccio Italien, Op. 15. Dedicated to K. J. Davydov. Composed Jan. 16 to May 15, 1880. First performed Dec. 6, 1880. Moscow. Conducted by N. G. Rubinstein. Published Sept., 1880. Jurgenson.
"Romeo and Juliet," Overture Fantasia (third version). See 1869.
"1812" Overture Solonnelle, Op. 49. Composed Sept. 30, to Nov. 7, 1880 (on occasion of consecration of the Church of Christ the Saviour in Moscow). First performed Aug. 8, 1882, Moscow. Conducted by I. K. Altani. Published May, 1882. Jurgenson.

1883

Coronation March. Composed March 8 to 31, 1883. (Commissioned by the city of Moscow on the occasion of the coronation of Alexander III). First performed May 23, 1883, Moscow, at Coronation Fete in Sokolniki Park. Conducted by S. I. Taneyev. Published July, 1883, Jurgenson.
Second Suite, Op. 53. Dedicated to P. V. Chaikovskaya. 1. Play of Sounds. 2. Waltz. 3. Humorous Scherzo. 4. A Child's Dreams. 5. Wild Dance (in the style of Dargomyzhsky). Composed June 27 to Oct. 13, 1883. First performed Feb. 4, 1884. Conducted by M. Erdmansderfer. Published Jan., 1884, Jurgenson.

1884

Third Suite, Op. 55. Dedicated to M. Erdmansderfer. 1. Elegy. 2. Melancholy Waltz. 3. Scherzo. 4. Theme and variations (12). Composed April 17 to July 19, 1884. First performed Jan. 12, 1885, St. Petersburg. Conducted by H. von Bülow. Published Jan. 1885, Jurgenson.

1885

"Manfred," Symphony (Symphonic Poem), in 4 scenes after Byron. Op. 68. Dedicated to M. A. Balakirev. 1. Lento Lugubre. 2. Vivace con spirito. 3. Andante con moto. 4. Allegro con fuoco. Composed April to Dec. 22, 1885 (at suggestion and after programme of M. A. Balakirev). First performed March 11, 1886, Moscow. Conducted by M. Erdmansderfer. Published Feb., 1886, Jurgenson.

March of the Law School Students. Composed Oct. 27 to Nov. 5, 1885. Published Oct., 1894, Jurgenson.

1887

"Mozartiana," Fourth Suite, Op. 6. 1. Gigue. 2. Minuet. 3. Preghiera (after transcription by F. Liszt). 4. Theme and variations (10). Composed June 17 to July 28, 1887. First performed Nov. 14, 1887, Moscow. Conducted by author. Published Nov., 1887, Jurgenson.

1888

Fifth Symphony (E-minor). Op. 64. Dedicated to T. Ave-Lalleman. 1. Andante. Allegro con anima. 2. Andante cantabile con alcuna licenza. 3. Valse. 4. Finale. Composed May 19, to Aug. 14, 1888. First performed Nov. 6, 1888. St. Petersburg. Conducted by author. Published Oct., 1888, Jurgenson.

"Hamlet," Overture-fantasia after Shakespeare, Op. 67. Dedicated to Eduard Grieg. Composed June 22 to Oct. 7, 1888. First performed Nov. 12, 1888, St. Petersburg. Conducted by author. Published July, 1890, Jurgenson.

1891

"Voyevoda," symphonic ballad after Mickiewicz-Pushkin (Op. 78). Composed Sept. 28, 1890, to Sept. 22, 1891. First performed Nov. 6, 1891. Moscow. Conducted by author. Published 1897. Bel. (score destroyed by author; restored for publication according to orchestral parts).

1892

"Nutcracker Suite" from ballet, Op. 71-bis. 1. Miniature Overture. 2. Character Dances: a) March, b) Dance of the Sugar Plum Fairy, c) Russian Dance (Trepak), d) Arabian Dance, e) Chinese Dance, f) Dance of Shepherds. 3. Waltz of the Flowers. Composed Jan. 28 to Feb. 9, 1892. First performed March 7, 1892, St. Petersburg. Conducted by author. Published May, 1892, Jurgenson.

1893

Sixth Symphony (Pathetique) (B-minor), Op. 74. Dedicated to V. L. Davydov. 1. Adagio. Allegro non troppo. 2. Allegro con grazia. 3. Allegro molto vivace. 4. Finale. Composed Feb. 4 to Aug. 19, 1893. First performed Oct. 16, 1893, St. Petersburg. Conducted by author. Published Feb., 1894. Jurgenson.

For Small Symphony Orchestra

1863–1864

Andante ma non troppo. Composed 1863–1864 (student piece). Not published.

Agitato. Composed 1863–1864 (student piece). Not published.

1865

Overture (F-major). Composed Aug. 15 to Nov. 14, 1865 (first version). First performed Nov. 14, 1865, St. Petersburg. Conducted by author. Not published.

1872

Serenade for N. G. Rubinstein's birthday. Composed Dec. 1, 1872. First performed Dec. 6, 1872. Conducted by N. G. Rubinstein. Not published.

For String Orchestra

1880

Serenade, Op. 48. Dedicated to K. K. Albrecht. 1. Piece in the form of sonatina. 2. Valse. 3. Elegy. 4. Finale (on Russian themes). Composed Sept. 9 to Oct. 27, 1880. First performed Jan. 16, 1882, Moscow. Conducted by M. Erdmansderfer. Published Jan., 1881, Jurgenson.

1884

Elegy in honour of I. V. Samarin. Composed Nov. 3–6, 1884. Published Dec., 1890, Jurgenson (dedicated to memory of I. V. Samarin).

For Military Band (two flutes, two oboes, trumpet, 2 clarinets, bass clarinet).

1863–1864

Adagio. Composed 1863–1864 (student piece). Not published.

For Mixed Septet
(2 violins, viola, violoncello, double bass, two flutes)

1863–1864

Allegro (small Allegro with introduction). Composed 1863–1864 (student piece). Not published.

For Piano Sextet
(2 violins, viola, violoncello, double bass, piano)

1863–1864

Allegro. Composed 1863–1864 (student piece). Not published.

For String Sextet
(2 violins, 2 violas, 2 violoncellos)

1892

"Memories of Florence," Sextet. Op. 70. Dedicated to the Society of Chamber Music in St. Petersburg. 1. Allegro con spirito. 2. Adagio cantabile e con moto. 3. Allegro moderato. 4. Allegro vivace. Composed June 13 to end of July, 1890 (first version); Dec., 1891, to Jan., 1892 (second version). First performed Nov. 25, 1892, St. Petersburg. Society for Chamber Music. Published June 1892, Jurgenson.

For Mixed Quintet
(2 violins, viola, violoncello, harp)

1863–1864

Adagio molto. Composed 1863–1864 (student piece). Not published.

For String Quintet

(2 violins, viola, violoncello, double bass; with episode
for 4 violoncellos)

1863–1864

Allegro ma non tanto. Composed 1863–1864 (student piece). Not published.

For String Quintet

(2 violins, viola, violoncello, double bass)

1863–1864

Prelude. Composed 1863–1864 (student piece). Not published.

For String Quartet

(2 violins, viola and violoncello)

1863–1864

Andante molto (fragment). Composed 1863–1864 (student piece). Not published.
Allegro vivace. Composed 1863–1864 (student piece). Not published.

1865

Quartet B-major (one-movement). Composed Aug. 15 to Oct. 30, 1865. First performed Oct. 30, 1865, St. Petersburg. K. Pushilov (first violin), D. Panov (2nd violin), B. Bessel (viola), A. Kuznetsov (violoncello). Published 1940. State Music Publishers.

1871

First Quartet D-Major. Op. 11. Dedicated to S. A. Rachinsky. 1. Moderato e semplice. 2. Andante cantabile. 3. Scherzo.
4. Finale. Composed Feb. 1, 1871. First performed March 16,
1871, Moscow. Chamber Section of Russian Musical Society.
Published Dev., 1872, Jurgenson.

1874

Second Quartet F-major. Op. 22. Dedicated to Grand
Duke Constantine Nikolayevich. 1. Adagio. Moderato Assai.
2. Scherzo. 3. Andante ma non tanto. 4. Finale. Composed Jan.
18 to March 10, 1874. First performed March 10, 1874, Moscow. Chamber Section, Russian Musical Society. Published
March, 1876, Jurgenson.

1876

Third Quartet E-flat Minor. Op. 30. Dedicated to the
memory of F. G. Laub. 1. Andante sostenuto. 2. Allegretto
vivo e scherzando. 3. Andante funebre e doloroso, ma con
moto. 4. Finale. Composed Jan. to Feb. 18, 1876. First performed March 18, 1876, Moscow. Chamber Section Russian
Musical Society. Published Nov., 1876, Jurgenson.

For Brass Quartet
(4 French horns at different pitch)

1863–1864

Allegretto. Composed 1863–1864 (student piece). Not published.

For Piano Trio
(Violin, violoncello, piano)

1882

Trio, Op. 50 (A-minor). Dedicated to "Memory of a Great Artist" (N. G. Rubinstein). 1. Pezzo elegiaco. 2. a) Theme with variations (11), b) Final variation and Coda. Composed Dec. 15, 1881, to Jan. 28, 1882. First performed Oct. 18, 1882, Moscow. I. V. Grzimali (violin), V. F. Fitzenhagen (violoncello), S. I. Taneyev (piano). Published Sept., 1882, Jurgenson.

For String Trio
(Violin, viola, violoncello)

1863–1864

Allegretto. Composed 1863–1864 (student piece). Not published.

For Piano Duet

1877

Funeral March (on motifs from opera "Oprichnik"). Composed March 7–16, 1877. (Commissioned by N. F. von Meck). Not published.

Solo
(For piano duet and symphony orchestra)

1875

First Concerto (B-flat minor) Op. 23. Dedicated to Hans von Bülow. 1. Allegro non troppo e molto maestoso. 2. Andantino semplice. 3. Allegro con fuoco. Composed middle Nov., 1874, to Feb. 9, 1875. First performed 1875, Boston, H. von Bülow. Nov. 1, 1875, St. Petersburg, G. G. Kross. Published Aug., 1879, Jurgenson.

1880

Second Concerto (G-major), Op. 44. Dedicated to N. G. Rubinstein. 1. Allegro brillante. 2. Andante non troppo. 3. Allegro con fuoco. Composed Oct. 10, 1879, to April 28, 1880 (first version); Aug. 20, 1893 (second version, A. I. Ziloti and author). First performed May 18, 1882, Moscow. S. I. Taneyev. Published Feb., 1881 (first version), Jurgenson, Sept., 1897 (second version), Jurgenson.

1884

Concert Fantasia, Op. 56. Dedicated to S. Menter. 1. Rondo. 2. Contrasts. Composed June 16 to Sept. 24, 1884 (additional version of end of first movement for separate performance appended). First performed Feb. 22, 1885, Moscow, S. I. Taneyev. Published March, 1893, Jurgenson.

1893

Second Concerto (G-major) Op. 44 (second version). See 1880.

Third Concerto (E-flat major) Op. 75 (one movement). Dedicated to L. Diemer. Composed May 20, 1892, to July 10, 1893 (from esquisses for unfinished symphony E-flat major). First performed Jan. 7, 1895, St. Petersburg. S. I. Taneyev. Published Dec., 1894, Jurgenson.

Andante and Finale. Op. 79. 1. Andante. 2. Finale. Composed Oct. 3, 1893 (from esquisses for unfinished symphony E-flat major) (Orchestrated by S. I. Taneyev). First performed Feb. 8, 1896, St. Petersburg, S. I. Taneyev. Published 1897, Belyaev.

For Piano (two hands)

1854

Waltz. Dedicated to A. P. Petrova. Composed Aug., 1854. Not published.

1862

Piece (on theme of "By the River, by the Bridge"). Dedicated to H. A. Laroche. Composed Oct.-Dec., 1862. Not published.

1863–1864

Allegro (fragment). Composed 1863–1864 (student piece). Not published.

Theme and Variations (9). Composed 1863–1864. Published Feb., 1909, Jurgenson.

1865

Sonata (C-Sharp minor) Op. 80. 1. Allegro con fuoco. 2. Andante. 3. Scherzo. 4. Allegro vivo. Composed 1865. Published Jan., 1901, Jurgenson.

1867

Two pieces, Op. 1. Dedicated to A. G. Rubinstein. 1. Russian Scherzo. 2. Impromptu. Composed March 8, 1867. (No. 2, 3, 1863–1864) (No. 1 on suggestion of N. G. Rubinstein). Published 1868, Jurgenson.

"Memories of Hapsale," 3 pieces. Op. 2. Dedicated to V. V. Davydova. 1. Ruined Castle. 2. Scherzo. 3. Song Without Words. Composed June, July, 1867 (No. 2, 1863–1864). Published 1868, Jurgenson.

1868

Valse Caprice, Op. 4. Dedicated to A. K. Dobr. Composed Oct., 1868. Published Dec., 1868, Jurgenson.
Ballad, Op. 5. Dedicated to D. Artôt. Composed Nov., 1868. Published Dec., 1868, Jurgenson.

1870

Valse-Scherzo (A-major), Op. 7. Dedicated to A. I. Davydova. Composed Feb. 3, 1870. Published April, 1870, Jurgenson.
Capriccio, Op. 8. Dedicated to K. Klindworth. Composed Feb. 3, 1870. Published April, 1870, Jurgenson.
3 Morceaux, Op. 9. Dedicated to N. A. Muromtseva (No. 1). A. O. Zorgraf (No. 2), A. I. Dubuque (No. 3). 1. Reverie. 2. Salon Polka. 3. Salon Mazurka. Composed Oct. 26, 1870. Published March, 1871, Jurgenson.

1871

2 Morceaux, Op. 10. Dedicated to V. S. Shilovsky. 1. Nocturne. 2. Humoresque. Composed Dec., 1871. Published Feb., 1876, Jurgenson (separately No. 1, May, 1874, Jurgenson; No. 2 April, 1875, Jurgenson).

1873

6 Morceaux, Op. 19. Dedicated to N. D. Kondratyev (No. 1), V. V. Timanova (No. 2), A. K. Abramova (No. 3),

M. Y. Terminskaya (No. 4), E. L. Langer (No. 5), H. A. Laroche (No. 6). 1. Evening Reverie. 2. Humorous Scherzo. 3. Leaf from an Album. 4. Nocturne 5. Capriccioso. 6. Theme and Variations (13). Composed Oct. 2, 1873. Published April, 1874, Jurgenson (separately Jan., 1874, Jurgenson).

6 Morceaux on one theme, Op. 21. Dedicated to A. G. Rubinstein. 1. Prelude. 2. Fugue for Four Voices. 3. Impromptu. 4. Funeral March. 5. Mazurka. 6. Scherzo. Composed Oct.-Nov., 1873. Published 1873, Bessel.

1876

"The Four Seasons," 12 Character Pictures, Op. 37-bis. 1. January. By the Fireside. 2. February. Shrove-tide. 3. March Song of the Skylark. 4. April. The Snowdrop. 5. May. White Nights. 6. June. Barcarolle. 7. July. Song of the Reaper. 8. August. Harvest. 9. September. Hunting.˙ 10. October. Autumn Song. 11. November. Troika. 12. December. Christmas Eve. Composed 1875–1876 (commissioned by N. M. Bernard). Published 1876, Bernard, St. Petersburg; October, 1885, Jurgenson.

1878

"Russian Volunteer Fleet" ("Skobelev March"). Composed April 24, 1878 (commissioned by V. I. Jurgenson). Published May, 1878, Jurgenson (under pseudonym Simonov).

12 Morceaux of medium difficulty, Op. 40. Dedicated to M. I. Tchaikovsky. 1. Etude. 2. Sad Song. 3. Funeral March. 4. Mazurka. 5. Mazurka. 6. Song without Words. 7. In the Village. 8. Waltz (two versions). 10. Russian Dance. 11. Scherzo. 12. Interrupted Reverie. Composed February 12 to July 13, 1876 (No. 9, first version, 1876) (No. 10, 1876). Published Jan., 1879, Jurgenson.

Sonata (Large Sonata) (G-major), Op. 37. Dedicated to K. Klindworth. 1. Moderato e risoluto. 2. Andante non troppo quasi moderato. 3. Scherzo. 4. Finale. Composed March 1 to July 26, 1878. First performed Oct. 21, 1879, Moscow, N. G. Rubinstein. Published Feb., 1879, Jurgenson.

Children's Album, 24 Easy Pieces, Op. 39. Dedicated to Vladimir Davydov. 1. Morning Prayer. 2. Winter Morning. 3. Gee Up, Horsey. 4. Mama. 5. March of the Wooden Soldiers. 6. Dolly is Ill. 7. Doll's Funeral. 8. Waltz. 9. New Doll. 10. Mazurka. 11. Russian Song. 12. Peasant Playing Accordion. 13. Kamarinskaya. 14. Polka. 15. Italian Song. 16. Old French Song. 17. German Song. 18. Neapolitan Song. 19. Nursey's Story. 20. Baba-Yaga. 21. Sweet Reverie. 22. The Skylark's Song. 23. The Song of the Organ-Grinder. 24. In Church. Composed May 1 to July 29, 1878. Published Oct., 1878, Jurgenson.

1882

6 morceaux, Op. 51. Dedicated to M. S. Kondratyeva (No. 1), A. L. Davydova (No. 2), A. N. Merkling (No. 3), N. A. Plesskaya (No. 4), V. L. Rimskaya-Korsakova (No. 5), E. I. Menton (No. 6). 1. Salon Waltz. 2. Polka (Polka peu dansante). 3. Menuet Scherzoso. 4. Natalie-Waltz (two versions). 5. Romance. 6. Sentimental Waltz. Composed Aug. to Sept. 15, 1882 (No. 4, first version, 1878). Published Nov., 1882, Jurgenson.

1884

Caprice Impromptu. Dedicated to S. I. Jurgenson. Composed Sept. 18 to 20, 1884 (at suggestion of French newspaper *Gaulois*, Paris). Published 1885 in album of *Gaulois* (Paris). Published March, 1886, Jurgenson.

1886

"Dumka," Russian village scene. Op. 59. Dedicated to A. F. Marmontel. Composed Feb. 15–24, 1886. Published May, 1886, Jurgenson.

1889

Valse Morceau (A-major). Composed Aug. 16, 1889 (at suggestion of magazine "Artist"). Published 1889 in "Artist," No. 1 (Moscow). Published Oct., 1894, Jurgenson.
Impromptu. Dedicated to A. G. Rubinstein. Composed Sept. 20–30, 1889 (for album of former students of St. Petersburg Conservatory). Published July, 1897, Jurgenson.

1893

18 morceaux. Op. 72. Dedicated to V. I. Maslova (No. 1), P. Moskalev (No. 2), A. A. Gerke (No. 3), A. I. Galli (No. 4), V. I. Safonov (No. 5), E. P. Jurgenson (No. 6), S. A. Pabst (No. 7), E. I. Laroche (No. 8), A. I. Maslova (No. 9), A. I. Ziloti (No. 10), V. D. Kondratyeva (No. 11), A. P. Jurgenson (No. 12), A. I. Brullova (No. 13), in memory of Vladimir Sklifasovsky (No. 14), S. M. Gomezov (No. 15), N. K. Lentz (No. 16), N. S. Zveryev (No. 17), V. L. Sapelnikov (No. 18). 1. Impromptu. 2. Cradle Song. 3. Tender Reproaches. 4. Character Dance. 5. Meditation. 6. Mazurka pour le danse. 7. Concert Polonaise. 8. Dialogue. 9. Un poco di Schumann. 10. Scherzo-fantasia. 11. Valse bluette. 12. L'espiegle. 13. Village Echo. 14. Elegiac Song. 15. Un poco di Chopin. 16. Waltz in 5/8 time. 17. Distant Past. 18. Invitation to a Trepak. Composed April 7–22, 1893. Published Sept. 1893, Jurgenson.
Military March. Dedicated to the 98th Yuryev Infantry Regiment. Composed March 24 to May 5, 1893 (at suggestion of A. P. Tchaikovsky). Published Oct., 1891, Jurgenson.

Impromptu (Momento lirico). Composed 1893 (finished by S. I. Taneyev). Published Nov., 1898, Jurgenson.

For Violin and Symphony Orchestra

1875

Melancholy Serenade, Op. 26. Dedicated to L. S. Auer. Composed Jan. to Feb. 13, 1875. First performed Jan. 16, 1876, Moscow. A. D. Brodsky. Published Nov., 1879, Jurgenson.

1877

Valse-Scherzo, Op. 34. Dedicated to I. I. Kotek. Composed beginning of 1877 (at suggestion of I. I. Kotek). First performed Sept. 8 (20), 1878 (Paris), S. K. Bartsevich; Dec. 1, 1879, Moscow, S. K. Bartsevich. Published April, 1895, Jurgenson.

1878

Concerto, Op. 35. Dedicated to A. D. Brodsky. 1. Allegro moderato. 2. Canzonetta. 3. Finale. Composed March 5–30, 1878. First performed (1879) New York, L. Damrosch; 1881, Nov. 22 (Dec. 4), Vienna, A. D. Brodsky; August 8, 1882, Moscow, A. D. Brodsky. Published June, 1888, Jurgenson.

For Violin and Piano

1878

"Memories of Beau Geste," three pieces, Op. 42. Dedicated to A. Bailov (name of N. F. von Meck's country estate). 1. Meditation. 2. Scherzo. 3. Melody. Composed March 11 to Aug. 13, 1878. Published May 1879, Jurgenson.

For Violoncello and Symphony Orchestra

1876

Variations on Rococo Theme (8), Op. 33. Dedicated to V. F. Fitzenhagen. Composed Dec. 15–31, 1876. First performed Nov. 18, 1877, Moscow, V. F. Fitzenhagen. Published Nov., 1889, Jurgenson.

1887

"Pezzo Capriccioso," concert piece, Op. 62. Dedicated to A. A. Brandukov. Composed Aug. 12–19, 1887. First performed Nov. 25, 1889, Moscow. A. A. Brandukov and orchestra conducted by author. Published July, 1888, Jurgenson.

Arrangements of Own Compositions
Orchestration
For Mixed Chorus and Symphony Orchestra

1863 1864

"The Vision Beyond," chorus (originally for mixed chorus a cappella). Arranged 1863–1864. Not published.

For Three Voices and Symphony Orchestra

1889

"Dawn," duet, Op. 46, No. 6 (originally for two voices and piano). Arranged Dec. 17, 1889. Not published.

For Voice and Symphony Orchestra

1884

"Legend," Song for Children, Op. 51, No. 5 (originally for voice and piano). Arranged April 2, 1884 (at suggestion of D. A. Usatov). Published 1889, Jurgenson.

250 RUSSIAN SYMPHONY:

"Were I But a Blade of Grass in the Field," Op. 47, No. 7 (originally for voice and piano). Arranged Sept. 25, 1884 (at suggestion of E. A. Lavrovskaya). Published 1884, Jurgenson.

1888

"Is It Day?" Ballad, Op. 47, No. 6 (originally for voice and piano). Arranged Feb. 12, 1888. First performed Feb. 16 (28), 1888, Paris; M. P. Benardachi and orchestra conducted by author. Not published.

For Violoncello and Symphony Orchestra

1866–1888

Andante cantabile from First Quartet, Op. 11, Part 2 (originally for two violins, viola and violoncello). Arranged, 1886–1888. Not published.

"Nocturne," Piece, Op. 19, No. 4 (originally for piano). Arranged 1886–1888. Not published.

Transpositions
For Voice and Piano (Pianoforte Arrangement)

1868

"Voyevoda," opera, Op. 3. Rearranged Sept., 1868. Not published (autograph destroyed by author).

1872

"Oprichnik," opera. Rearranged Feb., 1872, to middle of April. Published 1874, Bessel.

Cantata for opening of Polytechnic Exhibition in Moscow. Rearranged May 3, 1872. Not published.

1873

"The Snow Maiden," music for spring fairytale, Op. 12. Rearranged April 20, 1873. Published Dec., 1873, Jurgenson.

1874

"Vakula, the Smith," opera, Op. 14 (see also "The Little Shoes"). Arranged Oct. 19 to Nov. 9, 1874 (in collaboration with A. I. Hubert) (instrumental numbers for piano duet). Published 1876, Jurgenson.

1878

"Eugene Onegin," opera (lyrical scenes), Op. 24. Arranged Oct. 17, 1877, to Jan. 28, 1878. Published Sept., 1878, Jurgenson.

1879

"The Maid of Orleans," opera. Arranged Aug. 27 to Sept. 22, 1879 (First and Second Acts—J. Messer, Third Act—I. I. Kotek, edited by author). Published July, 1880, Jurgenson.

1883

"Moscow," Cantata. Rearranged March, 1883. Published Dec., 1885, Jurgenson.

"Mazeppa," opera. Rearranged April 16 to May 33, 1883. Published Aug., 1883, Jurgenson.

"The Little Shoes," opera. Rearranged March 23, 1885 (after opera "Vakula, the Smith"), in collaboration with A. I. Hubert. Published July, 1885, Jurgenson.

1887

"The Enchantress," opera. Rearranged Oct. 1, 1886, to
Feb. 11, 1887. Published April, 1887, Jurgenson.

1890

"The Queen of Spades," opera, Op. 68. Rearranged March
4–24, 1890. Published June, 1890, Jurgenson.

For Mixed and Children's Chorus and Piano

1869

Chorus of Flowers and Insects (from opera "Mandragora").
Originally for mixed and children's chorus and symphony
orchestra. Rearranged Dec. 27, 1869. Published June, 1902,
Jurgenson.

For Mixed Chorus a cappella

1889

"Legend," Song for Children, Op. 54, No. 5 (originally
for voice and piano). Rearranged Dec. 15, 1889. Published
Jan., 1890, Jurgenson.

For Two Pianos, Four-Hand Arrangements

1874

First Concerto for Piano and Symphony Orchestra, Op. 23.
Rearranged Nov. to Dec. 21, 1874. Published Dec., 1875, Jurgenson.

1880

Second Concerto for Piano and Symphony Orchestra, Op. 44. Rearranged Feb. 5–20, 1880. Published Oct., 1880, Jurgenson.

1884

Concert Fantasia, Op. 56 (originally for piano and symphony orchestra). Rearranged June 16 to Sept. 24, 1884. Published Dec., 1884, Jurgenson.

1893

Third Concerto for Piano and Symphony Orchestra (Op. 75). Rearranged Sept. 27 to Oct. 3, 1893. Published Nov., 1894, Jurgenson.

Andante and Finale (Op. 79), originally for piano and symphony orchestra. Rearranged Oct. 3, 1893. Published 1893, Belyaev.

For Piano Four-Hand Arrangements

1866

Overture to Children's Hymn, Op. 15 (originally for symphony orchestra). Rearranged Nov. 12 to Dec. 10, 1866. Published April, 1878, Jurgenson.

1867

Entr'acte and Dance of Village Girls from Opera "Voyevoda," Op. 3 (originally for symphony orchestra). Rearranged summer of 1867. Published 1868, Jurgenson.

1873

Second Symphony, Op. 17 (originally for symphony orchestra). Rearranged Dec. 26, 1872, to April 24, 1873 (first version); Dec. 21, 1879, to Jan. 4, 1880 (second version). Published 1874, Bessel.

1879

First Suite, Op. 43 (originally for symphony orchestra). Rearranged April 15 to 22, 1879. Published Nov., 1879, Jurgenson.

1880

Second Symphony, Op. 17 (originally for symphony orchestra) (second version). See 1873.

Capriccio Italien, Op. 45 (originally for symphony orchestra). Rearranged Oct. 12–16, 1880. Published Sept., 1880, Jurgenson.

Serenade for String Orchestra, Op. 48. Rearranged Oct. 10 to 23, 1880. Published April, 1881, Jurgenson.

1883

Second Suite, Op. 63 (originally for symphony orchestra). Rearranged Sept. 6 to Oct. 11, 1883. (First Part by A. I. Hubert). Published 1884, Jurgenson.

1884

Third Suite, Op. 56 (originally for symphony orchestra). Rearranged May 25 to Aug. 19, 1884. Published Feb., 1885, Jurgenson.

1885

"Manfred," Symphony (symphonic poem), Op. 58 (originally for symphony orchestra). Rearranged July 8 to Sept. 22, 1885 (in collaboration with A. I. Hubert). Published April, 1885, Jurgenson.

1893

Sixth Symphony, Op. 74 (originally for symphony orchestra). Rearranged July 20 to Aug. 19, 1893. Published Nov., 1893, Jurgenson.

For Piano Two Hand Arrangement

1868

Potpourri of opera "Voyevoda," Op. 3. Rearranged 1868. Published 1868, Jurgenson (under pseudonym of Kramer).

1873

Cradle Song, Op. 16, No. 1 (originally for voice and piano) (two versions). Rearranged 1873. Published 1873, Bessel.
"Oh, Sing That Song Again," Ballad, Op. 16, No. 4 (originally for voice and piano). Rearranged 1873. Published, Bessel.
"What Then?" Ballad, Op. 16, No. 5 (originally for voice and piano). Rearranged 1873. Published 1873, Bessel.

1876

Slavonic March, Op. 31 (originally for symphony orchestra). Rearranged Sept. to Nov. 25, 1876. Published Oct., 1876, Jurgenson.

1878

Liturgy of St. Chrysostomus, Op. 41 (originally for mixed chorus a cappella). Rearranged June 24 to July 29, 1878. Published Jan., 1879, Jurgenson (with score).

1882

Vesper Mass, Op. 52 (originally for mixed chorus a cappella). Rearranged Jan. 30 to March 7, 1882. Published Nov., 1882, Jurgenson (with score).

1883

Coronation March (originally for symphony orchestra). Rearranged March 21–31, 1883. Published Aug., 1883, Jurgenson.

1885

Hymn in Honour of St. Cyril and Methodius (originally for mixed chorus a cappella). Rearranged March 6–8, 1885. Published March, 1885, Jurgenson (with score).

Nine pieces of Sacred music (originally for mixed chorus a cappella). Rearranged Nov. 3 to 17, 1884. (Nos. 1–3; March to April, 1885 (Nos. 4–9). Published Feb., 1885, Jurgenson (Nos. 1–2); Aug., 1885, Jurgenson (Nos. 4–9) (with score).

1892

Suite from "Nutcracker" ballet, Op. 71-bis (originally for symphony orchestra). Rearranged Aug. 12–29, 1892. Published Oct., 1897, Jurgenson.

"Nutcracker" ballet, Op. 71. Rearranged Aug. 12–29, 1892. Published Nov., 1892, Jurgenson.

For Violin and Piano

1873

"Oh, Sing that Song Again," Ballad, Op. 16, No. 4 (originally for voice and piano). Rearranged 1873. Published 1873, Bessel.

1875

Melancholy Serenade, Op. 26 (originally for violin and symphony orchestra). Rearranged Jan. to Feb. 13, 1875. Published April, 1876, Jurgenson.

1877

Valse-Scherzo, Op. 34 (originally for violin and symphony orchestra). Rearranged 1877. Published June, 1878, Jurgenson.
"Humoresque," morceau, Op. 10, No. 2 (originally for piano). Rearranged 1877. Published April, 1877, Jurgenson.
Andante Funebre from Third Quartet, Op. 30, Part 3 (originally for two violins, viola and violoncello). Rearranged 1877. Published April, 1877, Jurgenson.

1878

Concerto for Violin and Symphony Orchestra, Op. 35. Rearranged March 17 to 24, 1878. Published Oct., 1878, Jurgenson.

For Violoncello and Piano

1876

Variations on Rococo Theme, Op. 33 (originally for violoncello and symphony orchestra). Rearranged Dec. 15–31, 1876. Published Oct., 1878, Jurgenson.

1877

"Pezzo Capriccioso," concert piece, Op. 62 (originally for violoncello and symphony orchestra). Rearranged Aug. 15–17, 1887. Published March, 1888, Jurgenson.

Rearrangements of Works of Other Composers
Recitatives and Choruses for Operas

1868

D. Auber—"Black Domino," recitative and choruses. Composed Oct., 1868 (commissioned by Merelli). Not published.

1875

W. A. Mozart, "The Marriage of Figaro," recitatives. Composed 1875 (at suggestion of N. G. Rubinstein). First performed May 5, 1876, Moscow Conservatory. Published April, 1884, Jurgenson.

Orchestration
For Mixed Chorus and Symphony Orchestra

1883

M. Glinka—Couplets on "Glory" theme from opera "Life for the Tsar," ("Ivan Susani"). Rearranged Feb. 2–4, 1883. (Commissioned by N. A. Alexeyev). First performed May 10, 1883, Moscow. Red Square (on entry of Alexander III). Published 1883, Jurgenson (choral scores).

For 3 Voices and Symphony Orchestra

1870

A. Dargomyzhsky, "The Golden Cloud Went to Sleep,"

Trio (originally for two voices and piano). Rearranged 1870 (at suggestion of N. G. Rubinstein). Not published.

For Voice and Symphony Orchestra

1870

A. Stradella, "O del mio dolce," aria. Rearranged Oct. 29, 1870 (at suggestion of N. G. Rubinstein). Not published.

1874

R. Schumann "Dream Forboding," ballad (originally for voice and piano). Rearranged 1874. Not published.

F. Liszt, "The King of Thule," ballad (originally for voice and piano). Rearranged Oct. 22, 1874 (at suggestion of I. A. Melnikov). Not published.

For Symphony Orchestra

1863–1864

L. van Beethoven—1st part from Sonata for piano Op. 31, No. 2. Rearranged 1863 (four versions) (student work). Not published.

L. van Beethoven—1st part from Sonata for violin and piano, dedicated to Kreutzer, Op. 47. Rearranged 1863–1864 (student work). Not published.

K. M. v. Weber—Scherzo from sonata for piano, Op. 39. Rearranged 1863–1864 (student work). Not published.

R. Schumann—two versions from "Symphonic Etudes" (Adagio and Allegro brillante) (originally for piano). Rearranged 1863–1864 (student work). Not published.

I. Hungi—"The Return," waltz (originally for piano). Rearranged 1863–1864. Not published.

1866

A. Dubuque—"Mario Daghmar" polka (originally for piano). Rearranged 1866. Not published.

1867

K. Kral—Ceremonial March (originally for piano). Rearranged May, 1867 (on occasion of arrival of Slavonic guests to Moscow). Not published.

1874

"Gott erhalte Franz, den Kaiser," Austrian national anthem (originally for piano(?)). Rearranged Feb. 12, 1874 (on occasion of visit to St. Petersburg of Emperor Franz Josef). Not published.

1887

W. A. Mozart—three pieces for piano and chorus "Ave verum" (see Mozartiana, p. 12).

1888

H. Laroche—Overture-Fantasia (originally for piano). Rearranged Aug. 15 to Sept. 15, 1888. First performed Nov. 5, 1888, St. Petersburg, conducted by Tchaikovsky. Not published.

For Piano and Symphony Orchestra

1893

S. Menter—"Ungarische Zigeunerweisen," Hungarian Rhapsody (originally for piano). Rearranged Jan. 23, 1893.

First performed Jan. 23, 1893, Odessa, S. Menter and orchestra conducted by Tchaikovsky. Not published.

Transposition
For Male Chorus and Piano

1874

"Gaudeamus Igitur" ("Let us be merry, friends"), students' song (originally for chorus). Text by N. V. Bugayev (from Latin). Rearranged Jan., 1874. Published Jan., 1874, Jurgenson.

For Vocal Quartet and Piano

1893

W. A. Mozart—Fragment from Fantasia for Piano (C-minor). See "Night," p. 6.

For Piano, Four-Hand Arrangement (Piano Duet)

1868

E. Tarnovskaya—"I Remember All," ballad (from transcription for piano by A. I. Dubuque). Rearranged 1868. Published 1868, Jurgenson.

50 Russian folk songs (originally for chorus). Rearranged Nov. to Dec., 1868 (Nos. 1–25); March 13 to Oct. 2, 1869 (Nos. 26–50). Published Jan., 1869, Jurgenson (Nos. 1–25); Nov., 1869, Jurgenson (Nos. 26–50).

A. Rubinstein—"Ivan the Terrible," musical character picture (originally for symphony orchestra). Rearranged Oct. 6 to 30, 1869. (Commissioned by V. Bessel.) Published 1869, Bessel.

1870

A. Rubinstein "Don Quixote," musical character picture (originally for symphony orchestra). Rearranged 1870. (Commissioned by V. Bessel.) Published 1870, Bessel.

For Piano Two-Hand Arrangements

1868

A. Dargomyzhsky—"Cossack Dance," fantasia (originally for symphony orchestra). Rearranged 1868. Published 1868, Jurgenson (Tchaikovsky's first published work).

1874

K. M. v. Weber—"Perpetuum Pobile" from Sonata for piano, Op. 39. Arranged for left hand alone. Dedicated to A. O. Zograf. Rearranged April, 1874. Published April, 1874, Jurgenson.

Edited
For Mixed Chorus a cappella

1881

D. Bortnyansky—Complete collection of sacred music. Ten volumes, rearranged June 21 to Oct. 27, 1881. (Commissioned by P. I. Jurgenson.) Published May, 1885, Jurgenson (separately Jan., 1882–Feb., 1883, P. Jurgenson).

For Voice and Piano

1873

V. Prokunih—66 Russian folk songs. Rearranged Oct., 1872 (Nos. 1–33); Feb., 1873 (Nos. 34–66). Published Oct., 1872, Jurgenson (Nos. 1–33); May, 1873, Jurgenson (Nos. 34–66).

1877

M. Mamontova—Children's Songs on Russian and Little Russian Airs. Rearranged April 26, 1872 (first edition—24); May, 1877 (second edition—10) (at suggestion of author). Published 1872 by author, Aug., 1888, Jurgenson (first edition).

LITERARY WORKS
(Abridged Index)

Textbooks

1871. Guide to Practical Study of Harmony.
1874. Brief Textbooks on Harmony adapted for reading sacred music in Russia.

Articles and Notes on Music

1868–1891. 50 articles and comments on musical criticism.
1888. Autobiographical description of foreign tour in 1888.
1889. Autobiography.

Opera Librettos

1868. "Voyevoda" (in collaboration with A. N. Ostrovsky).
1872. "The Oprichnik."
1878. "Eugene Onegin" (in collaboration with K. S. Shilovsky).
1879. "The Maid of Orleans."
1883. "Mazeppa" (rearrangement of libretto by V. P. Burenin).
1890. "The Queen of Spades" (in collaboration with M. I. Tchaikovsky).

Texts of Vocal Compositions
Two fragments for opera "Voyevoda"

1869. Duet "Softly the Moon will Rise."
1868. Quartet "Dark Night."

Four fragments for opera "The Queen of Spades"

1890. Chorus "Now, Mashenka."
1890. Aria "I Love You."
1890. Chorus "The Sun Shines Red."
1890. Aria "Ah, how Weary am I."

Four Choruses

1881. "Evening" (Tchaikovsky's authorship doubtful).
1885. Hymn in honour of St. Cyril and Methodius.
1885. Song of the Law School Students.
1889. "Nightingale."

Three vocal ensembles

1870. Trio "Nature and Love."
1877. Quartet M. I. Glinka "The Prayer."
1893. Quartet "Night."

Three Romances

1872. "What Now?"
1875. "Awful Moment."
1886. "Simple Words."

Verses

1861. Verse on the occasion of birth of T. L. Davydova.
1875. To M. A. Golovina.
1877. "Cry of a Sick Fool to Fifi."
1877. Verse on the occasion of T. L. Davydova's birthday.
1878. Lilies of the Valley.
1880. Verse on the occasion of T. L. Davydova's birthday.
1880. To A. I. Maslova.
1882. (Verse about Beetles).
1886. "What Sashenka and Lenochka Wanted."

Translations:

Musical Theory

1865. "Guide to Orchestration," by A. F. Gevaert (from the French).
1868. "Vital Rules and Advice to Young Musicians," by R. Schumann (from the German).
1869. "Musical Catechism," by I. Lobe (from the German).
1868. Aria of the page from Meyerbeer's opera, "The Huguenots" (from the Italian).
1869. "Persian song," A. G. Rubinstein (from the German).
1870–1871. 19 ballads by A. G. Rubinstein (from the German).
1875. Libretto for opera "Marriage of Figaro," by Mozart (from the German).
1877. (5 Italian arias), M. I. Glinka (from the Italian).
1878. Florentine song "Pimpinella" (from the Italian).

Musical Texts edited

1892–1893. Dictionary of the Russian language (two editions).

Childhood Works

1844. "Our Mama is in St. Petersburg," a song (written together with his sister A. I. Tchaikovskaya).
1847. Translation of fragment from schoolbook "L'education maternelle," by T. Tasteau (from the French).
1847–1848. 18 verses (in French).
1847–1848. 3 prose compositions (in French).
1854. Article "History of Literature in our class."
1854. Verses.

INDEX